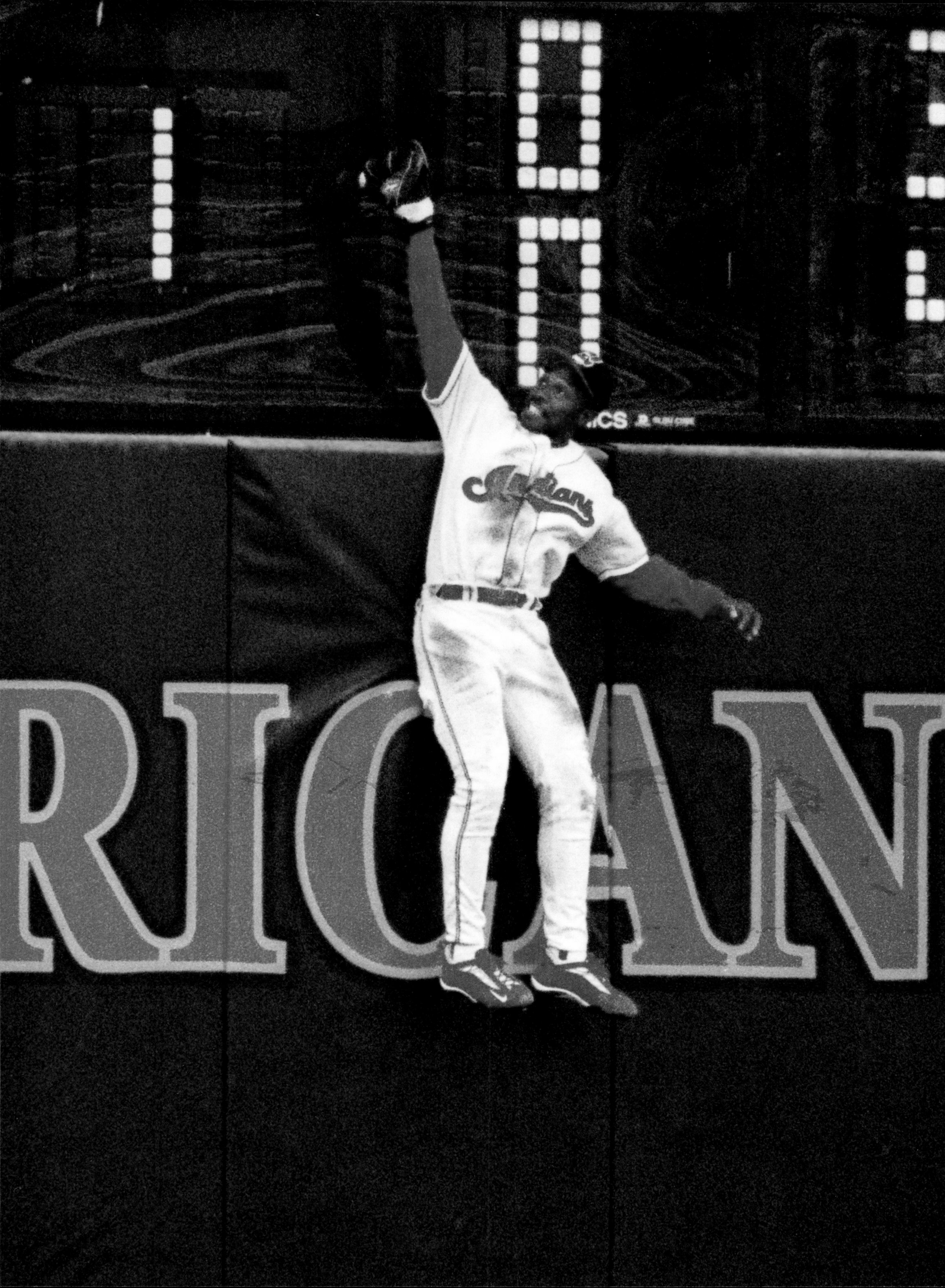
RICAN

LEGENDS OF THE
TRIBE

An
Illustrated
History of the
Cleveland
Indians

Morris Eckhouse

PRODUCED BY BOB MOON

TAYLOR PUBLISHING COMPANY, DALLAS, TEXAS

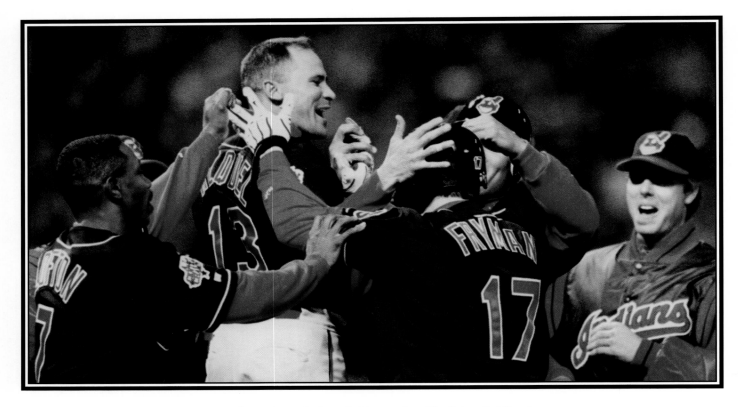

Published by Taylor Publishing Company
1550 West Mockingbird Lane
Dallas, Texas 75235

Edited, Designed and Produced by
Bob Moon, SporTradition Publications
798 Linworth Rd. East
Columbus, Ohio 43235

Library of Congress Cataloging-in-Publication Data

Eckhouse, Morris
    Legends of the tribe : an illustrated history of the Cleveland Indians / Morris
Eckhouse.
      p.   cm.
    ISBN 0-87833-197-2 (cloth)
    1. Cleveland Indians (Baseball team)—History. 2. Cleveland Indians (Baseball team)—Pictorial works.

GV875.C7 E34 2000
796.357'64'0977132—dc21   00-044682

PHOTOS (i–xvii):

(i) A leaping catch by Kenny Lofton. (ii) Bartolo Colon sights the mitt. (iii) Lou Boudreau breaks for first following a base hit. (iv) Kenny Lofton, Omar Vizquel, Travis Fryman and others celebrate. (vi) Manny Ramirez steps into the pitch. (viii) Home run slugger Hal Trosky. (ix) The powerful swing of David Justice. (x) The winning delivery of Charles Nagy. (xi) Sudden Sam McDowell. (xii) Hall-of-Fame pitcher Addie Joss. (xiii) The home run stride of Jim Thome. (xiv) Rapid Robert Feller on the mound at League Park. (xv) Rocky Colavito and Herb Score. (xvi) Omar Vizquel jumps high to avoid the slide.

The most memorable dates in my life are October 29, 1959, October 25, 1986, and August 6, 1989. The first is my debut date; the second is the debut date of Morris Eckhouse and Maria Valenti Eckhouse as husband and wife; and the third is the debut date of Allen Eckhouse. This book is dedicated to my father, Melvin and my late mother, Eleanor, who are responsible for the first debut; Maria, who is responsible for the second and third debuts; and Allen who is reasonably responsible for a ten-year-old.

Contents

Acknowledgments

First and foremost, sincere thanks to Fred Schuld and Joe Simenic for serving as readers and fact checkers for the text of *Legends of the Tribe*. Their efforts made the text substantially better and kept several errors from getting through to the final manuscript. Any errors that remain can be charged to the author. Joe and Fred are both distinguished members of SABR, Society for American Baseball Research. SABR membership should be part of any baseball writer's tools. SABR's networking ability and resources are a great benefit for baseball professionals and fans alike. SABR's staff (John Zajc and Vanetta Ellis) and Publications Director Mark Alvarez do a great job in assisting baseball writers and researchers.

Bob Moon of SporTradition deserves special thanks for his efforts to make *Legends of the Tribe* as good as possible. As producer of the book, he provided a clear vision for the content. Bob's photographic research and design expertise provide a visual presentation that Indians fans will greatly enjoy and his insightful editorial work adds clarity to the text.

The support of family and friends is sincerely appreciated. There are too many individuals to name separately, but you know who you are. Special thanks to Maria Eckhouse and Allen Eckhouse who patiently put up with the author through thick and thin.

—Morris Eckhouse

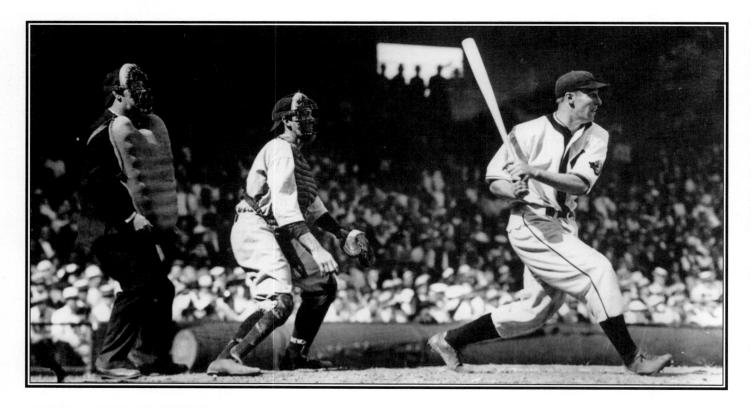

Introduction

The 1990s became the second golden era of Cleveland Indians baseball. Beginning with their 1994 move to Jacobs Field, a transformation has occurred that now finds the Indians as one of baseball's premier franchises. With five straight division titles, two World Series appearances and five seasons of consecutive sellouts, "The Tribe" is the toast of northeast Ohio. It is perhaps the most dramatic turnaround in baseball history. For much of more than three decades prior to 1994, the Indians had been a bottom-dwelling franchise on the field and at the gate.

"The Curse of Rocky Colavito" became a moniker for the unfulfilled promise and sorrowful finishes to the 34 seasons following the trade of the popular slugger to the Detroit Tigers prior to the 1960 campaign. The years 1960-1993 produced 28 losing seasons and only seven finishes higher than fifth.

Season after season, promising players would arrive to intrigue the faithful—a Sam McDowell, a Ken Harrelson, a Buddy Bell, a George Hendrick, a Wayne Garland, a Len Barker, a Bert Blyleven or a Joe Carter—but a winning mix never developed. Twenty different managers and numerous owners and general managers could not free the Tribe from the morass.

Such was the story of the Cleveland Indians: a losing team in a rust-belt city playing in the ancient, cavernous and baseball-unfriendly Municipal Stadium.

In a time when "Cleveland jokes" had gained national attention, the Indians were another reason to snicker. Their fans, however, were not laughing. They had developed their own cynical, yet steadfastly hopeful attitude. Tribe fans of the 1960s, '70s, '80s and early '90s became a curious blend of high optimism, realistic expectations and low support at the gate.

Attendance remained among the league's worst, but the general consensus was that a winner would produce a boon at the turnstiles on par with the years following World War II when the Tribe was a winner and major league baseball was at an all-time peak in popularity. Just the possibility of a contender made a difference at the gate. After the Tribe held first place briefly

early in 1986 and stayed in the pennant race for much of the campaign, home attendance climbed to the highest total in 27 years.

On the heels of an 84-78 record, the Indians, with their impressive lineup of young hitters, were declared the "best team in baseball" in *Sports Illustrated's* 1987 baseball preview issue. But the Tribe reverted to previous form and lost 101 games to touch off a streak of seven more losing seasons.

The 1960-93 era aside, the history of the Indians is surprisingly rich in contending clubs. In fact, through their first six decades, they finished in the first division of the American League—fourth place or higher—42 times. The 1920 and 1948 teams were World Series champions and the 1954 club won the AL pennant. The teams surrounding those champions were outstanding as well. The 1918, 1919 and 1922 Indians finished in second place as did six Indians clubs of the 1950s: 1951, 1952, 1953, 1955, 1956 and 1959.

The 1908 Naps lost the AL pennant by a half game to Detroit who, according to rules of the time, were not required to make up an August rainout with Washington and, thus, finished with one less loss. The 1940 Indians finished second to Detroit by a game. The 1952 and 1955 teams finished just two and three games, respectively, behind the Yankees.

Though lacking in championships, the 100-year history of the Cleveland Indians is dotted with special players and outstanding performances.

On the pitching mound, Addie Joss (1908) and Len Barker (1981) threw perfect games. Bob Feller struck out a record 18 batters against Detroit in 1938 and threw a no-hitter on opening day of 1940 versus Chicago, one of three in his career. In 1941, Al Smith and Jim Bagby Jr. combined to stop Joe DiMaggio's 56-game hitting streak at Cleveland Municipal Stadium. Johnny Allen (1937) and Gaylord Perry (1974) won 15 consecutive games. Early Wynn won his 300th game in 1963 and Cy Young won No. 500 with the 1910 Naps. Joss, Young, Feller, Wynn and Perry are Hall of Famers, as are Stan Coveleski, Bob Lemon and Satchel Paige.

Offensively, Napoleon Lajoie (1914) and Tris Speaker (1925) became the third and fifth players, respectively, to record 3,000 hits. Eddie Murray got his 3,000th as a designated hitter with the Tribe in 1995. Rocky Colavito hit four homers in a game against Baltimore in 1959. Earl Averill (1929) and Jay Bell (1986) hit home runs in their first major league at-bats. Indians players have won seven batting, six home run and eight RBI titles. Lajoie and Speaker are Hall of Famers along with shortstops Joe Sewell and Lou Boudreau, and outfielders Elmer Flick, Earl Averill and Larry Doby.

Defensively, shortstop Neal Ball executed an unassisted triple play in 1909. Second baseman Bill Wambsganss did likewise in the 1920 World Series.

Doby became the AL's first black player in 1947. Frank Robinson became baseball's first black manager in 1975. Robinson was one of several playing managers who put their imprint on Cleveland history along with Boudreau, Lajoie and Speaker.

Al Lopez played briefly as a catcher with the Tribe in 1947, but his managerial contributions helped make him a Hall of Famer. From 1951 through 1956, Lopez guid-

ed the Tribe as they battled the Yankee dynasty, winning the 1954 pennant and finishing second five times before moving on to the White Sox where he won another pennant in 1959. Among his accomplishments, Lopez will forever be remembered as the architect of the Tribe's 1954 pitching staff, one of the best in baseball history. Other managers were memorable as well, occassionally bordering on infamy. Oscar Vitt, for example, was so disliked by his players that they petitioned owner Alva Bradley to fire the feisty manager. Vitt was retained and the 1940 Indians became known as the "Cleveland Crybabies." Twenty years later, the Tribe's Joe Gordon and the Tigers' Jimmy Dykes were traded for each other, the only swap of managers in major league history.

Born as the Bluebirds (later shortened to Blues) in the minor American League of 1900, the Cleveland franchise then became an original American League entry in 1901. The name was changed to "Bronchos" in 1902, then "Naps" in 1903 in honor of their Hall-of-Fame second baseman Napoleon Lajoie. Following a last-place finish in 1914 and Lajoie's subsequent departure for the Athletics, the team was renamed one final time as the "Indians," a nickname first applied to the National League's Cleveland Spiders in 1897, the season in which outfielder Louis Sockalexis, a Penobscot Indian, joined the team. Sockalexis, who played from 1897-99, had died in 1913.

Another Hall of Famer, center fielder Tris Speaker joined the Tribe in 1916 and, like Lajoie, soon became a player-manager. For most of The Gray Eagle's tenure, which lasted from 1919 through 1926, the Indians were one of the league's top teams, winning the 1920 World Series and finishing in the second division only twice.

Following an ownership change in 1927, the Indians continued to produce quality seasons and solid players through the early Depression years, but could not match the performance of pennant winners from Philadelphia, Washington, New York or Detroit. From 1927-35, the Tribe could finish no better than third place in 1935.

One highlight, however, came not on the field, but was the field itself. On July 31, 1932, the Indians played their first game in Cleveland Municipal Stadium. Before a crowd of 80,154, Tribe pitching ace Mel Harder lost a 1-0 duel with the Athletics' Lefty Grove. Baseball on the lakefront became a tradition for six decades.

Then in 1936 came the arrival of arguably the greatest player in franchise history, the 17-year-old Iowa schoolboy and fire-balling right-hander, Bob Feller. For the better part of two decades, "Rapid Robert" became the shining symbol of Indians baseball and the pitching equivalent to his legendary hitting contemporaries, Ted Williams and Joe DiMaggio.

Feller won 266 games in 18 seasons, this in spite of 44 months in the Navy during World War II that caused him to miss the 1942-44 seasons, and most of 1945. He returned full time in 1946 to win 26 games—one of six times he would break the 20-win plateau. Feller led the American League in strikeouts seven times, threw three no-hitters and 12 one-hitters. He was elected to the Hall of Fame in 1962, his first year of eligibility.

One of Feller's few sub-par years (by his standards) was 1948, when he was 19-15. Ironically, it was also the season of the most-recent World Series title. The 1948 Tribe is the most celebrated team in franchise history.

Guided on the field by their Hall-of-Fame shortstop and manager Lou Boudreau, and off the field by the pro-motion-minded owner and general manager Bill Veeck, the Tribe emerged from a fourth-place finish in 1947 to capture their first World Series in 28 years.

They did it by beating both Boston teams—the Red Sox in a one-game playoff and the Braves in the Series, four games to two. They did it with a solid, but unspectacular, lineup whose offensive strength came from the infield where second baseman Joe Gordon and third baseman Ken Keltner hit 32 and 31 home runs, respectively, and Boudreau won the MVP award with a .355 average. And they did it with the unlikely pitching heroics of Gene Bearden, a minor-league pick-up from the Yankees who won 20 games that season, beat the Red Sox in the playoff, then won Game 3 and saved Game 6 of the World Series.

Bearden, who pitched with an aluminum plate in his head and a screw in his knee resulting from injuries suffered when his ship was sunk in World War II, was never the same again after 1948. He was 8-8 in 1949 and 1-3 in 1950 before being sold to Washington.

The Tribe was never quite the same after 1948 either. The next incarnation of the Yankee dynasty, which had begun in 1947, was in full bloom by 1949. The Indians averaged 92 victories from 1949-53, but they dropped to third in '49, fourth in 1950 and second the next three seasons. Continual retooling by general manager Hank Greenberg and a productive farm system kept the Tribe in contention, but it was not until 1954 that they would

eradicate the Yankee nemesis, if only for one season. The 1954 Indians, arguably the best in franchise history, won 111 games to finish eight ahead of the Yankees. Hall-of-Fame manager Al Lopez was at the helm by then as the Tribe's starting rotation of Bob Lemon, Early Wynn, Mike Garcia, Art Houtteman and Bob Feller combined for 93 victories. Second baseman Bobby Avila won the batting title and outfielder Larry Doby led the AL with 32 homers and 126 RBI. An unlikely combination of veteran Hal Newhouser and rookies Don Mossi and Ray Narleski formed the league's best bullpen.

But the history of the Indians is filled with triumph linked with heartache and 1954 was no exception. The Tribe had overcome one New York obstacle, but then failed to do likewise in the World Series—a four-game sweep by the Giants.

After 1954, the Tribe finished behind the Yankees four more times, then staged a memorable pennant race with Chicago's "Go-Go White Sox" through five months of the 1959 campaign. Behind Chicago by per-

centage points in late August, the Indians were swept in a four-game series by the Sox at Municipal Stadium, failed to recover and finished five games out. Not until the 1990s would they remain this closely in the hunt this deep into the season.

With 89 wins in 1959, the Indians appeared to be on the brink of another pennant as they approached the 1960 campaign. But general manager Frank "Trader" Lane, who had joined the organization in 1957,

was forever anxious to disturb the status quo. A revolving door of players was Lane's trademark wherever he went and his 38-month tenure in Cleveland was no exception, much to the eventual dismay of Tribe fans.

Following the 1959 season, Lane tinkered with the roster, making several significant trades, then made two deals too many just prior to opening day of 1960. On April 12, Lane dealt first baseman Norm Cash to Detroit for third baseman Steve Demeter. Five days later, he traded outfielder Rocky Colavito, the Indians' most popular player and one of the league's premier young sluggers, also to the Tigers, for outfielder Harvey Kuenn, the 1959 American League batting champion. The Indians dropped to fourth in 1960 at 76-78—21 games behind the Yankees. Symbolically, the Colavito trade marked the beginning to the downslide that lasted more than 30 years.

It was a gradual descent, not a dramatic drop-off. Through the rest of the 1960s, the Indians were mostly a sub-.500 ball club, finishing higher than fourth only once—third in 1968. There was a flash of brilliance in 1966 when they opened the season with 10 straight victories, had a 27-10 record and 4.5-game lead by Memorial Day, then collapsed. By June 20 they had fallen to third place and were 10 games behind Baltimore by the All-Star break. They finished fifth at 81-81.

After an 87-75 record in 1968 under new manager Alvin Dark, a 25-year plunge began with a 62-99 mark in 1969, dead last in the Tribe's first season in the American League East. From 1969-93, the Indians never finished higher than fourth, losing at least 90 games in a season nine times. Although highlights are few and far between during that period, there were some memorable events such as the debut of Frank Robinson as baseball's first black manager in 1975, the meteoric, but brief rise to stardom of the eccentric "Super Joe" Charboneau in 1980, Len Barker's perfect game in 1981 and the inspirational career of Andre Thornton.

The latter years of that span saw the beginning of the makeover that would lift the Tribe to elite status in the mid 1990s. The Jacobs brothers, Richard and David, purchased the franchise in 1986. John Hart, an assistant under general manager Hank Peters, succeeded Peters in 1991. Also in '91, Mike Hargrove replaced John McNamara as manager in the midst of the worst losing season in team history—105 defeats and a seventh-place finish. In 1992, ground was broken for construction of Jacobs Field, the jewel of Cleveland's downtown redevelopment project known as "Gateway."

With the Jacobs brothers signing the checks, Hart began a rebuilding process designed to acquire quality young players from other organizations, combine them with farm system hopefuls, then sign the best of the bunch to long-term contracts. The result would be a talented young team to occupy—and contend for the pennant—in the Indians' new Jacobs Field home in 1994. What became known as "The Cleveland Plan" has since become a successful model for other major league organizations to emulate.

Hart's trade acquisitions included catcher Sandy Alomar Jr., second baseman Carlos Baerga, shortstop Omar Vizquel and center fielder Kenny Lofton. They were joined by farm system products such as pitcher Charles Nagy, third baseman Jim Thome and outfielders Albert Belle and Manny Ramirez.

The Indians won 66 games in the strike-shortened 1994 season, their first winning campaign since 1986, then overpowered the American League in 1995 with 100 victories for their first pennant in 41 years. From 1995-99, the Tribe won five straight division championships and two American League pennants, although losing the World Series both times—to the Atlanta Braves in 1995 and to the Florida Marlins in 1997.

Hart's ongoing player moves and a continually productive farm system have kept the Tribe in contention, but pitching has remained a trouble spot. The seeds of frustration were sewn when the Indians were eliminated from the 1999 playoffs by Boston after leading the series 2-0. The result was the firing of Mike Hargrove.

Hargrove's successor, Charlie Manuel and the sale of the franchise to Larry Dolan have cast a new light on Indians baseball in the year 2000. What's not likely to change is the fan support. Although their expectation level has risen, their optimism, patience and enthusiasm remain intact. In the Tribe's 100th season, the Yankee nemesis still exists and the White Sox and Royals are coming on strong in the Central. But with an arsenal featuring some of the greatest names in the game, the fans remain hopeful that the Indians will get several more title shots and win their first World Series championship since that glorious and memorable season of 1948.

The Forest Citys and Spiders

1869–1900

Baseball in Cleveland existed well before the creation of the American League and the American League club now known as the Cleveland Indians. Evidence of baseball in Cleveland dates back at least as far as 1845, when ball playing was banned in Cleveland's Public Square. The ban did not last long. One hundred and fifty years later, Cleveland's baseball Mecca was just south of Public Square and a major contributor to the resurgence of the city. The beginning of professional baseball in Cleveland is generally pegged at June 2, 1869. On that date, the Cleveland Forest Citys played the legendary Cincinnati Red Stockings. Recognized as the first team to be comprised entirely of professional (paid) players, Cincinnati lived up to its reputation with a 25-6 triumph over Cleveland. The Red Stockings won another contest against Cleveland, later in 1869, by a 43-27 score. Other notable matches for the 1869 Forest Citys included a 41-27 loss to the Eckfords of Brooklyn and a split of two games with the Haymakers of Troy, New York. In another memorable game on May 17, 1870, Cleveland outscored the Atlantic & Great Western Railways club in a five-inning contest, 132-1.

Professional baseball's evolution continued with the creation of the National Association of Professional Baseball Players in 1871. Cleveland was one of nine teams in the NA in 1871 along with the Athletics of Philadelphia, Boston Red Stockings, Chicago White Stockings, Mutuals of New York, Olympics of Washington (DC), Union Club of Troy (New York), Kekiongas of Fort Wayne (Indiana) and Forest Citys of Rockford (Illinois). In its opening game on May 4, 1871 (the first game in NA history), at Fort Wayne, Cleveland suffered a 2-0 loss to Bobby Mathews. Cleveland's home opener in 1871 came on May 11, against Chicago, in a new park at Willson Avenue (now East 55th Street) and Garden Street (now Central Avenue).

Patsy Tebeau hit .282 for the 1889 Spiders, then jumped to the Cleveland entry in the Players' League along with several teammates. He returned in 1891 for eight more seasons as the Spiders' first baseman and manager before being transferred to the NL's St. Louis Browns by Frank Robison, who owned both franchises.

PYRIGHTED 1888 BY
ODWIN & CO. N.Y.

LEGENDS OF THE TRIBE

When the Cleveland team felt it was getting unfair treatment from umpire James L. Haynie, an experienced umpire but also a Chicago sportswriter, the home team vacated the field and left Chicago to an 18-10 victory. Cleveland finished seventh among the nine teams that completed the season, winning 10 games and losing 19. Shortstop John Bass led the Association with 10 triples. Pitcher Al Pratt is credited with all 10 of Cleveland's wins and led the circuit in strikeouts (34). Cleveland's legacy in the NA ended on August 19, 1872. Following an 18-7 to loss to Boston, and with six wins against 16 losses, Cleveland dropped out of the league.

The National League, established in 1876, admitted Cleveland on December 4, 1878. A young Cleveland businessman, William Hollinger, organized the club. The city's first NL team had two players of particular note, pitcher Jim McCormick and Jack Glasscock, a second baseman in 1879 who moved to shortstop in 1880. Outfielder Charlie Eden led the league with 31 doubles and hit three home runs. McCormick pitched in 62 of 82 games with 59 complete games and 546.1 innings pitched.

Cleveland finished sixth in the eight team league in 1879, but jumped to third in 1880 (47-37), adding star players in second baseman Fred Dunlap, outfielder Ned Hanlon, and outfielder Pete Hotaling. McCormick, five-feet 10-inches tall, weighed in at some 220 pounds, making him one of the great heavy pitchers of all time. Jumbo Jim led the NL with 45 wins, 72 complete games, and 657.2 innings pitched. Dunlap led the league with 27 doubles and hit four home runs.

Led by McCormick and Glasscock, Cleveland continued in the NL until 1884 with mixed results. Its best season came in 1883. With 28 wins from McCormick and 23 from "One Arm" Hugh Daily, Cleveland finished at 55-42, 7.5 games behind first-place Boston. When Daily jumped to the Union Association and McCormick followed during the season, the team fell to seventh place (35-77) in 1884.

The first, but not last, association between Cleveland and St. Louis clubs came in 1885 when Henry V. Lucas, creator of the Union Association, purchased the Cleveland club and put his St. Louis club in the NL. The 1885 St. Louis NL team featured such familiar Cleveland faces as Dunlap and Glasscock. The club finished last in the NL in 1885 (36-72). Major league baseball was absent from Cleveland in 1885 and 1886.

Frank DeHaas Robison became determined to bring major league baseball back to Cleveland. To Robison, a trolley car magnate, baseball was a way to put riders on his transit line and to collect from them again at the ballpark. Robison landed a franchise in the American Association, then a major league.

The new team would play in a park near Robison's trolley line, bounded by East 39th Street, East 35th Street, Euclid Avenue and Payne Avenue. Cleveland was less than a rousing success in the AA, but showed sufficient promise to earn another berth in the National League, replacing Detroit in the senior circuit at the start of the 1889 campaign. The team would be known as the Spiders, due to the thin, wiry, nature of many of its players.

In 1890, the upstart Players' League placed a team in Cleveland. The new league, created by players who hoped to take control of the game, rather than serve outside owners, lured star players from the NL and the AA. Top players from Cleveland's 1889 NL team, including third baseman Oliver Wendell "Patsy" Tebeau, outfielder Larry Twitchell and rookie outfielder Jim McAleer, jumped to the new league. Both

Catcher Chief Zimmer joined the Spiders for their first season in the American Association in 1887, became the starter a year later and remained in the lineup until moving on to Louisville in 1899. Zimmer batted a career-high .340 in the championship season of 1895.

The Forest Citys and Spiders

The 1895 Spiders finished in second place, three games behind Baltimore in the National League race, then beat the Orioles, four games to one, for the Temple Cup championship.

Cleveland teams suffered. The Spiders ran seventh (44-88), as did the Players' League club (55-75). Financial losses were felt all the way around. Ultimately, the backers of the new league bailed out on the players and what amounted to a one-year experiment of employee-owned ball clubs came to an abrupt end.

The return of Tebeau and McAleer to the Spiders bolstered an up-and-coming team that included shortstop Ed McKean, outfielder George Davis, catcher Chief Zimmer, and sophomore pitcher Denton True "Cy" Young. Born on March 29, 1867, in Gilmore, Ohio, Young had gone 9-7 for the Spiders in 1890. In 1891, Cy (short for cyclone) won 27 games and Cleveland moved up to fifth place.

Cleveland's big league ball clubs had many homes during the nineteenth century. The wooden park at Payne Avenue was severely damaged by fire in 1890. Finally, in 1891, just as major league baseball was taking a foothold in Cleveland, so too did a playing site. The site was further East along Robison's trolley line at East 66th Street and Lexington Avenue. League Park opened on May 1, 1891, when Young pitched the Spiders to victory. The new park, with a capacity of about 10,000, was heralded as an outstanding baseball facility. The east-side site would remain the home of major league baseball in Cleveland for more than half a century.

A taste of championship baseball finally came to Cleveland in 1892. The American Association had folded and the National League had bloated up to 12 teams. The NL adopted a new split-season format with the best team of the first half to face the best team of the second half in a championship series.

An outstanding Boston team, led by Hall-of-Fame manager Frank Selee, took the first half title with a 52-22 record. Cleveland took the second half title with a 53-23 mark. The National League World Series of 1892 began on October 17 in Cleveland before 6,000 fans. Young pitched shutout ball, but the Spiders could not score against "Happy" Jack Stivetts and the game was called due to darkness after 11 innings. Boston ran off five straight victories to win the series.

The 1892 championship series did not live up to expectations and no series was played the following season when the Spiders finished third (73-55). From 1894 to

1897, the Temple Cup series would be the equivalent of today's World Series, with the first and second place NL teams facing each other. The winner would receive a trophy donated by William C. Temple. Cleveland finished sixth in 1894, never challenging for the post-season series.

Cleveland's first truly great major league team emerged in 1895. Cy Young led the NL in wins (35) and outfielder Jesse "The Crab" Burkett led the league in batting average (.409) and hits (225) while scoring 153 runs. With a strong supporting cast including Tebeau, second baseman Cupid Childs, McKean, McAleer, Zimmer, and 26-game winner Nig Cuppy, Cleveland challenged the famed Baltimore Orioles for first place. Led by one time Cleveland rookie-turned-Hall-of-Fame-manager Ned Hanlon, the Orioles featured other Hall of Famers in third baseman John McGraw, catcher Wilbert Robinson and outfielder Willie Keeler. In the end, Baltimore topped Cleveland with 87 victories, but the Spiders' 84 wins were good enough for second place and a spot in the Temple Cup series.

Once again, Cy Young got the call for the series opener on October 2. With two runs in the ninth, the Spiders prevailed, 5-4, before 8,000 fans at League Park. Nig Cuppy pitched a five-hitter in the second game and three first-inning runs propelled the Spiders to a 7-2 victory in front of 10,000. Young was in top form for game three, a 7-1 Spiders win before a crowd of 12,000. The series moved to Baltimore where Duke Esper held Cleveland to five hits in a 5-0 Orioles win.

The fifth game became a scoreless duel between Young and Bill Hoffer for six innings. Young started a three-run rally in the seventh with a double. The Spiders added two runs in the eighth and Young earned his third win of the series, 5-2, and the Temple Cup championship for Cleveland, four games to one.

The two teams ran one-two again in the 1896 NL race with the Orioles (90-39) outdistancing the Spiders (80-48). In the Temple Cup series, Baltimore solidified its claim as professional baseball's top team by sweeping the series in four games.

Unlike the 1895 series, however, the rematch was marked by sizable apathy. The largest crowd was for the opener in Baltimore on October 2, 1896, when 4,000 fans saw Hoffer defeat Young, 7-1. Only 3,100 showed up the following day for the Orioles' 7-2 victory and just 2,000 came out for the third game when Hoffer won again, defeating Cuppy 6-2. Only 1,500 attended the lone game in Cleveland on October 8 when Joe Corbett won his second game of the series, beating Cuppy 5-0.

The 1897 season was notable for the arrival of outfielder Louis Sockalexis, a much-heralded athlete and Native American. Although he played just 94 major league games, all in a Cleveland uniform, his impact on Cleveland baseball far outweighs raw numbers. Sockalexis had been a star in two seasons at Holy Cross with an overall batting average of .444. According to Jay Feldman's article, "The Rise and Fall of Louis Sockalexis," (*Baseball Research Journal*, 1986), "Manager Patsy Tebeau signed Sock on sight for $1,500 a year." After Sockalexis's arrival, the Cleveland club was often referred to as the Indians.

Jesse Burkett led the National League with a .409 batting average in the championship season of 1895. Known as "The Crab," Burkett played eight of his 16 professional seasons in the Spiders' outfield. He was inducted into the National Baseball Hall of Fame in 1946.

Outfielder Louis Sockalexis joined the Spiders in 1897 as a former college baseball star from Holy Cross who then became the first native American to gain notoriety playing major league baseball. His popularity found the Spiders often referred to as the "Indians" during his brief career. When the Cleveland Naps sought a new nickname in 1915 following the departure of Napoleon Lajoie, the franchise was renamed "Indians," recalling that bygone era of baseball in Cleveland.

According to Feldman, at the beginning of the 1897 season Sockalexis was the "hottest gate attraction in baseball." The addition of such a talent should have strengthened Cleveland for another title run. Instead, the Spiders fell from contention to fifth place (69-62), despite another stellar season from Burkett.

"Chief" Sockalexis started brilliantly, then tapered off to a .338 batting average in 66 games. He played just 21 games in 1898 and his brief major league career ended with seven games in 1899. The Cleveland Indian would not be the last player to take the city by storm and then quickly fade from stardom.

By 1899, the Spiders had fallen from championship contention and from the favor of owner Robison. Also the owner of the NL club in St. Louis (ownership of multiple teams, not allowed by today's Major League Baseball rules, was permitted then), Robison transferred the best Spiders (Tebeau, Childs, Burkett, Young and Cuppy) to St. Louis. Cleveland was left with a hopeless collection of players, known by a variety of derogatory nicknames, most notably the Misfits. The 1899 Spiders won just 20 while losing 134, finishing dead last.

The franchise was dropped from the NL following the season as the league cut down from 12 teams to eight. Visionary baseball executive Ban Johnson seized the opportunity presented by the downsizing and the long-standing NL monopoly of major league baseball by moving to turn his minor league Western League into the major league American League.

Cleveland represented a major league city without a major league team. Johnson moved to fill the void by arranging to relocate the Western League's Grand Rapids franchise to Cleveland. The 1900 American League would be comprised of Cleveland, Milwaukee, Chicago, Kansas City, Minneapolis, Indianapolis, Detroit and Buffalo.

Johnson needed financial backing, much of which was provided by 30-year-old Charles W. Somers. The young man and his father had become wealthy in the coal business. Joining Somers to head up the financial backing for a new Cleveland club was another young Clevelander, John F. Kilfoyl, who owned a men's clothing store. He was also part of a family real estate business. Kilfoyl became the president and treasurer of the new club. Somers became vice president.

Somers's dollars not only got the Cleveland franchise off the ground, but later enabled Johnson's AL to compete head to head with the NL by also funding operations in Boston, Chicago, St. Louis and Philadelphia. In 1901 and 1902, Somers was recognized as owner of the Boston AL club at the same time he was an owner of the Cleveland club, much like Frank Robison's ownership in the Cleveland and St. Louis NL clubs in the 1890s. With Somers's money and Kilfoyl's business skill, Cleveland had the front office backbone to revive baseball in the city.

Key to the rebirth of major league baseball in Cleveland was a "peace" agreement between Johnson's American League and the established National League. Terms provided that the AL would be a minor league in 1900, that the NL would allow an AL club in Chicago and would allow Cleveland's AL team use of League Park.

Cleveland's only season in the minor American League was not a rousing success, but was sufficient to show there was a place for major league baseball in the Forest City. Managed by Jimmy McAleer, the team finished sixth at 63-73, but a solid foundation was in place for Cleveland's return to major league baseball. The city had been home to champion-caliber clubs and future Hall of Famers Ned Hanlon, George Davis, Cy Young and Jesse Burkett. If not as good as the clubs of 1895 and '96, the talent at the start of the 1900s was a great improvement from the dreadful 1899 Spiders. One star player could make the difference and bring Cleveland back into baseball's elite.

Jimmy McAleer joined the Spiders' outfield in 1889, jumped to the Players' League in 1890, then returned in 1891 for eight more seasons. McAleer became the first manager of the AL's Cleveland Blues in 1901, but after a seventh-place finish, he moved on to the St. Louis Browns (1902-09) and to Washington (1910-11).

The Forest Citys and Spiders

INNING 2

A New League and Nap Lajoie

1901–1915

The dawn of the American League as a major league began in 1901 with Cleveland looking for further improvement and with Napoleon Lajoie playing for the Philadelphia Athletics of Connie Mack. In 1901, the American League took on recognition as a major league alongside the 25-year-old National League. Gone from the AL's 1900 roster were the cities of Kansas City, Minneapolis, Indianapolis and Buffalo. In their place were Boston, Philadelphia, Baltimore and Washington. The AL and NL would compete head to head in three cities: Boston, Philadelphia and Chicago. Once Milwaukee shifted to St. Louis (1902) and Baltimore to New York (1903), creating two more head-to-head battles with the NL, the AL lineup remained unchanged for half a century. Cleveland's return to championship caliber baseball would hinge on Lajoie's future in Philadelphia.

Napoleon Lajoie began his major league career on August 12, 1896, with the Philadelphia Phillies as a 22-year-old first baseman, of French-Canadian descent, from Woonsocket, Rhode Island. In his first full season (1897), he led the National League in slugging percentage (.569) and batted .361. The following year, he moved to second base as Philadelphia completely overhauled its infield. In 1898, according to modern records, he led the NL with 127 runs batted in. By 1900, Lajoie was established as one of the major stars of major league baseball.

Following the 1900 season, American League teams took bold steps to lure established National League stars to the junior circuit. Lajoie accepted a substantial offer from Connie Mack and jumped to the new Philadelphia club of the American League. In his first season with the Athletics, Lajoie set an AL record by batting .426 and led the league in runs scored, hits, doubles, home runs, runs batted in, on base percentage and slugging percentage.

The 1901 Cleveland team of manager James R. McAleer finished seventh among eight teams. Baseball records credit pitcher Earl Moore with 16 of Cleveland's 54 victories (against 82 defeats) and outfielder Ollie Pickering with 102 of 667 runs scored. On May 9, 1901, Moore pitched no-hit ball at League Park for nine innings against Chicago, only to lose a 4-2 decision when Chicago got two hits in the 10th inning. Bill Bradley, snatched from the National League, was installed at third base and began a notable career in Cleveland. A native Clevelander, Bradley jumped at the opportunity to play for his hometown team. Home attendance for the year of 131,380 ranked last in both leagues, but was a substantial improvement from the attendance for the NL Cleveland team from 1897 to 1899. At least Cleveland was back in the major leagues.

For a nickname, the new team went in a new direction. For its first season in the major league American League, Cleveland's team would be called the Blues, reflective of the club's blue uniforms. For a home, the Blues remained at League Park. In 1901, Cleveland's home yard retained a basic capacity for about 9,000 fans, similar in size to its AL counterparts in Boston (Huntington Avenue Baseball Grounds), Detroit (Bennett Park) and Philadelphia (Columbia Park), but smaller than South Side Park, home of Chicago's AL club, which could hold some 15,000 fans.

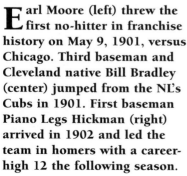

Earl Moore (left) threw the first no-hitter in franchise history on May 9, 1901, versus Chicago. Third baseman and Cleveland native Bill Bradley (center) jumped from the NL's Cubs in 1901. First baseman Piano Legs Hickman (right) arrived in 1902 and led the team in homers with a career-high 12 the following season.

Soon after Lajoie's jump to the AL, Phillies owner John Rogers filed for an injunction that would bar Lajoie (and pitchers Bill Bernhard and Chick Fraser) from playing for other teams. The Court of Common Pleas denied the action by the Phillies, but, on April 21, 1902, the Philadelphia Supreme Court overturned the lower court decision and ruled that Lajoie could not play for a team other than the Phillies. He was pulled out of the opening game of the 1902 season at Baltimore on April 23 when Mack was handed a temporary restraining order forbidding Lajoie from playing for Philadelphia's AL club. In appreciation for the financial help Somers gave Mack to start his franchise, the Athletics' owner-manager sent Lajoie to Cleveland where he hit .379 for his new club.

LEGENDS OF THE TRIBE

Under new manager William R. Armour, Cleveland improved by 15 games to finish fifth in 1902 with a 69-67 record. Attendance more than doubled to 275,395 and was fifth best among the 16 major league teams. Uninspired by the name Blues (or sometimes Bluebirds), the players chose the more forceful nickname of Bronchos for the 1902 season. With the arrival of Lajoie, the team was indeed stronger.

The legal wrangling continued and Lajoie was unable to play for Cleveland when the team went to Philadelphia. A grudging truce ultimately was adopted by the AL and the NL. No further action was taken against the players who jumped leagues.

The other dramatic Cleveland debut of 1902 belonged to Addie Joss. As a teenager, he had gained notice pitching in Wisconsin and signed with the minor league Toledo Mud Hens. With 19 wins in 1900 and 25 in 1901, Joss became a prized commodity. Bill Armour convinced Joss to sign with Cleveland. Born in Woodland, Wisconsin, on April 12, 1880, Joss was a rare college-educated player who took no time in displaying his brilliance at the major league level. In his first start for the Naps, Joss pitched a one-hitter. He won 17 games as a rookie, matching Bernhard and Moore for the club lead.

Also joining the 1902 Bronchos was outfielder Elmer Flick. Like Lajoie, Flick had played for Philadelphia's NL team, then jumped to Connie Mack's forces. Like Lajoie, Flick was barred from playing for Mack's team, but was kept in the junior circuit by being sent to Cleveland. A native of northeast Ohio (born in Bedford), the 26-year-old Flick hit .297 in his hometown debut.

That Lajoie was the dominant force in Cleveland baseball was reflected in 1903 when the nickname Naps, in Lajoie's honor, was applied to the club. In voting conducted by *The Cleveland Press*, Naps (or Napoleons) received 365 votes, Buckeyes 281, Emperors 276, Metropolitans 239, Giants 223 and Cyclops 214. The club set another attendance record (311,280).

In 1904, Lajoie became the first player-manager for the young franchise. (McAleer did play three games for the 1901 club while winding down his playing career.) Lajoie won the batting title in both seasons and the Naps showed steady improvement with 77

The newly-renamed Naps pose in their Sunday best before boarding the train for spring training of 1903. Their namesake, second baseman and future manager Nap Lajoie is seated third from the left.

A New League and Nap Lajoie

Bob Rhoads was one of three 20-game winners (22-10) for the Naps of 1906. He was joined by Addie Joss (21-9) and Otto Hess (20-17). Rhoads later won 18 games for the second-place Naps in 1908, including the second no-hitter in franchise history on September 18 against the Red Sox.

wins in 1903 and 86 in 1904. The 1904 club gave Cleveland its first taste of American League championship-caliber play, finishing fourth, 7.5 games out of first place.

While Lajoie was clearly the star, he was surrounded with other stars such as Joss, Flick and Bradley. The 1904 team led the AL with a .260 batting average and 647 runs scored. Six pitchers, Bernhard, Red Donahue, Otto Hess, Joss, Moore, and Bob Rhoads accounted for 152 of Cleveland's 154 games started and 140 complete games.

Joining Cleveland as Lajoie's keystone partner in 1904 was 23-year-old shortstop Terry Turner. Better with the glove than the bat, "Cotton" Turner would spend 15 seasons in Cleveland and become (and remain) the club's all-time leader with 1,619 games played (five more than Lajoie).

Lajoie's domination of the local baseball scene became complete when Armour stepped down as manager on September 9. Lajoie was appointed player-manager for the next season. In 1905, Lajoie's first full season in the position, Cleveland sprung from the gate quickly and led the AL on July 1. But on that day, Lajoie suffered a serious spike wound at second base resulting in blood poisoning. With the effectiveness of the Frenchman decreased by the injury, the Naps slipped out of pennant contention and below the break-even level in the won-loss ledger, despite having the league's batting leader in Flick with his .306 average. Another club attendance record was set (316,306). The one-season setback preceded the peak of the Lajoie era, a three-year run of topnotch baseball.

Cleveland, Chicago and New York battled for the AL pennant in 1906 as the Naps set a club record with 89 victories. Bob Rhoads led the team with 22 wins and Joss added 21. Lajoie batted .355 and set a club record with 214 hits. For all its talent, Cleveland could not keep pace when Chicago's "hitless wonders" embarked on a 19-game winning streak in August and September. The Naps finished third, five games off the pace.

By 1907, the Detroit Tigers had joined the elite AL clubs, led by young Ty Cobb, playing in just his second full season. Joss won a league-high 27 games for the Naps, but Cobb led the AL in batting average, hits, total bases, RBI, and stolen bases. Cleveland's 85-67 record ranked fourth behind the pennant-winning Tigers, Philadelphia and Chicago.

Cobb's talent was matched by his truculence. The idea of a more harmonious Detroit team gave rise to the idea of a trade between the Tigers and Naps that would exchange batting stars Cobb and Flick, both future Hall of Famers. Ultimately, there was no trade. As fate unfolded, Flick had peaked and would fade quickly. Cobb was just getting started.

For many fans, the 1908 season is an ideal. In the National League, Chicago, New York and Pittsburgh went down to the wire in a race defined by Fred Merkle's so-called "boner," a base running blunder which, in the minds of many, cost New York the pennant. The American League race was just as tight between Cobb's Tigers, the White Sox of workhorse spitball pitcher and 40-game winner Ed Walsh, and the Naps. Lajoie and Joss led the way for the Naps, but two other key players did not contribute much. Flick was ill and played just nine games. Turner was injured and played just 60 games. Bill Hinchman and George Perring picked up the slack at shortstop and Josh Clarke stepped in for Flick. While the offense held its own, the pitching staff was best in all the majors with a 2.02 earned run average. Addie Joss won 24 and "Dusty" Rhoads added 18.

On September 18, Rhoads pitched a no-hitter against Boston, giving the Naps their 12th victory in 14 games, part of a run of 15 wins in 18 games that vaulted the club into the pennant chase, one game behind first-place Detroit. By month's end, the Naps, Tigers and White Sox were neck, neck and neck, setting the stage for one of baseball's all-time great games.

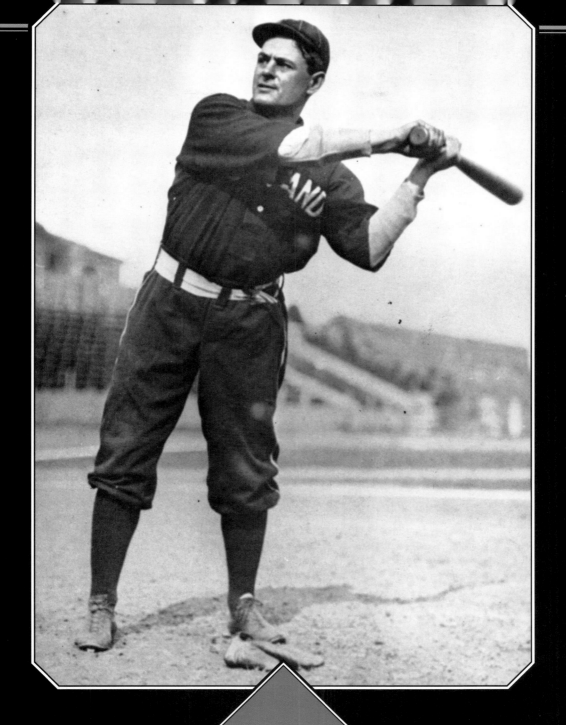

ELMER FLICK

OF • Bronchos/Naps • 1902-1910   National Baseball Hall of Fame, 1963

For the pitching matchup on Friday, October 2, 1908, it was Joss against Walsh. Almost 11,000 fans squeezed into League Park where "Big Ed" allowed just four hits and struck out 15 batters while Joss was perfect, facing 27 men and retiring them all. The lone run of Cleveland's 1-0 victory was scored in the third inning by Joe Birmingham who singled, stole second, took third on a wild throw by Walsh and came home when a wicked Walsh spitball eluded catcher Ossee Schreckengost. The Naps concluded the day a half game behind the Tigers.

The Joss-Walsh duel is still judged by many to be the greatest game of pitching in baseball history, especially considering the pressure-cooker playing conditions. Joss's perfect game was the fourth in major league history, following John Lee Richmond (against Cleveland) in 1880, John Montgomery Ward in 1880 and Cy Young in 1904.

On October 2, 1908, Addie Joss and Chicago's Big Ed Walsh (right photo, left-right) battled in a 1-0 pitchers duel in which Joss threw a perfect game and Walsh threw a four-hitter. Two days later, Bill Hinchman (above) was called out after failing to beat out a tie-breaking hit in the ninth inning at St. Louis. The game finished tied and was replayed the next day whereupon the Browns defeated the Naps to eliminate them from the race.

The following day, a huge crowd of 20,729 (twice the attendance for the Joss-Walsh matchup), packed League Park. Thousands of fans stood in the roped-off outfield. Another low-scoring game was 3-2 in favor of the White Sox when Cleveland loaded the bases in the seventh. Walsh emerged from the bullpen and struck out Lajoie to end the threat. Chicago prevailed while Detroit won its game and increased its lead over the Naps to a game and a half.

Cleveland traveled to St. Louis for its next game on Sunday, October 4, known for Bill Hinchman's "boner." In the ninth inning, Hinchman appeared to drive home Joss with a tie breaking run to give the Naps a 4-3 lead. Instead, Hinchman was ruled out at first on umpire Jack Egan's controversial call. Some viewers claimed that Hinchman was not running full speed to first and would have otherwise beaten the play. Others blamed Egan and questioned his work in Cleveland games during the season. Either way, the game remained tied after 11 innings and had to be replayed the following day.

The Browns ended Cleveland's pennant dreams with a 3-1 win on October 5, mathematically eliminating the Naps from the pennant race. Detroit held off Chicago and earned its second straight trip to the World Series. Cleveland's record of 90 wins and 64 losses left the club just a half game behind Detroit's 90-63 mark. Chicago finished a game back at 88-64. (The difference in games played by Cleveland, Detroit and Chicago resulted from the fact that baseball's rules of the times did not count tie games or require rain-outs to be made up despite the effect an unequal number of games

played could cause in the final standings.) The 1908 Naps set a franchise attendance record (422,262), cracking the 400,000 mark for the first time, and remained in the middle of the pack among big league gate attractions.

The 1908 season was the plateau of the Lajoie era of baseball in Cleveland. After the season, John Kilfoyl, unnerved by the pennant race, gradually bowed out of the picture. Charles Somers became club president and E.S. Barnard became vice president. With Somers's money and Barnard's acumen, a network of minor league clubs was built, including teams in the American Association, Pacific Coast League and Southern Association. An improved infrastructure, however, did not bring improvement in the standings for the remainder of the Somers ownership. Cleveland's best chance to win a pennant for Somers had come in 1908. For the following seven years, Cleveland came within 20 games of first place only once (1913).

Entering the 1909 season, fans had every reason to expect another pennant run with help from a familiar face. Cy Young was acquired by the Naps, returning to Cleveland after having spent the previous eight years in Boston. Young had won 241 games for the Spiders from 1890 through 1898. After two seasons in St. Louis, Young, like so many others, jumped from the NL to the AL. With Boston, he won 192 games, paced the AL in wins its first three seasons, and led the team to the World Series in 1903.

After winning 21 games for Boston in 1908, the 42-year-old Young won 19 for Cleveland in 1909, but lost 15. Lajoie regained his batting form, hitting .324, but Joss slipped from 24 victories to 14 and Flick was finished. Cleveland's run production slipped drastically and the Naps fell far off the pace in 1909 with 19 fewer victories than in 1908 as Detroit won its third straight American League pennant.

Elmer Flick played 24 games in 1910, his final major league campaign. In nine seasons with Cleveland, the local product hit .299. He led the American League in triples three consecutive seasons (1905-1907). Overshadowed by Lajoie, Flick was a model of consistency from 1902 through 1907, batting between .295 and .311 each season and in the top five in offensive production (according to *Total Baseball*, sixth edition) for four straight seasons starting in 1904. His all-around excellence was rewarded with induction into the National Baseball Hall of Fame in 1963.

Bill Bradley's career with the Naps also ended in 1910. He was released, spent three more seasons in the minor leagues and concluded his playing career with two seasons in the short-lived Federal League. The Cleveland native was rock-solid at third base for

The 1908 Naps nearly won the first pennant in club history, finishing at 90-64, a half game behind the Tigers (90-63) who, under baseball rules of the day, were not required to make up a rained-out game against Washington.

ADDIE JOSS

P • Bronchos/Naps • 1902-1910   National Baseball Hall of Fame, 1978

LEAGUE PARK.

Cleveland Sixth City

a decade (1901-1910), both offensively and defensively, establishing a standard for play at the hot corner that would be matched by few future Cleveland players. After Bradley's departure, Terry Turner began to see most of the action at third.

As Flick and Bradley left, a new, unique Cleveland baseball personality came onto the scene. John Gladstone "Jack" Graney began his baseball career as a pitcher, but wildness played a part in his moving to the outfield. Graney moved into the Naps' outfield in 1910 and became a dependable run producer. In 1914, he was the first batter to face rookie pitcher Babe Ruth of the Red Sox. Graney is recognized as being the first player to wear a uniform number (June 26, 1916) and, later, as the first player to make the transition from the playing field to the broadcast booth.

The strain of managing had seemingly taken a toll on Nap Lajoie. During the 1909 season, on August 17, he returned to player-only status (the team retained the "Naps" name) and the managerial chair became a hot seat. James McGuire took the reins from Lajoie. George Stovall, Cleveland's starting first baseman since 1907, added managerial duties and replaced McGuire in 1911, but was traded to the Browns following the season. Harry Davis began as manager in 1912 and lasted 125 games before giving way to the superb defensive outfielder, Joe Birmingham, who remained until being fired on May 21, 1915. Lee Fohl, a former minor league catcher, replaced Birmingham.

Following the 1909 season, the wooden version of League Park was torn down. In its place, a modern, concrete Cleveland baseball cathedral was constructed. A two-deck affair, the new League Park had a seating capacity of 21,000. The bench seats of the old park were replaced with individual seats for Cleveland's baseball patrons.

The new park had dimensions of 385 feet down the left field line, 505 feet to the deepest corner of the outfield (just left of center field), 420 feet to dead center field and 290 feet down the right field line. To compensate for the short distance from home plate to right field, a 20-foot-high wall, with a chicken-wire fence reaching up another 20 feet atop the wall, was built. Part of a wave of new steel-and-concrete ballparks, the new League Park, preceded by the openings of Shibe Park in Philadelphia (1909), Forbes Field in Pittsburgh (1909) and Comiskey Park in Chicago (1910), gave Cleveland one of the most modern facilities in baseball.

Rejuvenated at the plate without the burden of managing, Lajoie pursued Cobb for the 1910 AL batting championship, one of the most memorable in the annals of baseball. Cobb had rattled off three straight batting crowns (1907-09) and was out to match Lajoie's record of four in a row (1901-04). On October 9, Lajoie collected eight hits, seven of them bunts, in a doubleheader against the Browns. The effort gave him a .384

Shortstop Neal Ball (left) executed the first unassisted triple play in American League history on July 19, 1909, at League Park versus the Red Sox. In 1910, the Naps moved into the renovated League Park (above) with its steel-and-concrete stands and a seating capacity increased to 21,000.

average, one point better than Cobb's. Within the week, on October 15, AL President Ban Johnson adjusted Cobb's final average to .385 and awarded him the title.

The Chalmers Automobile Company, which provided a new car to the batting champion, compromised and gave cars to both Cobb and Lajoie. Decades later, researchers uncovered evidence that a record-keeping mistake had given Cobb additional hits and at-bats, adjusting his all-time hit record and, to some, the outcome of the batting race.

Despite an improved ballpark and the feats of Young and Lajoie, Cleveland finished a distant fifth in the 1910 AL pennant race, 32 games behind the world champion Philadelphia Athletics.

Stout Cy Young, with aging legs and an expanded waistline, won just seven games in 1910, but one was

Although Cy Young (left) was well past his prime when he joined the Naps in 1909, he did win 19 games. Young won the 500th of his career at age 43 in 1910, the same season that outfielder Shoeless Joe Jackson (right) arrived from Philadelphia.

memorable. On July 19, he was credited with his 500th victory by pitching Cleveland to an 11-inning, 5-2 victory against Washington. He started the 1911 season in Cleveland, then finished what was the last of his 22 major league seasons in Boston with the National League's Braves. No other major league pitcher has ever approached the 500-win plateau and Young's record of 511 career victories is among the most unreachable of baseball's achievements.

As the first decade of the twentieth century ended, Philadelphia's AL club was loaded with talent to the extent that Connie Mack's club had little need for a young, raw, outfielder named Joe Jackson. While Jackson gave plenty of evidence of being a budding hitting star, he also gave plenty of indication of being completely uncomfortable in a large eastern city like Philadelphia. Mack sent Jackson to the Naps where

"Shoeless" Joe would succeed Lajoie as Cleveland's dominant hitter and chief rival to Cobb for AL batting honors. In four full seasons (1911-14), Jackson became the best hitter in club history. For his entire tenure in Cleveland (1910-15), Jackson set a team record with a .375 batting average.

Bleak news came with the start of the 1911 season. Addie Joss, who won just five games in 1910 (including his second no-hitter for the Naps), proved to be suffering from tubercular meningitis. He was just 31 years old when he died on April 14, 1911, in Toledo. In his brief, but brilliant Cleveland career, Joss won 160 games, still one of the highest victory totals in franchise history. He remains the club's all-time leader in career earned run average (1.89), career shutouts (45) and career winning percentage (.623). He was inducted into the National Baseball Hall of Fame in 1978.

The entire team attended his funeral, causing a delay of the opening game of the season at Detroit. A revolt was avoided when AL president Johnson granted a postponement of the opener so that members of the Naps and the Tigers could travel to Toledo for the services. On July 24, 1911, the Cleveland club staged a benefit game to honor Joss and help his surviving family. The game, between the Naps and a group of major league stars, is one of the most memorable events in Cleveland baseball history.

A forerunner of today's All-Star Game, the Addie Joss Benefit Game was the brainchild of E.S. Barnard. Rival teams and players were all supportive. Ty Cobb was one of the first to indicate he would participate. Other future Hall of Famers that played included center fielder Tris Speaker of the Red Sox, second baseman Eddie Collins and third baseman Frank "Home Run" Baker of the Philadelphia Athletics, outfielder Sam Crawford of the Tigers, shortstop Bobby Wallace of the Browns and pitcher Walter Johnson of the Senators. Also on hand were Senators first baseman Germany Schaefer and Cleveland native Paddy Livingston, a catcher with the A's.

Cobb forgot to bring his uniform. Thus, he got two of the all-stars' 15 hits wearing borrowed Cleveland flannels. Hal Chase was the offensive star with three hits for the stars. Cy Young started for Cleveland and surrendered three runs in three innings as the

The Addie Joss Benefit Game on July 24, 1911, featured stars of the American League (above) against the Naps at League Park. Ty Cobb (first row) wore a Cleveland uniform after he forgot to bring his Detroit flannels. Future Indians on the AL roster included Smoky Joe Wood and Walter Johnson (standing, third and fourth from left) and Tris Speaker (seated, second from left).

NAP LAJOIE

2B-Mgr•Bronchos/Naps•1902-1914   National Baseball Hall of Fame, 1937

All-Stars beat the Naps, 5-3. With an overflow crowd of 15,272 fans at League Park, the event generated $12,931.60 for Mrs. Joss and the Joss family.

Another notable development of 1911 was the first professional baseball game played in Cleveland on a Sunday. State Representative Joseph Greeves sponsored legislation to permit baseball on the Sabbath in Ohio. The first Sunday game for the Naps in Cleveland came on May 14, 1911, with a 16-3 rout of the New York Highlanders.

As a rookie in 1911, Joe Jackson set a club record with a .408 batting average, still a full 12 points off Cobb's league-leading .420 mark. Rookie Vean Gregg, became the second left-hander in club history to win 20 games (23-7). Otto Hess was the first in 1906. Jackson and Gregg continued their success the following two seasons, but could not elevate the Naps as they finished fifth in 1912 and third in 1913.

A new challenge arrived in 1913 in the form of the Federal League which began play with six clubs. The Cleveland entry was managed by Cy Young. Despite the new competition, the Naps had a relatively successful season. Cy Falkenberg won 23 games with his emery ball. Ray Chapman, a 22-year-old sophomore, became the starter at shortstop. Record books indicate that the Naps established a new franchise standard with a home attendance of 541,000. Only the NL's New York Giants, and Chicago and Philadelphia in the AL, outdrew Cleveland in 1913 according to *Total Baseball* (sixth edition).

Somers acted decisively to stave off the threat of the Federal League. He moved Cleveland's farm club in the American Association from Toledo to Cleveland. Although the Federal League would continue to operate in 1914 and 1915, it did not maintain a team in Cleveland, but the league still took its toll on the Naps, most notably the defection of ace pitcher Falkenberg.

The departure of Falkenberg and the diminished performance of Vean Gregg, who was traded to the Red Sox in August, were key contributors to a tumble from 86 wins and third place to 51 victories and eighth place in 1914, the first last-place finish in franchise history and a club record 102 losses. Cleveland also fell to last in attendance in the American League with less than 200,000 paid admissions, the lowest mark for the club since 1901. Moreover, in a pattern that would repeat itself throughout the years, financial troubles of the owner were affecting the baseball operation.

With the 1914 season came an end to Napoleon Lajoie's career with the team named in his honor. He turned 40 years old in 1914 and batted just .258, but did achieve one of baseball's most hallowed milestones with the 3,000th hit of his major league career. Exactly when he reached the 3,000 hit mark is a matter of some historical dispute. Lajoie was given his release following the season. He returned to Philadelphia, spending the 1915 and 1916 seasons with Connie Mack's Athletics.

Nap Lajoie remains the all-time hit leader in the history of Cleveland's American League franchise with 2,046 hits. Only Terry Turner ranks higher on the club's all-time list of games played than Lajoie with 1,614 games played for Cleveland. He is also second in team history in doubles (424) and RBI (919). Lajoie's .339 batting average and 2,728 total bases are both third best in club history. One of the giants of baseball's early days, Lajoie became one of the first inductees to the National Baseball Hall of Fame at Cooperstown, New York, at the initial induction ceremony on June 12, 1939.

Terry Turner played third base, second base and in the outfield during a 15-year career in Cleveland (1904-18). He still holds the team record for most games played: 1,619.

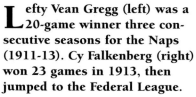

Lefty Vean Gregg (left) was a 20-game winner three consecutive seasons for the Naps (1911-13). Cy Falkenberg (right) won 23 games in 1913, then jumped to the Federal League.

Lajoie's departure prompted consideration of a new nickname for Cleveland's American League franchise. The adoption of the new name became one of the great issues in the history of the club.

On January 6, 1915, *The Plain Dealer* of Cleveland reported that Somers proposed a conference of Cleveland's baseball writers to choose a new nickname for his club that would be "short, expressive and appropriate." Over the next several days, numerous name suggestions were sent to the different papers, including Colts, Grays, Hustlers and Buckeyes.

On January 15, *The Cleveland Leader* reported that Grays was the favored nickname of E.S. Barnard. *The Leader* said, "A meeting of sport writers and officials of the club will be held this afternoon, when a name will be settled upon." On Sunday, January 17, *The Leader* and *The Plain Dealer* reported that Indians had been chosen to replace Naps as the team nickname. *The Leader, The Cleveland Press* and *The Cleveland News* provided no explanation for the choice of the name.

The *Plain Dealer* said, "President Somers invited the Cleveland baseball writers to make the selection. The title of Indians was their choice, it having been one of the names applied to the old National league club of Cleveland many years ago."

The writers also chose another historic Cleveland baseball nickname, Spiders, as a new name for the minor league (American Association) Cleveland club which had most recently been known as the Bearcats.

On Monday, January 18, the following appeared in *The Plain Dealer*:

Looking Backward

Many years ago there was an Indian named Sockalexis who was the star player of the Cleveland baseball club. As batter, fielder and base runner he was a marvel. Sockalexis so far outshone his teammates that he naturally came to be regarded as the whole team. The "fans" throughout the country began to call the Clevelanders the "Indians." It was an honorable name, and while it stuck the team made an excellent record.

It has now been decided to revive this name. The Cleveland's of 1915 will be the "Indians." There will be no real red Indians on the roster, but the name will recall fine traditions. It is looking backward to a time when Cleveland had one of the most popular teams of the United States. It also serves to revive the memory of a single great player who has been gathered to his fathers in the happy hunting grounds of the Abenakis.

The other papers had little, or nothing, to say about the new name and its origin. Much of the reporting leading up to the choice of the name "Indians" indicated that whatever nickname was used in 1915 might be temporary and that the team might "make its own nickname." But, the nickname that originated with the arrival of Louis Sockalexis in Cleveland in 1897 stuck—The Cleveland Indians.

Without Lajoie, Cleveland's attendance was even worse in 1915 than in 1914, with less than 160,000 paying customers. (The American League teams in Philadelphia and St. Louis fared worse still.) The Indians finished seventh in 1915 only because Connie Mack's Athletics had been decimated following their surprising loss to the "Miracle" Boston Braves in the 1914 World Series. Gone were four future Hall of Famers. Second baseman Eddie Collins was sold to the White Sox. Pitchers Eddie Plank and Chief Ben-der signed with the Federal League. Third baseman Home Run Baker sat out the season in hopes of breaking his contract to accept an offer from the rival league.

Between the struggles of the franchise, his coal business and failed investments, Charles Somers was forced to sell his club. He had become inclined to make moves based more on financial, rather than baseball, considerations. An example was Joe Jackson being sent to the Chicago White Sox for three players and cash. "Shoeless Joe" helped Chicago to a pair of American League titles, but is best known as one of the "Eight Men Out" from the "Black Sox" scandal of 1919-1920.

The Charles W. Somers story has a generally happy ending. His fortunes had well rebounded at the time of his death in Put-in-Bay, Ohio, on June 29, 1934, at age 65. He had retained one baseball franchise, the minor league New Orleans Pelicans. Cleveland's baseball fortunes would soon be on the rebound as well.

Joe Jackson, Ty Cobb and Nap Lajoie (l-r) had each batted .400 in their careers when they posed at League Park in 1913: Jackson, .408 in 1911; Cobb .420 in 1911 and .409 in 1912; and Lajoie, .426 in 1901.

INNING 3

The Tragedy and the Triumph

1916–1926

The shape of baseball in Cleveland was formed in large part by two new faces to the local baseball scene in 1916, Jim Dunn and Tris Speaker. Dunn became owner of the club on February 21, 1916. His new club had little to distinguish itself. But, in a recurrent theme of Cleveland Indians' history, a significant addition to the club would make for a rapid upswing in franchise fortunes.

The story of the Tris Speaker trade from Boston to Cleveland is a clear example that financial hassles and player-ownership disputes have long been a part of baseball. Legend has it that noted Cleveland sports writer Ed Bang set the wheels in motion for the acquisition of Speaker. After much haggling, the "Gray Eagle" became a member of the Indians. Just as Nap Lajoie, one of the true stars of the game in 1902, became available to the Cleveland club in 1902, so did a similar star, Tris Speaker of the Boston Red Sox. Born in Hubbard, Texas, in 1888, Speaker won the Texas League batting championship for Houston in 1907 and the Southern Association batting championship for Little Rock in 1908. After brief trials with Boston in 1907 and 1908, he became a fixture in the Red Sox outfield in 1909, batting .309 and leading the AL outfielders in putouts (319) and assists (35). Prematurely gray, Speaker became known as "The Gray Eagle," the greatest defensive outfielder of his day. "Spoke" led Boston to World Series wins in 1912 and 1915.

Speaker was baseball's premier center fielder and its highest-paid player, but he was unable to reach a contract agreement with Boston for 1916. Cleveland acquired Speaker on April 8, 1916, for pitcher Sam Jones, infielder Fred Thomas and cash. Speaker demanded, and received, a portion of the purchase price received by the Red Sox before the deal was finalized on April 15. Cleveland immediately moved back toward the top of the AL ladder.

In 1916, the Indians got back to the .500 mark (77-77). With a premier gate attraction, attendance at Dunn Field (the new name for League Park throughout the Dunn ownership) rebounded to the second-highest total (492,106) in Indians history. Dunn retained Lee Fohl as manager of the Indians. The 1916 club had Speaker, plus additional solid players in infielders Bill Wambsganss, Ray Chapman and Terry Turner, outfielders Bobby "Braggo" Roth and Jack Graney, plus catcher Steve O'Neill and pitchers Stan Coveleski and Jim Bagby. First baseman Arnold "Chick"

Jack Graney and Smoky Joe Wood were ex-pitchers who moved to the outfield. Graney (left) played 14 seasons (1908, 1910-22), but is better remembered as the Tribe's radio voice from 1932-53. Wood won 34 games for the Red Sox in 1912, but an arm injury slowed his career. He made a comeback with the Tribe (1917-22) mostly as a part-time outfielder.

Gandil gained greater notoriety later as a leader of the Chicago "Black Sox." Speaker won the American League batting title with a .386 average, led the AL with 211 hits and scored 102 runs. Graney matched Speaker with a league leading 41 doubles, scored 106 runs and walked 102 times.

Stanley Coveleski had pitched minor league ball since 1908, getting a brief trial with the Philadelphia A's in 1912, before securing a spot on the 1916 Indians. The right-hander from Shamokin, Pennsylvania, had three 20-win seasons to his credit in the minors. He had won 17 games for Portland (Pacific Coast League) in 1915 and led the league with 64 pitching appearances. The strong-armed spitball hurler won 15 games in his debut season with the Indians, the first of seven straight seasons in which he would win 15 or more games for the Tribe.

Cleveland also acquired Speaker's buddy "Smoky" Joe Wood from Boston. Wood was once a brilliant pitcher for the Red Sox, winning 34 games for the 1912 AL champions and 117 against just 52 losses for Boston from 1908 through 1915. Wood's ability on the mound had been ruined by arm trouble, but he was always a fine hitter. Like Jack Graney, Wood moved from the pitching staff to the outfield corps and added to the Cleveland offense.

The Indians showed further signs of improvement in 1917. Bagby won 23 games, Coveleski 19. Wambsganss, a Cleveland native, and Chapman emerged as a formidable keystone combination. The club's .571 winning percentage (88-66) was third best in team history, best since the near-miss of 1908 and good for third place, 12 games behind the world champion White Sox and three behind second place Boston.

Major league baseball, and many other diversions, was overshadowed by the grim reality of World War I in 1918. Baseball was ruled "non-essential" and many players left the diamond for the military or war-related jobs. The regular season would end on Labor Day, September 2, 1918, to be followed by the World Series. The war also overshadowed Cleveland's return to pennant-race baseball.

Cleveland had the most prolific offense in the American League in 1918, scoring 504 runs. Coveleski won 22 games, Bagby 17. Guy Morton added 14 wins and Fritz Coumbe had 13. Perhaps, had the season run to its normal conclusion, Cleveland would have overtaken the Babe Ruth-led Red Sox. Instead, Boston held off Cleveland by two and a half games and won the World Series against the Chicago Cubs, Boston's last World Series win of the century.

The combination of the end of World War I and the second-place finish of the Indians in 1918 led to the highest expectations yet for the Indians. A blockbuster trade with the Philadelphia Athletics further fueled high expectations. Star third baseman Larry Gardner, a former teammate of Speaker's in Boston, came west, along with pitcher Elmer Myers and young outfielder Charlie Jamieson in exchange for outfielder Braggo Roth. In the short term, Gardner gave Cleveland a great infield. In the long term, Jamieson proved to be one of the all-time outfield stars in club history. Cleveland also reacquired former Indians outfielder Elmer Smith, providing further offensive depth.

Cleveland's second place finish marked the second time Terry Turner had come within an eyelash of reaching the World Series. He is somewhat unlikely to hold the Indians' all-time record for games played (1,619). Steady, if not spectacular, Turner played in 50 or more games each season in Cleveland from 1904 through 1918. Versatility allowed him to start at short for Cleveland early in his career and at third base later on, but he could also play second base and the outfield. He spent one more season in the majors (with Connie Mack's Athletics in 1919) to conclude a 17-year big league career.

For all their talent, the Indians struggled to keep up with the league leaders in the first part of the 1919 season. Injuries to Chapman and Graney held the team back. On July 18, Cleveland met the defending world champions at Dunn Field (League Park was known as Dunn Field from 1916 to 1927). Despite a home run by Ruth, the Indians forged a 7-3 lead going into the ninth inning. Myers, pitching in relief of Hi Jasper, allowed one run and faced a precarious situation: bases loaded and Ruth at bat. According to *The Cleveland Indians* by Franklin Lewis (the first full-length history of the Indians, published by G. P. Putnam's Sons in 1949 as part of its famed series of team histories),

Guy Morton lost his first 13 games with the Naps in 1914, then recovered to win 16 the following season. Morton threw four one-hitters in his 11-year Cleveland career.

Speaker and Fohl had a system of signals regarding game strategy, including pitching changes. Fohl called on soft-throwing lefty Fritz Coumbe. Speaker wanted a right-hander. Ruth bashed a mighty home run over the short wall in right field and gave Boston an 8-7 win and a crushing defeat for Cleveland.

Immediately after the contest, Dunn informed Speaker that Fohl had resigned. Speaker was Dunn's choice to be the new manager. The Indians were third in the AL, five-and-a-half games behind a first-place Chicago team thought to be one of the best of all-time. Cleveland finished strong, going 40-21 under Speaker to finish second, three-and-a-half games behind Chicago.

A new age of baseball dawned in 1920, the "lively ball" era. Babe Ruth, one of baseball's best pitchers as a left-handed star with the Red Sox, twice winning more than 20 games in a season, was also emerging as the dominant slugger in the game, a new phenomenon. Fans wanted to see Ruth play ball daily and hit home runs, so he was used less often as a hurler and more as an outfielder. The Bambino hit a single-season record 29 home runs in 1919, 19 more than his nearest challenger and more than 10 other major league clubs. Ruth's development as a gate attraction and new rules banning pitches such as the spitball (a grandfather clause was permitted for active spitball pitchers), put the major league baseball focus on power. The home run rose from a happenstance to a happening. Ruth was sold by the Red Sox to the New York Yankees following the 1919 season. Neither team would ever be the same.

Chicago was still the team to beat in the AL, despite rumors of a possible fix of the 1919 World Series. Speaker's Indians looked to be a contender again to start the new decade. Added to the pitching staff was Ray Caldwell, a former 19-game winner with the Yankees. After nine seasons in New York, Caldwell had gone to the Red Sox in 1919 and to Cleveland soon after. A drinking problem had diminished Caldwell's effectiveness. According to legend, Speaker put a provision in Caldwell's contract that he must get drunk after each game he pitched. For whatever reason, Caldwell got back on track, even pitching a no-hitter against his former New York club in 1919, once again becoming a dependable starting pitcher in 1920.

Joining Bagby and Coveleski, Caldwell gave the Indians a starting pitching staff able to hold its own with any team. Each would enter the 20-win circle in 1920.

For all the offensive firepower of the Yankees and White Sox, it was Cleveland that scored the most runs in major league baseball in 1920, 857, crushing the old club record of 691 (1911). Only the 1911 Athletics had scored more runs in a single twentieth-century season (861).

Speaker led the way with 137 runs scored, but Wambsganss, Chapman and Smith all topped 80 runs scored. New first baseman Doc Johnston, Gardner, Jamieson and catcher Steve O'Neill all surpassed 60 runs scored.

Bill Wambsganss arrived in 1914 and became the starting second baseman in 1915, pairing with shortstop Ray Chapman to form one of the American League's top double-play combinations.

LEGENDS OF THE TRIBE

STAN COVELESKI

P • Indians • 1916-1924   National Baseball Hall of Fame, 1969

Duster Mails was a pitcher better known for his braggadocio when the Indians purchased his contract from Portland of the Pacific Coast League in August 1920. Mails lived up to his self-named moniker of "The Great One" by winning seven games down the stretch without a defeat in the Tribe's pennant-winning season.

Chapman, Gardner, Smith, Speaker, Jamieson and O'Neill hit over .300 and the team as a whole hit .303. Speaker's .388 batting average was second only to George Sisler of the St. Louis Browns (.407). With its potent offense and splendid pitching, Cleveland made off with the American League lead in early August. Four straight losses to the Yankees and a split of two games with St. Louis had brought the Indians back to the pack entering a three-game series against the Yankees at the Polo Grounds in New York starting on a rainy Monday, August 16. Pitching for the Yankees was Carl Mays, a generally grim-faced, submarine-throwing right-hander. He had been a 20-game winner for the Red Sox in 1917 and '18. Like teammate Ruth, Mays had gone from Boston to New York in a deal that brought cash to Red Sox owner Harry Frazee. He was 18-8 when he took the mound against Cleveland.

Steve O'Neill's home run staked the Indians to a 3-0 lead as Chapman led off in the fifth inning. The second pitch to the Cleveland shortstop rode inside, Chapman appeared to freeze and the pitch crashed into his left temple. Such was the force of the blow that the ball bounced to Mays who threw to first base, thinking the ball had been hit. Chapman crumpled at the plate, bleeding from his left ear. Harry Lunte ran for Chapman and Cleveland held on for a 4-3 victory.

Chapman was raced to St. Lawrence Hospital. By the next morning, he was dead from an intercranial hemorrhage. Chapman remains the only player to die as the result of a beaning in a major league game.

Of all the tragic events in the history of the Cleveland Indians, Ray Chapman's death may be the saddest. An immensely popular player, he had established near Hall-of-Fame credentials. By 1920, Chapman was nearly ready to retire and move into the business world with his father-in-law, Martin B. Daly, president of East Ohio Gas Company. But Chapman played the 1920 season in hopes of capping his career with a championship.

The combination of tragedy, the loss of a key player and the competition from Chicago and New York should have been enough to curtail Cleveland's pennant hopes. Speaker and his teammates, however, would not submit as the club moved to strengthen the roster. An August acquisition was a brash, left-handed pitcher, Walter "Duster" Mails from Portland of the Pacific Coast League. With an ego greater than his credentials, Mails called himself "The Great One." But "The Great Mails" became a valuable addition, winning seven games without a loss down the stretch.

Lunte briefly took Chapman's place, but he suffered a leg injury in a win against St. Louis. The Indians reached down to their farm club in New Orleans and called up young Joe Sewell to step in. Sewell later said, "I was more frightened than pleased, but as I traveled north I made up my mind that when I took the field in a Cleveland uniform I would forget that I was Joe Sewell and imagine I was Chapman, fighting to bring honor and glory to Cleveland." Faced with the daunting challenge of replacing a star and beloved player at one of the diamond's most important positions, Sewell provided more than Speaker and the Indians could have hoped for. In 22 games, he batted .329 and began his own Hall-of-Fame career.

The White Sox arrived in Cleveland to begin a three-game series on September 23. Back in Chicago, the front page of the *Chicago Tribune* front-page blared "BARE 'FIXED' WORLD SERIES." Ever since the 1919 World Series, rumors had persisted

TRIS SPEAKER

OF-Mgr•Indians•1916-1926   **National Baseball Hall of Fame, 1937**

Ray Chapman was a nine-year veteran and one of baseball's best shortstops when he was struck on the left temple by a pitch from Yankees submarine-style hurler Carl Mays at the Polo Grounds on August 16, 1920. Chapman died the following day at age 29, the only player to die as a result of a beaning in a major league game.

LEGENDS OF THE TRIBE

and grown that some Chicago players had conspired with gamblers to lose the World Series. More and more, evidence that prompted the *Tribune's* headline exposed the scandal.

The ruckus seemed to have little impact on the Sox who blasted the Indians, 10-3, routing 29-game winner Jim Bagby. In the second game, "The Great Mails" kept the Indians in first place with a 2-0 shutout. Chicago won the series finale, 5-1, before 30,625 fans at Dunn Field, on the pitching of Claude "Lefty" Williams and the hitting of Joe Jackson. Both teams left Cleveland with the Tribe still a half game ahead of the White Sox.

The outcome of the 1920 AL pennant race rested as much in courtrooms and law offices as on playing fields. On September 28, indictments were returned against eight members of the 1919 White Sox: first baseman "Chick" Gandil (no longer with the team), shortstop Charles "Swede" Risberg, pitchers Eddie Cicotte and "Lefty" Williams, utility infielder Fred McMullen, third baseman George "Buck" Weaver and outfielders Oscar "Happy" Felsch and Joe Jackson. Each was suspended immediately by team owner Charles Comiskey. On the same day, Jim Bagby won his 30th game of the season, a 9-5 win against the Browns.

In 1920, Babe Ruth emerged as a record-shattering slugger poised to change the face of the game. The Black Sox scandal also changed the game forever. But the Indians survived the tragic death of Ray Chapman and finally grabbed the prize they had sought since the franchise's inception.

On Saturday, October 2, 1920, in Detroit, Bagby won his 31st game. Tris Speaker collected three hits, including a bases-loaded triple in the seventh inning. When the Gray Eagle grabbed Clyde Manion's fly ball in the ninth, the Indians had a 10-1 win and the American League pennant. Cleveland's 98-56 record was the best yet in franchise history and two games better than the second place "Black Sox."

Tribe infielders (top photo) wear black armbands to honor Ray Chapman: (l-r) Bill Wambsganss, Doc Johnston, Larry Gardner, Joe Sewell and George Burns. Above, manager Tris Speaker watches as Jim Bagby Sr., a 31-game winner in 1920, warms up.

Doc Johnston, Steve O'Neill and Jim Bagby Sr. arrive at home plate following Bagby's three-run homer in the fourth inning of Game 5 of the 1920 World Series. Bagby's blast was the first ever by a pitcher in World Series history.

In its first World Series, the second of three straight series (1919-1921) using a best-of-nine format, Cleveland would face a Brooklyn team managed by Wilbert Robinson. "Uncle Robbie" had played against the Spiders for the old Baltimore Orioles in the 1895 and 1896 Temple Cup series. Brooklyn was led by batting star Zack Wheat and 23-game winner Burleigh Grimes.

The 1920 World Series began on October 5 in Brooklyn with veteran pitching star and native Clevelander Rube Marquard getting the call for the Dodgers and Stan Coveleski pitching for the Tribe. Cleveland scored first, in the second inning, when George Burns scored on a bloop single and first baseman Ed Konetchy's throwing error. A walk to Joe Wood and hits by Joe Sewell and Steve O'Neill gave the Tribe a 2-0 lead. In the fourth, doubles by Wood and O'Neill made it 3-0. Coveleski allowed just one run on five hits and the Indians took the series lead with a 3-1 win.

Grimes got the better of Bagby in the second game, pitching a seven-hit shutout as Brooklyn evened the series with a 3-0 victory. Caldwell was ineffective starting the third

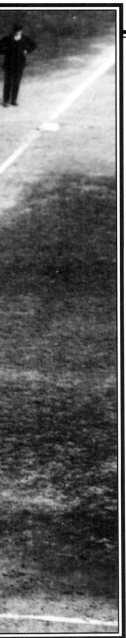

game, allowing two runs and not surviving the first inning. Mails and George Uhle pitched shutout relief, but the damage had been done. Speaker doubled and scored on Zack Wheat's error in the fourth inning, but Sherry Smith held Cleveland to just three hits and Robinson's squad took the series lead with a 2-1 victory.

The first home World Series game for the Cleveland Indians took place on October 9, 1920, with an overflow crowd of 25,734 at Dunn Field to see Coveleski start on three days rest against Leon Cadore. The Tribe scored twice in the first on a walk to Wambsganss, singles by Speaker and Elmer Smith and a sacrifice fly by Gardner. They followed with two more in the third when Burns, batting for Smith against relief pitcher Al Mamaux, singled home Wamby and Speaker. Coveleski pitched another five-hitter, scored Cleveland's final run himself and posted his second victory of the series, 5-1, leaving Cleveland and Brooklyn deadlocked at two wins apiece.

The fifth game, on October 10, 1920, at Dunn Field, remains one of baseball's most memorable games. Another huge crowd (26,884) saw history made in the first inning. Charlie Jamieson led off with a single to right, Wambsganss singled to center and Speaker beat out a bunt single to load the bases. Elmer Smith promptly unloaded with a home run off Grimes over the wall and screen in right field for the first grand slam in World Series history and a 4-0 Cleveland lead.

In the fourth, Doc Johnston singled, took second on a passed ball and third on Sewell's groundout. O'Neill was intentionally walked to bring up pitcher Bagby who then foiled the strategy with a three-run homer into the center field stands. It was the first ever for a pitcher in World Series history.

Down 7-0 in the fifth inning, Brooklyn tried to rally on singles by Pete Kilduff and Otto Miller. Relief pitcher Clarence Mitchell followed with a line drive toward right field. Wambsganss, moving toward second, intercepted the liner. He easily doubled off Kilduff by stepping on second. Turning toward first, he found Miller right in front of him and tagged him. Wambsganss had completed the only unassisted triple play in World Series history.

Bagby allowed 13 hits, but just one run, and Cleveland's historic 8-1 win put the Indians within two wins of the five necessary to be crowned world champions for the first time in team history.

For the sixth game, Speaker chose Duster Mails to pitch against Sherry Smith. A Fall Classic pitching duel ensued with Mails and Smith matching zeros into the sixth inning. With two out in the Indians' sixth, Speaker singled to left and Burns followed with a long double, also to left. Speaker sprinted around the bases with the only run of the game. Mails pitched a three-hit shutout and 27,194 fans at Dunn Field celebrated a 1-0 victory that gave the Indians a 4-2 advantage in the series.

Seeking to conclude the series in Cleveland and avoid a trip back to Brooklyn, Speaker sent Coveleski back to the mound on just two days rest for the seventh game of the best-of-nine series. Bolstered by a crowd of 27,525 at Dunn Field, Coveleski continued his hot pitching with his third five-hitter of the series. Larry Gardner scored on a double steal in the fourth

Right fielder Elmer Smith led the 1920 Indians in homers with 12, then hit the first grand slam in World Series history in the first inning of Game 5 on October 10 at Dunn Field.

Bill Wambsganss tags out a frozen Otto Miller for the third out of Wambsganss's unassisted triple play in the fifth inning of Game 5 of the 1920 World Series.

inning, Speaker tripled home Jamieson in the fifth and Jamieson doubled in Coveleski in the seventh. With two out in the Brooklyn ninth and Hy Myers at first base, Ed Konetchy grounded to Sewell at short who flipped the ball to Wambsganss to force Myers for the final out. The Cleveland Indians were world champions of baseball.

Coveleski had matched the World Series record with three wins and three complete games, two of them shutouts. O'Neill led Cleveland's batters with a .333 average. Speaker batted .320, had a team-high eight hits and a series-high six runs scored. A full winner's share of the financial pot was $4,168.

For the next six seasons, Speaker and the Indians were unable to recapture the magic of 1920. Babe Ruth's Yankees had become the team to beat in the American League. Wearing a somewhat ostentatious uniform with "World Champions" emblazoned across the front, the 1921 Indians nearly answered the challenge by posting the

second best record in club history (94-60), but that left them 4.5 games behind New York. The Indians set a club record with 925 runs scored that stood until 1996.

Jim Bagby never again approached his 31 wins of 1920 and Ray Caldwell won just six more games for the Tribe. George Uhle, a Cleveland native, emerged as a quality starter, leading the AL with 26 wins in 1923. Despite the presence of future Hall of Famers Speaker and Sewell, the Indians were no match for the Yankees of 1921-24 or the Walter Johnson-led Washington Senators of 1924-25.

Joe Sewell batted .299 or better in each of his first 10 seasons in Cleveland. The Alabama native led the AL in putouts four times, assists five times and twice drove in over 100 runs. Sewell was an uncanny bat handler. Twice he struck out only four times in seasons of 150 or more games played (1925 and 1929) and ultimately set a career record with just 114 strikeouts in 14 seasons.

"Sunny" Jim Dunn died in June 1922. Control of the franchise passed to his widow. The Indians floundered in the middle of the American League in 1922 and for the following three seasons. Aside from Uhle, no top-quality hurlers emerged on the pitching staff. While Speaker seemed to defy time, veterans like Gardner, Wood and Graney showed their age. Graney played the last of his 1,402 major league games, all with Cleveland, in 1922. Nine years later, he would return to the Cleveland baseball scene as the radio voice of the Indians.

A major trade after the 1923 season marked the end of two of the most notable playing careers by any members of the Indians when catcher Steve O'Neill and second baseman Bill Wambsganss were dealt to the Red Sox. Cleveland reacquired George Burns, along with catcher Roxy Walters and infielder Chick Fewster, for O'Neill, "Wamby,"

Wambsganss poses with the Brooklyn victims of his unassisted triple play: (l-r) Pete Kilduff, Clarence Mitchell and Otto Miller.

The Tragedy and the Triumph

George Uhle models the new uniform worn by the 1921 Indians following their World Series victory of 1920. Uhle won 147 games in 11 seasons (1919-28, 1936), eighth on the Tribe's all-time list. A Cleveland native, Uhle was a 20-game winner three times.

pitcher Danny Boone and outfielder Joe Connolly. O'Neill had not played less than 100 games in a season for Cleveland since 1914. The popular backstop was recognized in 1951 as the Indians' greatest catcher of the first half of the 20th century. He concluded his playing career with the Red Sox, Yankees and Browns, then made the transition to coach and manager that would bring him back to the Indians in 1935. Wambsganss likewise had become a baseball fixture in Cleveland. He played three more seasons before retiring to the Cleveland area.

Stan Coveleski had become a break-even pitcher. His earned run average jumped from an AL-leading 2.76 in 1923 to 4.04 in 1924. On December 12, 1924, he was traded to Washington for pitcher Byron Speece and outfielder Carr Smith. It was a mistake. Coveleski, winner of 172 games for the Tribe (fourth best in club history) and among Cleveland's all-time leaders in earned run average, shutouts, games pitched, innings pitched and winning percentage, made a big comeback in 1925. He won 20 games (matching Walter Johnson for the team lead), led the AL with a 2.84 ERA and helped the Senators to a second straight AL pennant. Coveleski pitched in another three seasons, finishing with 215 career victories (with just 142 defeats) and was inducted into the National Baseball Hall of Fame in 1969.

The 1925 Indians had some especially memorable moments in another otherwise disappointing season. In a remarkable opening game on April 14, they fell behind St. Louis, 13-9, only to rally with 12 runs in the eighth inning and gain a football-like 21-14 win.

On May 17, Tris Speaker, off to a great start himself, collected the 3,000th hit of his major league career. Only four other players (Ty Cobb, Honus Wagner, Nap Lajoie and Eddie Collins) had reached the hallowed hit plateau. The Indians, however, won just 70 games in 1925, losing 84, and finishing sixth. Garland "Gob" Buckeye was their top pitcher with a 13-8 record and a 3.65 ERA.

Led by Speaker, Sewell, Uhle and Burns, the Indians' final shot at glory during the Speaker-Dunn era came in 1926. Speaker made major league history on August 11 by hitting his 700th double. On August 28 against Boston, Emil Levsen became the last major leaguer to pitch complete-game victories in a doubleheader. He allowed just four hits in each contest, but did not record a strikeout in either game. The feat aided an eight-game winning streak capped by Uhle's 23rd win of the season, his ninth in a row, as the Tribe beat Detroit. The second-place Indians were 5.5 games behind the Yankees.

On September 18, Cleveland won its fourth straight game from the Yankees before 26,782 fans at Dunn Field, moving within 2.5 games of first place. The following day, another 29,726 fans packed the park, but Babe Ruth and Lou Gehrig hit home runs in an 8-3 Yankees victory.

Cleveland's pennant run was over. The Indians were mathematically eliminated on September 25, finishing the season three games behind the Yankees. George Burns, however, earned the Most Valuable Player award with a spectacular season including a .358 average, 216 hits, a major league-record 64 doubles and 114 RBI.

JOE SEWELL

SS-3B•Indians•1920-1930   National Baseball Hall of Fame, 1977

Outfielder Charlie Jamieson was an offensive force throughout the 1920s, batting .300 seven times. His .316 average over 14 seasons in Cleveland is ninth on the all-time list and his 1,753 hits is fifth.

Speaker resigned as manager following the 1926 season. Especially given the success of 1926, his resignation was a surprise. He told the Associated Press that he was planning to retire from playing as well. In late December of 1926, Cleveland's great star was embroiled in a betting scandal that rekindled memories of the Black Sox. Speaker and Ty Cobb, who had also resigned as player-manager of the Tigers after the 1926 season, were accused of fixing a game years earlier. Allegations by former American League pitcher Dutch Leonard, brought to AL President Ban Johnson, purported that Speaker and Cobb had fixed a game between Cleveland and Detroit in 1919.

Leonard's claims quickly came under fire. A battle between two other long-time rivals, Johnson and Commissioner of Baseball Judge Kenesaw Mountain Landis, focused on the status of Speaker and Cobb. Landis prevailed, and the two future Hall of Famers were reinstated. But, neither player returned to his former team. Both were allowed to become free agents by their clubs.

LEGENDS OF THE TRIBE

Cobb signed with Connie Mack's Philadelphia Athletics and had two more big seasons, ending his remarkable career in 1928. Speaker went to the Washington Senators for a year, then finished his career in 1928 as Cobb's 40-year-old teammate in Philadelphia, hitting .267 in 64 games.

During his 11 seasons in a Cleveland uniform, Speaker joined Nap Lajoie atop the legends of the Tribe. Speaker is Cleveland's all-time leader with 486 doubles (his 792 total doubles are a major league record) and he is second among the club's leaders in runs scored (1,079), batting average (.354) and hits (1,965).

Many experts claim Speaker was the greatest defensive center fielder in baseball history. His leadership carried the Indians to the first championship in club history. Fittingly, Speaker, Lajoie and another Cleveland baseball legend, Cy Young, were honored together at the initial National Baseball Hall of Fame induction ceremony in 1939.

Without Speaker, the Indians took a nosedive in the standings and at the gate in 1927. Attendance dropped from 627,426 in 1926 to 373,138 in 1927 as the Tribe struggled to a sixth-place finish with a 66-87 record, almost an exact reversal of the 88-66 mark of 1926. Jack McCallister, a coach for Speaker since 1920, led the Indians in his only season as a major league manager. George Uhle's fall from 27-11 to 8-9 was a major factor in Cleveland's return to the second division.

On the plus side, 21-year-old second-year pitcher Willis "Ace" Hudlin emerged as a dependable starter, finishing with an 18-12 record (although surrendering a league-high 291 hits). Despite never again equalling his 18-win total, Hudlin spent 15 seasons with the Tribe, winning 158 and losing 156 before moving on to Washington in 1940.

By the end of the 1927 season, Mrs. James Dunn was ready to surrender the franchise she had inherited from her late husband. The third ownership in Cleveland Indians history was around the corner, but unlike the Somers and Dunn ownerships, it would take significant time to build a championship contender.

The 1926 Indians (top photo) were Tris Speaker's last as manager, but also one of his best since 1920, finishing second, three games behind the Yankees. The following season (above), Speaker visited the Indians as a Senator, posing between the brother combo of Joe and Luke Sewell (l-r).

A New Home on the Lakefront

1927–1945

The Alva Bradley era of Cleveland Indians baseball began on November 17, 1927, when a syndicate led by Bradley purchased the club from the Dunn estate for $1 million. Bradley, a millionaire himself with family wealth from shipping and real estate, was not alone in the purchase of the Indians. His syndicate included Charles "Chuck" Bradley (Alva's brother), John Sherwin, Sr., George Martin, Percy Morgan, A.C. Ernst, Frank Hobson and others. The owners quickly set their sights on a new general manager to run the baseball operation, Billy Evans, who had been an AL umpire since 1906, working in the World Series numerous times. Evans was hired to succeed Ernest S. Barnard who had been elected president of the American League.

To manage the Indians for 1928, Bradley and Evans hired Roger Peckinpaugh, an Ohioan who had played briefly with the Naps in 1910 and 1912 before being traded to the Yankees after one game in 1913. In New York, "Peck" blossomed into one of baseball's star shortstops from 1913 to 1921. With the Washington Senators from 1922 to 1926, Peckinpaugh played on a pair of AL championship clubs. His playing career concluded with the White Sox in 1927.

With a new hierarchy in place, attention turned to the home of the Indians. Automobiles had increasingly replaced trolley cars as the way to get to the ballpark. Baseball's popularity was on the rise. Of the 15 major league ballparks in 1928 (the St. Louis Browns and St. Louis Cardinals shared Sportsman's Park), only Baker Bowl, home of the lowly Philadelphia Phillies, had a smaller seating capacity than League Park. Four parks (Comiskey Park in Chicago, Yankee Stadium and the Polo Grounds in New York, and Braves Field in Boston) had seating capacities in excess of 45,000. A bigger ballpark could bring increased revenues and a competitive advantage.

W es Ferrell was a 20-game winner four consecutive seasons with the Indians (1929-32), including a career-high 25 in 1930. One of baseball's toughest competitors, he pitched a no-hitter on April 29, 1931, against the Browns. Ferrell was traded to the Red Sox in 1934 where he won 25 once again in 1935.

Cleveland, itself, was also on the rise in the 1920s, in a league with New York and Chicago. Many civic leaders envisioned a new municipal stadium that could serve as a home for the Indians and a statement about Cleveland as a leading American city.

Various individuals had advocated the concept of a lakefront stadium in Cleveland throughout the 1920s. In particular, a stadium north of Cleveland's City Hall and other municipal buildings was thought to be a natural extension of the mall plan that had been developed in the early years of the twentieth century. Before leaving Cleveland, Barnard had also become a proponent of a municipal stadium to succeed League Park as home of the Indians. So was Cleveland's city manager, William R. Hopkins, a driving force in Cleveland's civic growth and namesake of Cleveland Hopkins International Airport. On August 21, 1928, the Cleveland City Council voted to submit a bond issue to the citizens for the purpose of funding a new stadium. On November 6, voters passed the issue with 112,448 votes in favor and 76,975 opposed.

Charged with making the new stadium a reality, and a statement, were the architectural firm of Walker and Weeks and the construction firm of the Osborn Engineering Company. Osborn was already a player in the ballpark business, having worked on the construction of New York's Yankee Stadium, Boston's Fenway Park, and Chicago's Comiskey Park. Stadium construction began on June 25, 1930, and, thanks to a mild winter, concluded on July 1, 1931.

As a new stadium began to emerge on the Cleveland lakefront, new stars emerged on the field for the Indians. Wes Ferrell had a "cup-of-coffee" in 1927, as did Mel Harder in 1928. Outfielder Earl Averill arrived with a bang in 1929. Joe Vosmik, a product of the sandlots of Cleveland, joined the Tribe in 1930. By 1931, Vosmik and Averill were a potent combination in the Indians' outfield.

A dismal 1928 season (62-92) ended a decade in Cleveland for workhorse right-hander George Uhle who had won 147 games for the Indians. At the time, only Stan Coveleski and Addie Joss had more victories for the franchise. Following the 1928 season, Uhle was traded to the Tigers for pitcher Ken Holloway and shortstop Jackie Tavener. Uhle "The Bull" won another 44 games for the Tigers, moved on to the Giants and Yankees, then pitched the final seven of his 513 major league games upon returning to the Indians in 1936, concluding his major league career with an even 200 wins.

Roger Peckinpaugh's managerial tenure started slowly, but he had the Indians playing respectable ball again in 1929. The 21-year-old Ferrell became Cleveland's new pitching ace and won 21 games. After Ferrell, 23-year-old Willis Hudlin added 17 wins and 31-year-old lefty Jake Miller added 14. The pitching staff ranked second to the world champion Philadelphia Athletics in earned run average in the AL, but only two clubs scored fewer runs than the Indians, despite the presence of first baseman Lew Fonseca who won the 1929 AL batting championship with a .369 batting average. Cleveland finished a distant third, 24 games out of first place.

Averill was known as "The Earl of Snohomish" in honor of his birthplace, Snohomish, Washington. His rookie season was one of the best in Tribe history.

One champ meets another at League Park in 1930. Tribe first baseman Lew Fonseca, the 1929 AL batting champion, greets ex-heavyweight boxing champion Jack Dempsey.

EARL AVERILL

OF • Indians • 1929-1939   National Baseball Hall of Fame, 1975

The outfielder hit a home run in his first major league at-bat (April 16, 1929) and went on to bat .332 with 198 hits, 43 doubles, 13 triples, 18 home runs, 96 RBI and 13 steals in 151 games. For a decade (1929-38), Averill was one of the best run-producers in major league baseball. With more than 100 RBI in five different seasons, he drove in 1,084 runs for the Indians, the only player in club history to reach the 1,000 mark. He also established a club record of 226 home runs that stood for decades.

With the major change of a new playing facility on the horizon, another quantum change in Cleveland baseball came in 1929 when Indians games were first broadcast on the radio. WTAM radio covered most home games from 1929 to 1931. Tom Manning, known for his field announcing at League Park, was the broadcaster.

Lew Fonseca suffered a broken arm in 1930, but Cleveland's offense still showed considerable improvement. First baseman Eddie Morgan, second baseman Johnny Hodapp and outfielders Averill and "twitchy" Dick Porter all batted over .330 and scored 100 or more runs. Only the Yankees had a higher team batting average than the Tribe's .304 mark. Ferrell won 25 games, but the rest of the pitching staff could not stem the offensive tide of 1930 and the Indians finished fourth. Peckinpaugh's 1930 Indians matched the 1929 club's win total (81).

Plans and good intentions aside, Alva Bradley and city officials could not agree to lease terms for the Indians to become a tenant at the new stadium. The Tribe played out another fourth-place finish (78 wins) in 1931, wasting a 22-win season by Ferrell (including a no-hitter at League Park against St. Louis on April 29), and began the 1932 season at League Park. Details were finally ironed out for the Indians to move to the stadium beginning with the game of July 31, 1932.

Willis Hudlin (left) and Oral Hildebrand (right) were two quality right-handed starting pitchers of the early 1930s. Hudlin spent 15 seasons in Cleveland (1926-40), winning in double figures nine times. His 157 wins are seventh on the Tribe's all-time list. Hildebrand was an Indian for six seasons (1931-36), the best of which was 1933 when he was selected to the first AL All-Star team, finishing at 16-11.

With Mel Harder on the mound, Philadelphia's Max Bishop comes to the plate for the first pitch of the first game at Cleveland Municipal Stadium on July 31, 1932. A crowd of 80,154 watched Lefty Grove out-duel Harder for a 1-0 Athletics victory.

The Indians' first game at Cleveland Municipal Stadium had all the trappings of a World Series or All-Star Game. Commissioner Landis was in attendance, part of a crowd numbering 80,154. Ferrell was to have started the historic game, but advised Peckinpaugh that his arm was not ready. Instead, Mel Harder got the call against Philadelphia ace Lefty Grove. Both pitchers were in top form. The world champion Athletics managed a lone eighth-inning run when Max Bishop walked, took second on a sacrifice and scored on Mickey Cochrane's single. Grove allowed just four hits and completed a 1-0 victory in just one hour and 50 minutes.

Cleveland played its final 32 home games of 1932 in the big, new, ballpark. Despite a good start, the Indians finished fourth again, though 87 wins were the team's best since 1926. Ferrell won 23 games, Clint Brown and Mel Harder each added 15 wins and Willis Hudlin had 12.

LEGENDS OF THE TRIBE

Total home attendance was 468,953, less than the 483,027 in 1931. The Cleveland Municipal Stadium era of Indians baseball was off to a lackluster start.

Returning to the scene in 1932 was Jack Graney. Ellis Vander Pyl had started the season as the broadcast voice of the Indians, but was replaced by Graney during the campaign. Graney made baseball history by becoming the first former player to move into the broadcast booth, then established himself as the voice of the Indians for more than two decades.

Departing in 1932 after 14 seasons with the Indians was outfielder Charlie Jamieson. With a lifetime batting average of .303 and a .316 mark with the Indians that ranks as one of the best in franchise history, he retired among Cleveland's all-time leaders in games played, hits, triples and total bases. One of Cleveland's most popular players ever, Jamieson was recognized as one of the Tribe's greatest outfielders when an all-time team was chosen during Major League Baseball's centennial celebration of 1969. When the twentieth century ended, only two players—Earl Averill and Tris Speaker—had scored more runs for the Indians than the Patterson, New Jersey, native.

When the Indians settled to the middle of the pack again early in 1933, Peckinpaugh was dismissed as manager. The choice to replace him was the legendary pitcher, Walter Johnson. "The Big Train" had managed the Senators from 1929 through 1932, leading Washington to a second-place finish in 1930 and third in 1931 and 1932, winning 90 or more games each season, but not enough to surpass the two great American League powerhouse teams, the Yankees and Athletics. Following the 1932 season, Johnson was replaced by Joe Cronin.

Johnson entered an awkward situation in Cleveland. While the new stadium offered more seats and more parking, the great size of the park was daunting to Cleveland's hitters. The Indians hit just 50 home runs in 1933 with only Averill (11) and Odell Hale (10) reaching double figures. The stadium also had plenty of empty seats.

Conversely, the stadium did help the pitchers lead the AL in shutouts (12) and ERA (3.71). Oral Hildebrand was the ace of the 1933 staff with a 16-11 record, but Wes Ferrell's sore arm limited him to just 11 wins. The Great Depression was affecting the finances of many teams, including the Tribe. Especially unhappy, due to a salary cut, was Ferrell.

Over the years, Cleveland had gained a reputation as "the graveyard of managers," a city in which the fans had unrealistic expectations and the sportswriters felt they were as much responsible for running the ball club as the manager. Johnson's chances to survive such an environment hardly improved when the 1933 Indians finished fourth again, won just 75 games and drew only 387,936 fans to the Stadium.

One highlight of the 1933 season was the first mid-season All-Star Game. The brainchild of Chicago sportswriter Arch Ward, the game was created as an event to complement the 1933 World's Fair in Chicago. The game was played at Comiskey Park on July 6.

Infielder Johnny Burnett played eight seasons with the Tribe (1927-34), but is best remembered for two offensive efforts in 1932. On July 10 at League Park, he collected a major league-record nine hits in an 18-17, 18-inning loss to Philadelphia. On August 7, he hit the first-ever home run in Cleveland Municipal Stadium in a 7-4 win over Washington.

Three Indians—Ferrell, Hildebrand and Averill—were selected to an AL roster that was loaded with future Hall of Famers including Averill, Lefty Grove, Lefty Gomez, Bill Dickey, Rick Ferrell, Jimmie Foxx, Lou Gehrig, Tony Lazzeri, Charlie Gehringer, Joe Cronin, Babe Ruth and Al Simmons. The American League won, 4-2.

Averill made a return trip to the 1934 All-Star Game. Joining him was Mel Harder who began an unmatched record by pitching five scoreless innings in the American League victory. Harder never allowed a run in All-Star Game competition.

Choosing not to continue leasing Cleveland Municipal Stadium, the Indians moved back to the team-owned League Park for the 1934 season. The Tribe played all but one home game in League Park from 1934 through 1936 and home attendance remained below 400,000 in 1934 and '35. One who benefitted from League Park was rookie first baseman Hal Trosky. A big, left-handed hitter, Trosky's first full season in the majors was one of Cleveland's best. He batted .330 with 206 hits, 142 RBI, 117 runs scored and 35 home runs. Harder blossomed into a 20-game winner in 1934. Monte Pearson added 18 wins and Willis Hudlin had 15.

The unhappy Wes Ferrell was sent to the Red Sox, along with Dick Porter, for pitcher Bob Weiland, outfielder Bob Seeds and cash. Ferrell was rejuvenated in Boston while Cleveland gained nothing. A productive Ferrell might have put the Tribe into the 1934 pennant race, rather than a distant third, 16 games behind the AL champion Detroit Tigers. Ferrell added a pair of 20-win seasons in Boston (including a league-leading 25 in 1935) to the four he had in Cleveland. He led the American League in complete games and innings pitched three times after leaving the Indians. His big league career concluded with 193 wins and a .601 winning percentage. Meanwhile, criticism of the team's leadership steadily increased.

Cleveland's reputation as a brutal place for managers took a giant leap forward in 1935 when an advertisement appeared in three Cleveland newspapers on June 6 in which the players announced their opposition to manager Johnson. The discontent reached a zenith when Johnson released catcher Glenn Myatt and suspended third baseman Willie Kamm, accusing both of leading the anti-Johnson group. Alva Bradley appointed Kamm a scout and Myatt signed with the New York Giants.

The uprising took a back seat to the 1935 All-Star Game, the third annual mid-summer classic and first to be played in Cleveland. The big game was played in big Cleve-

American League selectees gather at Comiskey Park in Chicago for the first All-Star Game on July 6, 1933. Indians on the roster are pitchers Oral Hildebrand and Wes Ferrell (standing, fifth and 13th from left) and outfielder Earl Averill (kneeling, seventh from left).

Opposite page, Hall-of-Fame umpire Billy Evans (left) and Hall-of-Fame pitcher Walter Johnson (right) had different rolls with the Depression-era Tribe. Evans was general manager from 1927-35 and Johnson was manager from 1933-35.

J oe Vosmik, The Blond Viking, batted over .300 in four of his six full seasons with the Tribe. The Cleveland native's best year was 1935 when he led the league in hits, doubles and triples, but lost the batting crown to Washington's Buddy Myer by a point (.349 to .348).

land Municipal Stadium, with a big, record, crowd of 69,831 in attendance. Appropriately, Joe Vosmik was one of Cleveland's three representatives and the first Tribe player to start in an All-Star Game. Mel Harder was a Cleveland selection for the second straight season and pitched three shutout innings in relief of starter Lefty Gomez. "Master Melvin" wrapped up a third straight victory for the American League, 4-1, aided by a Jimmie Foxx home run.

Johnson's reprieve ended soon after the All-Star Game. The Indians were in fifth place with a 46-48 record on August 4 when Bradley relieved Johnson and replaced him with coach Steve O'Neill. Apparently satisfied with the change, Cleveland's players carved out a 36-23 mark under the ex-Tribe catcher to finish third, 12 games behind the pennant-winning Tigers. Billy Evans was less satisfied. Weary of financial problems and managerial turmoil, he quit, later to be hired as farm director of the Red Sox.

Undaunted by the controversy of 1935, Vosmik made a charge at the AL batting championship. "The Blond Viking" finished at .348, second to the .349 of Washington's Buddy Myer. Vosmik led the league in hits (216), doubles (47) and triples (20) and achieved one of the best offensive seasons in Indians history.

By the end of its eighth season, the Alva Bradley ownership had not produced a team that finished better than third in the eight-team American League or closer than within 12 games of first. Charles Somers had acquired Napoleon Lajoie and barely missed the 1908 pennant. Jim Dunn had acquired Tris Speaker and won the 1920 World Series. The most notable aspect of the Bradley ownership had been the construction of Cleveland Municipal Stadium. The timing was far from perfect as the effects of the Great Depression took their toll on Cleveland baseball.

Steve O'Neill revived memories of the 1920 world champions. As a catcher, he had handled great pitchers like Stan Coveleski, Jim Bagby and George Uhle. He had played in the same lineup with stars such as Tris Speaker, Ray Chapman, Joe Sewell and Larry Gardner. As a manager, he would have a chance to groom the greatest pitching star in Indians history, Bob Feller.

Cy Slapnicka, the legendary baseball scout who signed Feller, became Cleveland's top administrator late in 1935 when he succeeded Billy Evans. Of all of Slapnicka's scouting conquests, the greatest became Robert William Andrew Feller, 16 years old when signed by Slapnicka on July 25, 1935, to pitch for the Tribe's Fargo-Moorhead (North Dakota) farm club of the Northern League.

With a bright star for the future, Cleveland also had several stars of the present. The 1930s were a hitting-dominated decade and the 1936 Indians, in League Park, fit right in. Had all of Cleveland's home games been played at League Park, the team might have broken the club record of 925 runs scored (1921), instead falling just short with 921. Hal Trosky hit 42 home runs and set a club record with a league leading 162 runs batted in. Earl Averill led the league in hits (232), triples (15) and batted .378

(second only to Chicago's Luke Appling). The Indians led the American League in hits (1,715), doubles (357) and batting average (.304).

Cleveland's pitching in 1936 was less successful. Harder and Hudlin both suffered from arm trouble. Harder won 15 games, but Hudlin managed just one win in six decisions. Johnny Allen, known as much for temper tantrums as for winning games, had been acquired from the Yankees following the 1935 season for pitchers Monte Pearson and Steve Sundra. Allen carried his weight with 20 of Cleveland's 80 wins, fifth best in the AL standings for 1936. Cleveland's liveliest baseball season in years was reflected at the gate with a home attendance of 500,391, the best mark since 1930.

The Tribe's 1936 offensive explosion came despite a sub-par performance, by his standards, for Joe Vosmik who batted .287 with 94 RBI. After the season, he was traded to the Browns with shortstop Bill Knickerbocker and pitcher Oral Hildebrand for shortstop Lyn Lary, pitcher Ivy Andrews and outfielder Moose Solters.

First baseman Hal Trosky emerged as a premier slugger in 1934 with 35 home runs and 142 RBI. His best season came two years later with 42 homers, an AL-leading 162 RBI and a .343 batting average. Entering the 2000 season, Trosky's 216 home runs and 911 RBI were third on the Tribe's all-time career lists.

Former catcher Steve O'Neill replaced the fired Walter Johnson as manager during the 1935 season. The catcher for the 1920 world champions, O'Neill became Bob Feller's first major league catcher in Feller's exhibition debut versus the Cardinals on July 6, 1936. In spite of two winning seasons, O'Neill was fired after the 1937 campaign.

Vosmik hit .325 for St. Louis, earning a trade to the Red Sox where he hit .324 with a league-leading 201 hits and 121 runs scored in 1938. In all, he batted .307 for a career covering 13 seasons and 1,414 games in the major leagues.

Feller never did go to Fargo-Moorhead. After finishing his 1935-36 high school year in May, the young right-hander was brought directly to Cleveland. Baseball rules of the day, however, prohibited the signing of a sandlot player to a major league contract. Commissioner Landis charged Slapnicka and the Indians with intentionally circumventing the rule. Fortunately for Cleveland baseball, young Feller and his father persuaded Landis to allow Feller to remain with the Indians.

The legend of Bob Feller began to grow with an exhibition-game appearance against the St. Louis Cardinals on July 6 at League Park. With his combination of blazing speed and disconcerting wildness, Feller struck out eight Cardinals in three innings. His regular-season debut came on July 19 in a mop-up role against the Senators in Washington.

Feller's first major league start came on August 23, 1936, at League Park against the Browns. He struck out 15, just one short of the existing AL record and two short of the major league record as the Tribe won, 4-1. Feller won five games in 1936 with 76 strikeouts in 62 innings pitched.

Much more was expected from Feller in 1937, but a sore arm curtailed his season and threatened his career. Ultimately, he won nine games in 1937 with 150 strikeouts in 148.2 innings pitched.

The nearly unbeatable pitcher for the 1937 Indians was Johnny Allen. "The Spitfire" won his first 15 decisions of the season. On the final day, he bid to tie the AL record of 16 straight wins in a season, a mark shared by Walter Johnson, Lefty Grove, Smoky Joe Wood and Schoolboy Rowe. Allen's opponent was the Tigers and pitcher Jake Wade, who pitched a masterpiece, allowing just one hit, a seventh-inning single by Hal Trosky. Big first baseman Hank Greenberg drove in Detroit's only run and the Tigers curtailed Allen's streak with a 1-0 victory.

Harder matched Allen's 15 wins but also lost 12. Hudlin won 12 games. Cleveland's 83 victories were good for fourth place, 19 games out of first, but not good enough to save Steve O'Neill's job as manager.

The Indians arranged to play weekend and holiday games at Cleveland Municipal Stadium in 1937. For the remainder of the Bradley ownership, the Indians, to a large extent, were always traveling. When the team was not on the road, it was moving between old League Park and the new Stadium.

Following the 1937 season, O'Neill became the next managerial casualty. For his successor, Bradley and Slapnicka looked to capture some Yankees magic. The Indians hired Oscar Vitt, manager of the Yankees farm club at Newark. O'Neill was judged to have been too laid back. Vitt would not be accused of the same attitude.

If Vitt did not win any friends, he did, indeed, seem to bring renewed spark to the Indians and a slightly improved record of 86-66. Home atten-

dance jumped to 652,006, best for the club since 1921. Feller blossomed into an all-star pitcher, winning 17 games to match Harder for the team lead and winning his first strikeout title with 240. Leading the offense were Averill, Trosky, outfielder Jeff Heath and third baseman Ken Keltner.

Keltner's rookie season in 1938 included 26 home runs and 113 RBI. The Milwaukee, Wisconsin, native became a fixture at third base. After a pair of trials, Heath's first full season was stunning with 21 homers, 31 doubles, 18 triples, 104 runs scored, 112 RBI and a .343 batting average. Heath's passion matched his ability, making the Canadian from Fort William, Ontario, an appropriate ingredient for Vitt's Indians.

A highlight of the 1938 season came on June 7 at Fenway Park in Boston. The temperamental Allen was pitching when Red Sox batters complained that the right sleeve

Bob Feller makes his first major league start on August 23, 1936, at League Park. The rookie struck out 15 Browns, just one short of the existing AL record and two shy of the major league record as the Indians won, 4-1.

Bob Feller demonstrates his classic kick. By 1938, the 19-year-old Feller had become one of the game's most intimidating pitchers. On the final day of the season against Detroit, he broke Dizzy Dean's major league strikeout record by fanning 18 Tigers.

Johnny Allen (opposite page) is often remembered for his hot temper, but the right hander from North Carolina kept a measure of calm long enough to win 20 games in 1936, his first season with the Tribe, followed by 15 straight victories against only one defeat in 1937.

of his undershirt was torn and distractive. Allen refused umpire Bill McGowan's directive to change the undershirt or cut off the torn sleeve and stormed off the mound. Vitt fined Allen $250 and Allen threatened to quit the team. A measure of calm was restored when Bradley arranged for the undershirt to be displayed at Higbee's department store. According to legend, the store paid $250 for the garment and, in turn, paid the fine.

Shortstop Lou Boudreau and second baseman Ray Mack were called up late in the 1938 season and in time to glimpse Bob Feller's brilliance. On October 2, Feller represented a major obstacle for Detroit's Greenberg in his bid to set a new single-season major league home run record. He had 58, two short of Babe Ruth's mark, entering a season-ending doubleheader at the Stadium. Feller pitched the first game and stole the show by striking out 18 to set a new single-game major league record. He struck out Greenberg twice and center fielder Chet Laabs five times. The 19-year-old Feller did not get the win, however, as Harry Eisenstat pitched Detroit to a 4-1 victory. Greenberg failed to homer in either game and finished the season with 58.

Boudreau and Mack became the keystone combination during the second half of the 1939 season as the Indians ran third again with an 87-67 record. Mack was a Cleveland native. Boudreau had been an amateur star in Illinois.

As newcomers Mack and Boudreau arrived, Cleveland's all-time-leading home run hitter, Earl Averill, was traded to the Tigers for Eisenstat and cash on June 14. After 10 seasons as a mainstay in the outfield, Averill was reportedly dissatisfied with Cleveland and requested a trade. At the time, he was the only player to have hit 200 or more home runs as an Indian. He left as the Tribe's all-time leader in RBI (1,084), triples (121), extra-base hits (724), runs scored (1,154) and total bases (3,200).

Averill hit 10 homers for the Tigers in 1939 and two in 1940 when he reached the World Series for the only time in his career. He finished with eight games for the Red Sox in 1941. Averill received two of the greatest honors in baseball in 1975 when his uniform number 3 became the third retired by the Indians and he was inducted into the National Baseball Hall of Fame.

In his fourth season, Feller became the dominant pitcher in baseball. He led the 1939 AL in games won (24), complete games (24), innings pitched (296.2) and strikeouts (246). With 15 victories from Harder, 14 from lefty Al Milnar and nine each from Allen and Hudlin, the Indians won 87 games to match their highest total since 1921, but still finished 20.5 games out of first place as the Yankees won their fourth straight world championship.

Night baseball arrived on the lakefront in 1939. Lights were never installed at League Park, but Municipal Stadium was equipped for night contests on June 27. Fittingly, Feller was the pitcher in the Indians' first home night game. Difficult enough to hit during the day, "Rapid Robert" was virtually untouchable against the Tigers. For five innings, Feller did not allow a hit. In the sixth, Earl Averill singled to spoil the no-hit bid. Detroit did not get another hit and Feller had the third one-hitter of his career, a 5-0 victory.

Entering the 1940 season, the Indians featured baseball's best pitcher in Bob Feller, a solid supporting pitching staff and a formidable offense and defense. Right out of the gate, Feller made baseball history on opening day by pitching a no-hitter against the White Sox at Comiskey Park. Boston took the early lead in the AL race, but Cleveland remained close. The Indians were hot on the field as ill feelings toward Oscar Vitt were heating up.

Vitt was accused of saying one thing to a player's face and something else behind his back. In his history of the Indians, Franklin Lewis wrote, "Vitt was despised by most of the Redskins. His tongue continued to wag in criticism of his players." The manager was on no better terms with general manager Cy Slapnicka. According to Lewis, Slapnicka had developed an intense hatred of Vitt.

For the first time in years, the Indians were a legitimate pennant contender. The players, however, had become convinced that winning the pennant would require a change in managers. On June 13, numerous players went to Bradley and asked the owner to remove Vitt. Bradley declined to take any immediate action and, worse, the players' revolt immediately made newspaper headlines in Cleveland and around the country. The Indians soon became known as the "Crybabies."

If anything, the revolt seemed to spark the Indians who continued to keep winning despite the unsuccessful effort to unseat Vitt. Boston started strong in 1940, but faded in the second half. The Yankees got off to a very un-Yankee-like start of 50-51.

By early August, Cleveland and Detroit emerged as the teams most likely to end New York's string of four straight championships. The Indians and Tigers were even with 64-44 records entering a two-game series in Cleveland starting on August 12. Feller beat Hal Newhouser in the first game, earning his 20th win of the season and Eisenstat won the second to give the Tribe a two-game lead. The next night, 59,068 saw Al Smith throw a one-hitter and shut out the White Sox at the Stadium. With two more victories, Cleveland opened a three-game lead. Suffering a six-game losing streak, the second-place Tigers fell to 5.5 games behind.

When Cleveland and Detroit next met head to head in a three-game series starting September 4, the Indians were four games in front. But the motor city club roared back into the race with three straight wins featuring heavy razzing of the Indians by the Detroit fans. The Yankees had also charged back into contention with 21 victories in 25 games, moving within two games of the Tribe. On September 7, Cleveland fell into a virtual tie for first place when the Tigers won again and the Indians lost again.

As the final month of the season wore on, the Indians fell into a severe batting slump. Pressure increased on the pitching staff and Vitt added to the pressure by pushing his pitchers, especial-

New manager Oscar Vitt (left) and general manager Cy Slapnicka confer during spring training of 1938. The feisty Vitt had been hired to instill a fighting spirit in the Indians, contrasting with the laid-back style of Steve O'Neill. But the fighting turned to infighting as the "Crybabies" affair resulted in Vitt being ousted after the 1940 season.

ly Feller, harder and harder. On September 13, Milnar pitched a three-hit shutout and Cleveland defeated Boston, 1-0, even though Jim Bagby Jr. allowed just two hits for the Red Sox. The anemic Indians fell to second place on September 17 with a second straight loss to the last-place Athletics. A day later, the Tribe returned to first place when Allen and Feller pitched the Indians to a doubleheader sweep of the Senators.

Cleveland and Detroit were deadlocked again, with 85-61 records, when a three-game series began in Detroit. Harder took the mound for the Indians and carried a 4-1 lead into the eighth inning. When Harder appeared to tire, Vitt brought Feller out of the bullpen. A tired Feller allowed three hits and was pulled in favor of Joe Dobson, but the move was too late. Detroit scored five runs and held on for a 6-5 victory. Vitt was roundly criticized for using Feller. Detroit won the following game

Bob Feller delivers a pitch during his no-hitter on opening day at Comiskey Park in Chicago on April 16, 1940. Feller and the Indians beat the White Sox, 1-0. It remains the only opening-day no-hitter in major league history.

A rookie double-play combination arrived in 1939 when second baseman Ray Mack (left) and shortstop Lou Boudreau (right) were promoted in August from Class AA Buffalo. They were a tandem into the 1944 season when the light-hitting Mack began sharing time with Rusty Peters.

to take a two-game lead. Feller salvaged the final game, hitting a home run and taking a 10-5 decision for his 27th win of the year. Detroit would add a game to its lead before a pennant showdown in Cleveland on the final weekend of the regular season.

Needing a sweep of three games to capture its second AL pennant, Cleveland went with its ace, Bob Feller. Needing just one win, Detroit manager Del Baker gambled and sent an unknown rookie, Floyd Giebell, to the mound. In the fourth inning, the Tigers broke a scoreless tie when Rudy York hit a 320-foot home run, his 33rd of the season, just inside the left field foul pole and just into the seats. The Indians threatened against Giebell, but could not score. The 30-year-old rookie held on for a 2-0 win, the third and last major league victory of his career. The Tigers, not the Indians, would go to the World Series against Cincinnati. Two meaningless wins gave the Tribe an 89-

65 record, one game behind the Tigers (90-64) and one ahead of the third-place Yankees (88-66). The Indians also barely missed setting a club attendance record. Their home attendance of 902,576 was just short of the 1920 club record and fourth best in the majors behind the Tigers, Yankees and Dodgers.

The bitter disappointment of finishing second overshadowed Cleveland's most successful season since 1920 and numerous individual achievements. Feller led the majors with 27 wins and 261 strikeouts. (No other pitcher came close to 200.) He led the AL in games pitched (43), starts (37) and complete games (31). Al Milnar won 18 games, Al Smith 15 and Mel Harder 12. Boudreau led the club with 101 RBI and hit .295. Trosky also hit .295 and led the club with 25 homers. Outfielder Roy "Stormy" Weatherly's .303 batting average led the team.

The failure to win the AL pennant in 1940 sealed the fate of Oscar Vitt, who was fired on October 28 and would never again manage in the major leagues. For the 1941 season, Bradley returned Roger Peckinpaugh to the managerial position. He was chosen over coach Luke Sewell, the players' choice to replace Vitt during the 1940 rebellion. Feller had another great year in 1941, but the rest of the team collapsed, as if in continuation of the disastrous conclusion of the 1940 season. Cleveland fell back to fourth place (tied with Detroit) and posted its worst record since the Bradley ownership took over and Peckinpaugh first managed the Indians in 1928.

While disappointing in Cleveland, elsewhere the 1941 season was one for the ages in major league baseball and has been written about for years since. One of the feats of the campaign, Joe DiMaggio's 56-game hitting streak, became one of the most hallowed and unbreakable records in major league history.

When "Joltin' Joe" came to Cleveland at the beginning of June, he had a modest 16-game hitting streak. In three games against the Tribe, DiMaggio extended the streak to 19 games with four hits in the series. The Indians and Yankees next met June 14-16 at Yankee Stadium. In three more games, "The Yankee Clipper" extended his streak to 29 games with one hit in each contest. By July 16, when the Yankees returned to Cleveland, DiMaggio's hitting streak was the talk of the nation.

The 1940 Indians nearly won the AL pennant, finishing second to Detroit by one game. But a great season on the field was overshadowed by activities off the field as a group of players attempted unsuccessfully to convince owner Alva Bradley to fire manager Oscar Vitt. The players soon became known as the "Cleveland Crybabies."

The pitching of Al Smith (left) and Jim Bagby Jr. (right), plus defensive gems by Ken Keltner and Lou Boudreau combined to stop Joe DiMaggio's 56-game hitting streak on July 17, 1941, at the Stadium.

DiMaggio had obliterated the previous record of 44 straight by Willie Keeler days earlier and extended his new record with each game. On the afternoon of July 16, League Park was the setting and 15,000 fans were in attendance to see if Al Milnar could stop the streak. In the first inning, DiMaggio's hitting streak reached 56 games when he singled to center field. DiMaggio had two more hits, one off Milnar and one off Joe Krakauskas as New York routed Cleveland, 10-3.

The Indians-Yankees game of July 17 was played at Cleveland Municipal Stadium where the largest crowd of 1941 could be accommodated. With 67,468 fans packing the park, lefty Al Smith took the mound for the Indians. In the first inning, DiMaggio smashed a Smith pitch down the third base line. Ken Keltner, playing so deep at third that he was almost in left field, made a tremendous backhanded stop and threw to first to retire DiMaggio. Smith walked DiMaggio in his next plate appearance, prompting boos from the fans that wanted an Indians' win and a continuation of the streak.

In the seventh, DiMaggio hit another smash down the third base line. Keltner was appropriately positioned again and made another dazzling play to keep DiMaggio hitless. The Yankees gave him one last chance with a rally in the eighth inning. New York led, 4-1, when DiMaggio faced relief pitcher Jim Bagby, Jr. On a two-ball, one-strike pitch, DiMaggio hit a hard grounder at shortstop Boudreau. The ball took a bad hop, but Boudreau made the play that began a 6-4-3 double play to thwart DiMaggio again. When a Cleveland rally fell short in the ninth, New York had a 4-3 victory, but DiMaggio's amazing hitting streak was over at 56 games.

BOB FELLER

P•Indians•1936-1941, 1945-1956   National Baseball Hall of Fame, 1962

The Indians' two games against the Yankees on July 16 and July 17 accounted for more than 11 percent of home attendance in 1941. While attendance fell to 745,948 it was still the best for any major league city outside of New York (following the AL Yankees and the NL Dodgers and Giants).

Like Charles Somers, Alva Bradley would never enjoy a championship season as Indians owner. His best chance had come and gone in 1940. And just as the Great Depression had altered the course of Bradley's ownership at the start of the 1930s, national and world events would sidetrack his Indians early in the 1940s.

The disappointment of 1940 followed by the fall of 1941 brought another wave of changes to Cleveland's baseball leadership. Cy Slapnicka, more comfortable and more successful as a scout than as a general manager, resigned on September 27, 1941, moving on to the Browns as a scout, then later working in a similar capacity for the Cubs. In 1946, Slapnicka returned to scout for the Indians.

Filling the vacancy left by Slapnicka was Roger Peckinpaugh, the two-time Tribe manager. Veteran manager Burt Shotton was rumored to be a candidate to succeed Peckinpaugh on the field. Candidates also included a young shortstop who was just beginning to make his mark on the Cleveland baseball scene.

Lou Boudreau's decision to apply for the managerial job reflected a combination of youthful confidence and enthusiasm that had been missing from the Indians' picture. While skeptical, the Cleveland ownership was ultimately persuaded to give the 24-year-old shortstop a chance. On November 25, 1941, Boudreau was named player-manager, the first since Tris Speaker and the fifth different manager for the Bradley ownership regime. Concerns existed about Boudreau's young age and the difficulty of playing and managing, but were balanced by his already apparent leadership ability as well as his background as a leader. It was hoped that Boudreau would strike a balance between the laid-back approach of O'Neill and the abrasive style of Vitt. As insurance, Boudreau was surrounded with veteran coaches. Shotton was hired to assist Boudreau. George Susce was retained from Peckinpaugh's staff and Ski Melillo, a coach for Vitt in 1939 and 1940, returned to the staff.

Within days of his appointment, Boudreau lost his most potent weapon, Bob Feller. If December 7, 1941, is a day that lives in infamy for all history, December 9, 1941, is a day that lives in infamy for Indians history. Two days after the Japanese invasion at Pearl Harbor, Feller enlisted in the United States Navy. For the next three seasons and most of 1945, the Tribe would have to compete without their ace pitcher, the best in major league baseball.

Next came the retirement of slugger Hal Trosky. The performance of the left-handed hitting first baseman had slipped drastically in 1941 after seven straight seasons with 93 or more RBI and an average of over 121 RBI per year during those seasons. Trosky, however, increasingly suffered from migraine headaches and played only 89 games in 1941. Just 29 years old, he retired due to the migraines.

Only Earl Averill had hit more home runs for the Indians than Trosky's 216. Only Averill and Lajoie are credited with more RBI for the Tribe than Trosky's 911. Trosky never again played for the Indians,

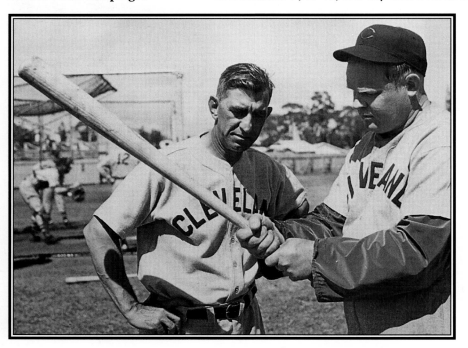

Roger Peckinpaugh (left) gives hitting instructions to Murray Howell during spring training of 1941. Replacing the fired Oscar Vitt, Peckinpaugh had previously managed the Indians from 1928-33. He provided a more stable atmosphere than Vitt, but the Tribe fell to fourth place, 26 games behind New York, and Peckinpaugh was replaced by Lou Boudreau for the 1942 campaign.

LEGENDS OF THE TRIBE

but he did make a brief comeback with the White Sox in 1944 and 1946, adding 12 more home runs and 101 more RBI to his career totals.

Baseball hardly seemed a priority in 1942, but it was judged to be of importance by President Franklin Delano Roosevelt. On January 15, 1942, he issued the "Green Light" letter and informed Commissioner of Baseball Kenesaw Mountain Landis that the 1942 major league baseball season should proceed. President Roosevelt felt professional baseball was good for America's morale.

Lou Boudreau could count on himself and little else for the 1942 season. He was classified 4-F due to a pair of bad ankles. Familiar faces Mel Harder, Al Smith and Al Milnar returned to the pitching staff. Boudreau's double-play partner, Ray Mack, was back, along with Ken Keltner at third.

Cleveland, with its loss of Feller, and Detroit, with its loss of Hank Greenberg, were arguably the two teams hit hardest in 1942 by the entry of the United States into World War II. Jim Bagby Jr., acquired from the Red Sox after the 1940 season, came up as the ace pitcher for the Indians, winning 17 games. Harder added 13 victories. Les Fleming took over from Trosky at first base and led the team with a .292 batting average, 14 home runs and 82 RBI.

Migraine headaches forced a premature finish to the career of Hal Trosky (left) in 1941, although he later made a comeback with the White Sox in 1944. Outfielder Roy Weatherly (right) played seven seasons, leading the Tribe in hitting in 1940 with a .303 average.

LOU BOUDREAU

SS-Mgr • Indians • 1938-1950   National Baseball Hall of Fame, 1970

Boudreau's first season as manager finished with Cleveland running fourth, two games ahead of the Tigers and 28 games behind the American League champion Yankees. Many teams suffered at the gate in 1942, but Cleveland was hit hardest with a drop of almost 40 percent to 459,447.

Not counting in the attendance was a crowd of 62,094 on July 7. The event was an exhibition game to benefit the war effort. Landis directed that the winning team from the July 6 All-Star Game would immediately travel to Cleveland for a benefit game against the United States Service team. The American League squad earned a trip from New York to Cleveland by defeating the National League, 3-1, thanks in part to a first-inning Boudreau home run. Feller led the Service team and, no doubt, helped attract the large crowd. A stirring pre-game ceremony was followed by a 3-0 win for the AL stars. The game succeeded where it mattered most, earning gross receipts of $143,571 (of which $62,094 was for the purchase of war savings stamps) to support the war effort.

World War II leveled the major league baseball playing field, to an extent, in 1942, 1943 and 1944. Most notably, the St. Louis Browns, a dreadful franchise, managed to capture the 1944 AL pennant with Luke Sewell, the former Indians coach, as manager. The 1943 and '44 seasons were forgettable for the Indians. As a concession to the war, teams trained closer to home in 1943, 1944 and 1945. Cleveland's chosen site, after three years in Fort Myers, Florida, was Purdue University in West Lafayette, Indiana.

Having lost Hal Trosky in 1942, the Tribe lost his replacement, Les Fleming, to a military job in 1943. Mickey Rocco became Fleming's replacement.

The 1943 Indians were short on offense, but had a pair of 17-game winners in Al Smith and Jim Bagby. Rookie Allie Reynolds showed promise with 11 victories and veteran Vern Kennedy added 10. Cleveland had six representatives in the All-Star Game including Bagby, Smith, Boudreau, Keltner, Jeff Heath and catcher Buddy Rosar.

The building blocks of the 1948 world champions continued to arrive in the early 1940s. Catcher Jim Hegan (left) and third baseman Bob Lemon (right) joined the Tribe in 1941. Lemon, of course, eventually became a Hall-of-Fame pitcher.

The Indians started fast in 1943 and held second place in August. As New York pulled away to the pennant, the Tribe slipped behind Washington to finish third with a record of 82-71.

Boudreau won the AL batting title in 1944 with a .327 average, but the Indians fell to fifth place (tied with Philadelphia).

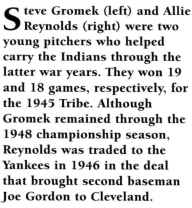

Steve Gromek (left) and Allie Reynolds (right) were two young pitchers who helped carry the Indians through the latter war years. They won 19 and 18 games, respectively, for the 1945 Tribe. Although Gromek remained through the 1948 championship season, Reynolds was traded to the Yankees in 1946 in the deal that brought second baseman Joe Gordon to Cleveland.

Mel Harder rebounded from an injury to lead the team with just 12 wins, one of which was the 200th of his career, making him the first to win 200 with the Tribe.

Steve Gromek emerged as a 10-game winner in 1944 and a husky outfielder, Pat Seerey, hit 15 home runs, second to Roy Cullenbine's 16. Keltner led with 91 RBI, followed by 80 from Cullenbine. George Susce came off the coaching staff and, at age 37, caught in 29 games after having appeared in just six games the previous three years.

The 1945 season was largely over before it started. Keltner and Mack were called into military duty. Feller was still in the Navy. Harder took a military-related job. When Heath suffered a serious knee injury, Boudreau was left as the only established star in the everyday lineup. And then he was lost to a broken ankle on August 13.

The following day, August 14, 1945, marked the end of World War II. Bob Feller's return to the Indians was cause for civic celebration in Cleveland. For his first start since 1941, 46,477 fans came to Cleveland Municipal Stadium and saw him strike out 12 and beat Hal Newhouser and the Tigers, 4-2. Despite Feller's return and outstanding pitching by Gromek (19-9) and Reynolds (18-12), the Tribe hovered around the break-even point throughout the season. Greenberg's return to the Tigers propelled Detroit to the AL pennant, 11 games ahead of the fifth-place Indians (73-72).

A golden age of baseball was in store following the end of World War II. A golden age was also on the horizon for the Indians, but not without a major shakeup in operations. With almost 20 years invested and only one real shot at a pennant in 1940, the Alva Bradley ownership was looking to sell out.

Ken Keltner was firmly established at third base by the mid 1940s. In his rookie season of 1938, he hit 26 home runs and drove in 113. In 1941, he made two outstanding defensive plays to help stop Joe DiMaggio's 56-game hitting streak. The best offensive season of his 12-year Tribe career came in 1948 when he batted .297 with 31 homers and 119 RBI.

A New Home on the Lakefront

INNING 5

The Best of Times for the Tribe

1946–1956

The Bill Veeck era in Cleveland is the one by which all others are measured. In just three years, Veeck's Indians created memories to last a lifetime. Indeed, as the 2000 season commenced, the memories of the Veeck era in general, and the 1948 season in particular, still waited to be matched by another world championship. Veeck was a showman and a baseball man. He is revered by many for bringing the unexpected and unusual to baseball. He is criticized by others for detracting from "pure" baseball. Either way, for a brief moment, he made Cleveland the most exciting baseball town around.

By 1946, several of the investors in the Alva Bradley group that purchased the Indians in 1927 were deceased, their stock in the team inherited by their widows. The Indians generally garnered more bad press than good, even in 1940 when the team came closest to bringing the Bradley ownership a championship. Constant negative publicity made brothers John and Francis Sherwin inclined to sell their interest in the club. If owners of the Cleveland Indians were looking to sell, Bill Veeck was looking to buy. Unlike the Bradley ownership, Veeck came from baseball bloodlines. William Louis Veeck, Sr., became vice president and treasurer of the Chicago Cubs in 1918. The following year he became club president and ran the team until his death in 1933.

Bill Veeck, Jr., began working around Wrigley Field at an early age, doing a variety of jobs. He is credited with hanging the ivy on the outfield fence. By 1941, at age 27, he had risen to the post of treasurer of the Cubs. But his upward mobility was limited in Chicago. He moved into ownership by purchasing the Milwaukee Brewers of the American Association. In Milwaukee, Veeck did two things that would mark his career—putting on unique, sometimes outrageous, promotions, and putting a winning team on the field. The Brewers won three consecutive AA pennants (1943-45).

Bob Feller's first full season after returning from World War II was his best. Winning 26 games, his 348 strikeouts were a career high and his 2.18 ERA was a career low. He pitched his second no-hitter (above) on April 30, a 1-0 win over New York at Yankee Stadium.

From December 1943, until spring 1944, Veeck served in the Marines. He suffered a severe injury when a recoiling antiaircraft gun crushed his right foot on Bougainville. Ultimately, part of Veeck's right leg would be amputated.

Veeck sold the Brewers following the 1945 season and went in search of a major league team. His two leading candidates were the Indians and the Pittsburgh Pirates. In Cleveland, he found a team languishing from poor performance, poor promotion and an uninspired ownership. The growth potential was substantial.

On June 21, 1946, a syndicate headed by the 32-year-old Veeck purchased the Indians. As head of the fourth ownership group in franchise history, Veeck was a dramatic departure from Alva Bradley, Charles Somers and Jim Dunn. He was, to a much greater extent, a man of the people, sensing that Cleveland fans would respond favorably to a more fan-friendly approach. Among his first moves was to establish the presence of the club on local radio. Indians games had not been broadcast in 1945. On June 28, 1946, four stations carried the game. Jack Graney and Bob Neal called the contest on WGAR, Earl Harper on WJW, Don Campbell on WHK and Tom Manning on WTAM.

Veeck's impact on the Cleveland baseball scene was recognized with a new award. He received the first Man of the Year Award from the Cleveland Baseball Writers. He is the only Indians owner to have ever received the annual award.

When Veeck took the keys from Alva Bradley and company, he took over a team that was about average at best. The 1946 team could hardly make that claim. Take away

Bob Feller's 26-15 record and the Tribe had a 42-71 (.372) record. Cleveland scored 255 runs fewer than first-place Boston and finished last in the AL with a .245 team batting average. The best offensive performance was Pat Seerey's 26 home runs.

Feller was out to prove that he was the same dominating pitcher he had been before World War II. He gave early indication on April 30, 1946, with a masterpiece in New York against the Yankees. He was at the top of his game and pitched a no-hitter, the second of his career. A home run by catcher Frankie Hayes provided the only run of the game, a 1-0 Cleveland victory. Within a month though, Boston had blown every club except New York out of the AL pennant race. The Red Sox won 104 games in 1946, 36 better than the sixth-place Indians.

Aiding Feller in his no-hitter was outfielder Bob Lemon, who had also shown ability as a pitcher. Boudreau sent the 25-year-old Lemon to the mound 32 times in 1946, five times as a starter. Lemon won just four of nine decisions, but convinced the Tribe's brain trust that his future was on the pitching mound.

Feller not only accounted for most of Cleveland's wins in 1946, but he also recorded strikeouts at a record-setting pace. In his first 19 appearances, he had 10 or more strikeouts 10 times and pitched nine or more innings 18 times while posting a 14-5 record. His strikeout pace slowed, but "Rapid Robert" entered the second half of September in striking distance of Rube Waddell's all-time single-season record. The mark, according to *The Little Red Book*, the accepted source for baseball's records at the time, was 343. But as Feller challenged the record, new research indicated that the record was actually 349. He finished the season with 348. Whether or not Feller is ultimately recognized as the record holder, his 1946 season ranks among the best turned in by any major league pitcher.

Looking at the bare statistics that make up the statistical history of major league baseball, it is surprising that the Indians would, in such a dreadful season, set a club attendance record and crack the one-million mark for the first time. Attendance increased for every major league team in 1946 and nearly doubled from 10,841,123 in 1945 to 18,523,288 in '46.

Among Veeck's early decisions was to make Cleveland Municipal Stadium the Indians' full-time home. The daunting size of the stadium was a challenge for Veeck and a chance for his broad entertaining to draw a big crowd. With a promoter like Veeck and a competitive ball club, the dream that the municipal stadium would put Cleveland on a par with the New Yorks and the Bostons and the Chicagos finally became a reality.

The final major league game at League Park took place on September 21, 1946. There were no civic celebrations or elaborate farewells. Only 2,772 fans attended the game, a 5-3 loss to the Tigers. The home of Cleveland's National League Temple Cup champions of 1895, the American League and world champions of 1920, plus numerous stars from Cy Young to Bob Feller, was forsaken for the lakefront facility.

One other significant occurrence of 1946 took place on July 14 during a doubleheader at Fenway Park. In the first game, Boston's great left-handed hitter, Ted Williams, had four hits in five at-bats. To defend against Williams, Boudreau unveiled what became known as the "Williams shift," putting three infielders (first baseman Jimmy Wasdell, second baseman Jack Conway and himself at shortstop) between first base and second base. Third baseman Ken Keltner was positioned behind second, leaving the entire left side of the infield open.

Pat Seerey's brief stint as a promising home run slugger peaked in 1946 when the 23-year-old outfielder hit a career-high 26 for the Indians. He was eventually traded to the White Sox for outfielder Bob Kennedy in 1948.

Gene Bearden was one of Bill Veeck's earliest and best acquisitions. The 26-year-old minor league pitcher came to the Indians from the Yankees in a December 1946 deal that sent veteran second baseman Ray Mack to New York.

Left fielder George Case was pulled in toward the infield while center fielder Pat Seerey moved to right-center field and right fielder Hank Edwards played near the right-field line. The strategy dared Williams, perhaps the greatest pure hitter in baseball history, to hit the ball to the opposite field.

Boudreau gambled that the stubborn Williams would try to hit the ball through or over the shift and he was generally right. Still, Williams was Williams. He had one hit and scored two runs in that second game as Boston won, 6-4. But on September 13 at League Park, Williams did give in to the shift, punched a Red Embree pitch to left field and circled the bases for an inside-the-park home run. It gave Boston a 1-0 win to clinch the pennant.

Following the season, Veeck made three trades that would have a major impact on the Indians. On October 19, Veeck sent Allie Reynolds to the Yankees for second baseman Joe Gordon and third baseman Eddie Bockman. Gordon, a former Most Valuable Player with New York, provided the short-term benefits of bringing a power bat and a championship background to the Indians. In the longer term, Reynolds became a pitching mainstay on several Yankees World Series champions.

Veeck's next move came on December 6 when he sent second baseman Ray Mack and catcher Sherm Lollar to the Yankees for pitchers Gene Bearden and Al Gettel, and outfielder Hal Peck, who had been Veeck's personal good-luck charm from his days of running the minor league club in Milwaukee. Bearden would forever make his mark on Cleveland baseball in 1948.

Finally, on December 7, Veeck dealt outfielder Gene Woodling to the Pittsburgh Pirates for catcher Al Lopez. Although he only played one season (1947) with the Indians, Lopez remained in the Cleveland system as a minor league manager and eventually became the successor to Boudreau.

Veeck's first full season as owner dawned with a new optimism, a new team image in the form of a team logo and a new spring training site, Tucson, Arizona. New uniforms had been introduced in 1946, the first substantial change to Cleveland's home uniforms since 1929. The 1946 white home shirts featured "Indians" in red script with navy-blue trim, replacing the large red wishbone "C." Then in 1947, the animated face of an Indian sporting a toothy grin was added to the left shoulder. "Chief Wahoo" became a part of Cleveland baseball and, over time, increasingly controversial.

Cleveland's pitching staff showed improvement and more balance in 1947. Bob Feller was again the league leader in wins (20), innings pitched (299) and strikeouts (196). Al Gettel and Bob Lemon each won 11 games, Don Black added 10 and Eddie Klieman developed into a dependable reliever. Black pitched a no-hitter against the Philadelphia Athletics on July 10.

Mel Harder, age 37, won six games in his final big league season for a career total of 223 major league victories, then the most by any pitcher in Indians history and, at the close of the 1900s, second only to Feller. Master Melvin was Cleveland's all-time leader with 582 games pitched and, with Feller, is one of only two pitchers with more than 3,000 innings pitched for the Indians. Harder's distinguished pitching career was over, but he began a new and equally illustrious career in the coaching ranks when he was named first base coach just before the start of the 1948 season.

With second baseman Gordon, shortstop Boudreau and third baseman Keltner, the infield was as good as any in baseball. Eddie Robinson emerged as the starting first baseman. Jim Hegan was not an imposing batter, but his defense and handling of pitchers ranked with baseball's best and the native of Lynn, Massachusetts, became the full-time catcher. The outfield, consisting of Hank Edwards, George "Catfish" Metkovich, Dale Mitchell, Peck and Seerey, left room for improvement. Still, the Indians led the American League in doubles, topped by Boudreau's league-high 45, and finished fourth in runs scored, third in batting average and second in home runs with 112 behind New York's 115. Cleveland's fourth-place finish (80-74) was 17 games behind the first-place Yankees, but was a marked improvement from 1946. Fans responded with a record

Lou Boudreau completes a double play over a breakup attempt by Joe Gordon in 1946. After the season, Bill Veeck sent pitcher Allie Reynolds to the Yankees for Gordon, who then joined Boudreau as the short-stop-second base combination for the 1948 world champions.

The Best of Times for the Tribe

home attendance of 1,521,978. Once again, the Tribe was the top draw among major league clubs outside New York, following the Yankees, Dodgers and Giants.

The big story of major league baseball in 1947, certainly in its long-term impact, was integration. The Brooklyn Dodgers broke the long-standing color barrier when Jackie Robinson appeared in their opening-day lineup. Robinson was the first African-American to appear in a major league game since the nineteenth century. Like Branch Rickey, Veeck was a champion of integration, from both moral and business standpoints.

According to *Pride Against Prejudice, The Biography of Larry Doby* by Joseph B. Moore, Veeck assigned former big league catcher Bill Killefer to the task of finding an appropriate player to integrate the Indians and the American League. Veeck wanted an up-and-coming star with a future, rather than an older, established star of the Negro Leagues. The player who kept rising back to the top of Veeck's list was Larry Doby, a young second baseman for the Newark Eagles of the Negro National League. Doby, born December 13, 1924, in Camden, South Carolina, hit seven home runs for Newark in 1946 and was off to a blazing start in 1947.

Integration came to the American League on July 3, 1947, upon the announcement that the Indians had signed Doby to a major league contract. The Tribe's newest player traveled directly to Chicago and made his debut on July 5, suffering a strikeout as a pinch hitter against the White Sox. For the remainder of the season, Doby would see limited playing time. With Gordon on the roster, there was no place for Doby at second base. He played in four games at second, one at first and one at shortstop. Of his 32 at-bats in 29 games, 21 were as a pinch hitter.

Another event of 1947 was the installation of an interior fence at Cleveland Municipal Stadium that would reduce the playing field to more manageable distances, especially as far as the hitters were concerned. Distance from home plate to center field was cut from 468 feet to 410. The power alleys in left and right field, which had been 435 feet, were reduced to 365. For a time, the fence was portable—moved closer to, or further from, home plate at Veeck's direction, depending on the opponent. That practice was outlawed following the season.

From the moment Veeck arrived in Cleveland, speculation began about the future of player-manager Lou Boudreau. The issue reached a fever pitch with rumors of a trade that would send him to the Browns for their talented shortstop, Vern Stephens.

In his autobiography *Veeck-As In Wreck* (with Ed Linn), Cleveland's new owner said he felt the Indians should have done better in 1947, thought veteran catcher Al Lopez was the best managerial prospect in baseball and was ready to make the deal with St. Louis and make Lopez the manager.

In his autobiography, *Lou Boudreau, Covering All The Bases* (with Russell Schneider, 1993), Boudreau said, "I knew that he [Veeck] valued me as a shortstop, but it was also evident from the day he arrived in Cleveland that he didn't consider me a good manager."

Public opinion, which was substantial, heavily favored Boudreau. Veeck would likely not have been swayed from making a deal he thought best, but he could not come to terms with St. Louis owner Bill DeWitt and was also concerned DeWitt would turn around and send Boudreau to the already-loaded Red Sox. Ever the promoter, Veeck publicly obliged Indians fans by retaining Boudreau.

A solid infield, offensively and defensively, was an Indians trademark of the late 1940s. The starting infield of the 1948 world champions was (l-r) third baseman Ken Keltner, shortstop Lou Boudreau, second baseman Joe Gordon and first baseman Eddie Robinson.

In addition to Boudreau, the brain trust for the 1948 Indians included coaches Bill McKechnie, Herold "Muddy" Ruel and Mel Harder. McKechnie was a dependable major league infielder from 1907 through 1920 before embarking on a Hall-of-Fame career as a manager. He guided three different franchises, the 1925 Pittsburgh Pirates, 1928 St. Louis Cardinals and the 1939 and 1940 Cincinnati Reds into the World Series, winning in '25 and '40. After nine seasons with the Reds, McKechnie announced his retirement late during the 1946 season. Veeck quickly offered him a lucrative salary to assist Boudreau. Ruel was a catcher for 19 major league seasons from 1915 through 1934 and appeared in the 1924 and 1925 World Series for Washington. He managed the Browns to a 59-95 record and last place in 1947.

Another new, integral part of the operation was future Hall of Famer Hank Greenberg. The tall slugger had come to the Indians after 12 seasons with the Tigers and one with the Pirates. Throughout the spring, Greenberg was in uniform as a player-coach, serving as insurance at first base. By opening day, however, he was wearing a suit and handling front office duty as an aide to Veeck. Greenberg never did play in a regular-season game for the Indians.

Manager Lou Boudreau greets Larry Doby before his first game in the major leagues in 1947. The 22-year-old outfielder broke the AL color line on July 5 against the White Sox at Comiskey Park.

The Best of Times for the Tribe

BOB LEMON

P-3B-OF • Indians • 1941-1942, 1946-1958   National Baseball Hall of Fame, 1976

Boudreau, McKechnie, Ruel and Harder's team had some strong points and plenty of question marks entering the 1948 season. The infield could hold its own with any in baseball. The star of the outfield was line-drive-hitting Dale Mitchell. Larry Doby was making a transition from a second baseman to an outfielder. Pat Seerey remained a budding slugger with a penchant for strikeouts. Thurman Tucker, acquired in the off-season, was primarily known for defense. Behind the plate, Jim Hegan had no peers in catching and calling a game. The 1947 Indians led the majors with a .983 fielding average and trailed only the White Sox in double plays. But the Tribe could not match the powerful world champion Yankees in run scoring.

At the top of the plus column on the pitching staff was all-star Bob Feller, a 20-game winner in 1947. Backed up by Don Black, Bob Lemon, Red Embree (traded to the Yankees for outfielder Allie Clark after the season) and Al Gettel, Feller had led the Tribe to the second best team earned-run average in the major leagues. Paced by Ed Klieman's league-leading 17 saves, Cleveland also led the AL in that department, but tied for the major league lead in most walks allowed.

Entering 1948, Feller was the only proven commodity on the staff. Rapid Robert and Lemon, who had only converted to pitching from playing third base and outfield in 1946, were now counted on to combine for 40 wins. In addition to Black and Gettel, Gene Bearden was a possible contributor with his left-handed knuckleball.

The pitching staff got a much-needed boost on April 3 when Veeck purchased relief pitcher Russ Christopher from the Athletics. A frail looking, lanky pitcher with a heart condition, he had been an effective hurler for the A's in short stints. Christopher would prove to be a valuable partner for Klieman in the bullpen.

Veeck had already made dramatic changes since his 1946 arrival. In addition to the Gordon and Bearden deals, "the Sportshirt" dealt with the Browns to acquire pitcher Bob Muncrief, outfielder Walt Judnich and infielder Johnny Berardino.

The Indians migrated home from training camp with a mix of all-stars, established players and several newcomers—Tucker, Clark, Judnich, Berardino, Muncrief, Christopher and pitcher Butch Wensloff, acquired on April 12 from the Yankees.

Entering the 1948 season, the Yankees and Red Sox were considered the teams to beat, with the Tigers also expected to rank in the first division. The Indians were generally picked third or fourth by the pundits.

Bill Veeck (above photo, left) confers with Lou Boudreau at the Stadium. Veeck's lack of confidence in his young manager prompted him to add experienced coaches to the 1948 staff. One was Bill McKechnie (left), who had managed four National League pennant winners.

Satchel Paige was a 20-year legend of the Negro Leagues when he joined the Tribe for the second half of the 1948 season. The 40-something right hander erased skepticism about his abilities by contributing six wins as a starter and reliever.

Entering the broadcast booth in 1948 was Jimmy Dudley, who quickly became a fan favorite as the entire city seemingly tuned in to every Indians broadcast. Dudley teamed with Jack Graney to paint the word picture for six seasons, then remained through 1967. He later received the highest honor for a baseball broadcaster, the Ford C. Frick Award—the equivalent of the broadcasters wing of the National Baseball Hall of Fame.

The first television broadcast of an Indians game also took place in 1948, with Van Patrick calling the game on WEWS-TV.

The Tribe was a perfect 6-0 in April as the season began and a four-way battle for first place between the Indians, Yankees, Red Sox and Connie Mack's surprising Athletics took place during the first half of the season. With 39 wins in its first 62 games, Cleveland held first place at the end of June. Boudreau carried the team with his bat, defense and leadership.

Lemon and Bearden paced the team from the pitching mound as Feller opened with an uncharacteristic slow start. Veeck then turned to the Browns again and dealt for pitcher Sam Zoldak. whose ego was substantially inflated when the trade included $100,000 to St. Louis. The 29-year-old left-hander may not have been worth six figures, but he contributed nine vital wins to the Indians of 1948. Lemon closed out the month of June with a no-hitter to defeat the Tigers, 2-0, in Detroit.

In early July, the maverick Veeck struck again by signing Negro Leagues legendary pitcher Leroy "Satchel" Paige. The amazing Paige had been pitching in the Negro Leagues since 1927, was its most famous player and would become the first player inducted into the National Baseball Hall of Fame for his Negro Leagues accomplishments. A skeptical Boudreau was convinced of Paige's ability following a secret workout at the Stadium. J.G. Taylor Spink, editor of *The Sporting News*, then known as the "Bible of Baseball," was not convinced and blasted the signing as another of Veeck's promotional stunts. Paige proved Veeck right and Spink wrong. Paige was a great drawing card, but he also won six of seven decisions and, at 48 years old or older, became a candidate for the Rookie of the Year award.

As Cleveland suffered its only losing month of 1948 in July (14-15), Boston caught fire with 24 wins in 33 games. At the end of the month, the Red Sox were first and the Athletics second. The Indians and Yankees were both two games off the pace.

On August 1, with an attendance of 70,702 at the Stadium, Lemon and Zoldak pitched the Indians to a double-header sweep of the Red Sox and launched a stretch of 18 victories in 22 games. One of the most memorable in franchise history came on August 8 in the first game of a doubleheader against the Yankees. Boudreau was on the bench, resting his constantly-aching ankles and an injured finger. In the seventh inning with the Indians trailing, 6-4, and the bases loaded, Boudreau called on himself as a pinch-hitter. Encouraged by the large crowd of 73,484, he faced ace relief pitcher Joe Page and delivered with a two-run single to center as the fans went wild. The inspired Indians won the game, 8-6, and swept the doubleheader.

Cleveland took a three-game lead on August 20 when Paige pitched a three-hit 1-0 shutout against the White Sox with 78,382 fans at the Stadium, the biggest crowd ever to see a major league night game. Paige's win was the fourth straight shutout by Tribe pitchers. Lemon was on the verge of a fifth when ninth-inning home runs by Aaron Robinson and Dave Philley gave last-place Chicago a 3-2 win that sent the Indians reeling to 11 losses in 18 games and 4.5 games behind the first-place Red Sox.

The most joyous season in Cleveland Indians history was tempered by tragedy. On September 13, Don Black, the no-hit pitcher of 1947, relegated to the background in

1948, took the mound against the Browns. Batting in the second inning, Black suddenly slumped at home plate. He had suffered a cerebral hemorrhage and entered St. Vincent Charity Hospital in critical condition. He would recover, but would never again appear in a major league game. To assist Black and his family, Veeck designated the game of September 22 as Don Black Night at the Stadium.

The Indians' second seven-game winning streak of September culminated on the 22nd when Feller beat Boston, 5-2, before 76,772 at the Stadium to tie the Indians with the Red Sox for first place. Feller pitched Cleveland into first place on the 26th. His sixth consecutive win was a five-hit performance against the Tigers. Joe Gordon hit his 31st homer to help produce the 4-1 victory.

The next game featured one of Veeck's most memorable promotions. Indians fan Joe Earley had written to a local newspaper that there should be a night for a loyal fan, not just for players, former players, dignitaries and the like. The idea was perfect for Veeck, a champion of the fans and the owner for whom Tribe fans have always had the most affection. Veeck chose Earley as the honoree and at "Good Old Joe Earley Night" he was showered with gifts of both the gag and the practical variety.

After the festivities, the Indians got down to business against the White Sox. Dale Mitchell led off the game with a home run and Bearden coasted to his 18th win, 11-0, before 60,405 fans at the Stadium.

Trainer Lefty Weisman and coach Bill McKechnie assist Don Black after he dropped to one knee while batting in the second inning of a game against the Browns on September 13, 1948. The Tribe pitcher, who had thrown a no-hitter in 1947, suffered a cerebral hemorrhage and would never again pitch in a major league game.

G ene Bearden's pitch-ing heroics helped to carry the Indians to the 1948 world championship. The rookie left hander went the distance for his 20th win, 8-3, over the Boston Red Sox (right) in the one-game playoff. Then in the World Series, he shut out the Boston Braves, 2-0, in Game 3 and saved Game 6, the final contest, won by the Tribe, 4-3.

Cleveland completed September with 20 wins in 26 decisions and headed into the final weekend of the regular season needing two wins to clinch the pennant.

October began when Lemon suffered a loss to the Tigers. The next day, Bearden won his 19th game and clinched a tie for the pennant with an 8-0 victory. The Red Sox defeated the Yankees to eliminate New York from the race. On the final day of the season, 74,181 fans flocked to the Stadium in anticipation that Feller would deliver Cleveland its first pennant since 1920. His opponent was Hal Newhouser, his great rival of the 1940s. On Bill Veeck Day in Cleveland, "Prince Hal" had the upper hand and defeated the Tribe, 7-1. Boston routed New York, 10-5, and at the end of the day, the Indians and Red Sox had identical 96-58 records. For the first time in major league history, the pennant race would be decided with a one-game playoff.

Both managers had surprises in store with their starting pitching choices. Starting for Boudreau and the Indians would be Bearden with just one day's rest. Boston manager Joe McCarthy's choice was even more surprising—a well-rested Denny Galehouse, a 36-year-old right hander who won eight of 16 decisions in 1948, but who had been successful against the Indians.

Boudreau became the hero again in Boston. His first-inning home run off Galehouse opened the scoring. Boston tied the score in the first, but Boudreau ignited the Tribe offense again in the fourth with a lead-off single. Joe Gordon followed with another single and Ken Keltner broke the game open with a three-run homer over the "Green Monster" in Fenway Park's left field. Cleveland added another run in the fourth off relief pitcher Ellis Kinder when Larry Doby doubled and scored.

The Best of Times for the Tribe

Boudreau blasted another homer in the fifth inning and Cleveland led, 6-1. Boston scored a pair in the fifth on Bobby Doerr's two-run homer, but the Tribe added solo runs in the eighth and ninth innings. Bearden went the distance and was carried off the field with an 8-3 victory that gave Cleveland the pennant. Boudreau finished the game with four hits, two home runs and three runs scored.

From intimate Fenway Park to big Braves Field, the Indians remained in Boston to begin the 1948 World Series against the NL champions featuring pitchers Warren Spahn and Johnny Sain, shortstop Alvin Dark, second baseman Eddie Stanky, third baseman Bob Elliott and outfielder Tommy Holmes. Former Tribe star Jeff Heath was also with the Braves, but sidelined with a broken ankle. The Braves had finished a comfortable 6.5 games ahead of second-place St. Louis.

Bob Feller would make his first World Series appearance in the opening game of the 1948 classic. Braves manager Billy Southworth had Sain, the NL leader with 24 wins, ready to face Feller in a classic pitching duel. The 29-year-old Feller began by retiring the first 11 batters before walking Earl Torgeson in the fourth inning. He surrendered his first hit, to Marv Rickert, in the fifth and then retired another nine straight.

Cleveland, however, fared little better against Sain and the game was scoreless as Boston batted in the eighth inning. A lead-off walk to Bill Salkeld, sacrifice by Mike McCormick and an intentional walk to Stanky preceded one of the most memorable plays in World Series history.

Jubilant teammates carry Gene Bearden off the field at Fenway Park (opposite page) after the Tribe beat the Red Sox for the 1948 pennant in a one-game playoff, 8-3, on October 4. Below, Bill Veeck, Steve Gromek and Bearden (l-r) arrive in the clubhouse for more celebrating.

The Best of Times for the Tribe

Phil Masi's hand touches second base after Lou Boudreau tagged him on a pick-off play peg from Bob Feller in the eighth inning of Game 1 of the 1948 World Series. Masi was called safe and then scored the eventual winning run on a single by Tommy Holmes.

As pinch runner Phil Masi led off second base, Cleveland executed its well-rehearsed pick-off play. On a set count, Boudreau raced to second as Feller threw to the base. Masi dove back to second and was called safe by NL umpire Bill Stewart. Boudreau argued with Stewart to no avail. Photographs later showed Masi to be out, but the call had been made and the game continued. Feller retired Sain on a fly to right field, but Holmes followed with an opposite-field hit down the left-field line to score Masi with what became the only run of the game. Sain allowed just four hits in the 1-0 victory.

Lemon and Spahn were the starting pitchers in the second game. Boston scored first again, but the Braves' first-inning rally was held to a run when Lemon and Boudreau employed the pick-off play again and successfully caught Torgeson off second base. Lemon ended the inning with a strikeout of Rickert.

LEGENDS OF THE TRIBE

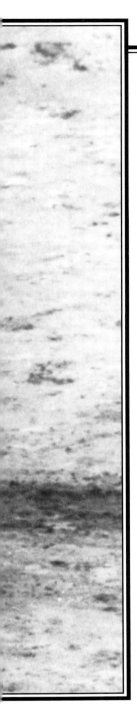

Cleveland's offense finally came alive against Spahn in the fourth inning. Boudreau started things again with a double into the right-field corner. Gordon singled home the first run for the Indians, then scored on Doby's hit. That was all the offense Lemon needed, but the Tribe added single runs on Boudreau's RBI hit in the fifth and Bob Kennedy's run-scoring bloop single in the ninth. Pitching shutout ball after the first, Lemon went the distance for a 4-1 victory to deadlock the series.

The first World Series game at Cleveland Municipal Stadium brought 70,306 fans to a Friday-afternoon showdown between Bearden and Vern Bickford. Cleveland's phenomenon surpassed his performance in the playoff against the Red Sox by pitching a five-hit shutout, getting two hits and scoring the game's first run in the third inning. Jim Hegan's fourth-inning single off Bickford scored Keltner with the other run in a 2-0 triumph.

Lou Boudreau congratulates Bob Lemon after his complete-game pitching performance in Game 2 of the 1948 World Series. The Tribe's 4-1 victory evened the series at 1-1.

The biggest crowd in World Series history to that point, 81,897 crammed into the Stadium for Saturday's fourth game. With the series lead, Boudreau selected Steve Gromek to face Sain and then provided Cleveland the lead with a first-inning double to score Mitchell. Doby doubled the margin in the third with a blast over the right field fence for the first home run of the series. The blow proved to be the winning margin after Marv Rickert homered in the Boston seventh.

Gromek pitched the game of his life, scattering seven hits and one run. After the game, photos of Doby and Gromek embracing and celebrating in the Cleveland clubhouse appeared in newspapers, thus providing another step in the progress of integrating major league baseball. Doby, Gromek and company had put the Indians within one win of a world championship.

Cleveland was set to celebrate on Sunday, October 10. For the fifth game, the Indians' record-setting flame thrower, Bob Feller, would go for the clincher before a World Series record crowd of 86,288, the largest ever to see an Indians' game in Cleveland. Feller had pitched many of the greatest games in franchise history, but the fifth game of the 1948 World Series was not one of them.

After four pitching duels, the fifth game was a slugfest. Tommy Holmes and Alvin Dark began the game with singles. One out later, Bob Elliott hit a three-run homer over the right-field fence. Dale Mitchell led off the Cleveland first with a homer off Boston's 37-year-old starter Nels Potter, but Elliott pulled a Feller pitch over the left field fence for another home run in the third.

The Indians, who had provided Feller just one run in 12 innings, came through in the fourth. After Joe Gordon singled and Ken Keltner walked, Walt Judnich looped a single to center that scored Gordon. One out later, Jim Hegan hit a three-run homer into the lower-left-field stands that gave the Indians a 5-4 lead.

Feller retired the next four batters he faced, but Bill Salkeld hit a game-tying homer just over the right-field fence in the sixth inning. Feller survived the sixth, but not the seventh when Holmes singled, Dark sacrificed and Earl Torgeson singled to put Boston back in front. Boudreau finally had to pull Feller from the game, but relief pitcher Eddie Klieman fared even worse. All three batters to face him reached base and Boston's lead grew to 8-5 before Boudreau could call on Russ Christopher. Hits by Mike McCormick and Eddie Stanky scored two more runs for the Braves. Finally, Boudreau called on Satchel Paige, making him the first African-American ever to pitch in the World Series.

Heroes embrace after the Tribe beat the Braves, 2-1, in Game 4 of the 1948 World Series. Steve Gromek (left) pitched a complete-game seven-hitter and Larry Doby (right) hit a solo homer in the third inning that became the game winner. The photo appeared in newspapers nationwide and helped to further the acceptance of African-Americans in major league baseball.

Paige put out the fire, but not before a sacrifice fly by Warren Spahn made the score 11-5. Spahn closed out five-and-two-thirds innings of one-hit relief pitching with a strikeout of pinch-hitter Joe Tipton to force a return trip to Boston.

Bob Lemon got the nod for game six and allowed one run through the first seven innings. Boudreau gave the Indians the lead with a third-inning double near the right-field line off Tommy Holmes's glove to score Dale Mitchell. The Indians regained the lead in the sixth when Joe Gordon homered off starter Bill Voiselle. A walk to Thurman Tucker, a single by Eddie Robinson and a groundout by Jim Hegan made the score 3-1, Cleveland.

Billy Southworth turned to Warren Spahn again in the eighth inning, but the star left hander struggled. Singles by Ken Keltner, Tucker and Robinson plated another run and made the score 4-1.

Boston then rallied against Lemon in the eighth. A single by Holmes, a double by Earl Torgeson and a walk to Bob Elliott loaded the bases. With the game in the balance, Boudreau replaced Lemon with Gene Bearden. The knuckleballer surrendered a sacrifice fly to pinch-hitter Clint Conatser that scored Holmes and moved Torgeson to third. Phil Masi, batting for Bill Salkeld, belted a drive off the left-field wall for a double as Elliott reached third. But Bearden finally snuffed out the rally, and preserved a 4-3 lead, when Mike McCormick grounded back to the pitcher for the final out of the inning. Spahn struck out the side (Bearden, Kennedy and Doby) in the top of the ninth

to set the stage for a dramatic ending. As 40,103 fans rooted for a rally, Stanky led off with a walk. Pinch hitter Sibby Sisti was called on to sacrifice. His bunt attempt popped up in front of home plate. Hegan charged out from behind the plate to make the catch and threw to first, easily doubling pinch runner Connie Ryan off first. The dynamic defensive play had put Cleveland an out from victory. Holmes hit a long fly to left field, but Bob Kennedy made the catch to end the game. The Cleveland Indians had a 4-3 victory and were world champions again. For the second time in a week, Bearden received a hero's ride in Boston as his happy teammates carried him off the mound.

Of all the great individual accomplishments in 1948, Lou Boudreau's overall play and leadership clearly ranks first. He was appropriately honored as the Most Valuable Player in the American League. His .355 batting average—a career high—led the Indians and trailed only Ted Williams in the AL.

Dale Mitchell finished third in the circuit with his .336 batting average. Larry Doby improved dramatically and sparkled in the World Series, leading the Indians with seven hits and batting .318. Joe Gordon led the club in home runs (32) and RBI (124). Bob Lemon and Gene Bearden were both second to Hal Newhouser with their 20 wins and Bob Feller was right behind them with 19. Lemon added two more wins in the World Series and Bearden was not charged with a run in his two appearances.

The world champion Indians exit Braves Field in Boston after defeating the Braves, 4-3, on October 11 in Game 6 of the 1948 World Series.

The Best of Times for the Tribe

Stars of Game 6 celebrate with manager Lou Boudreau after the Tribe won the 1948 World Series. From left to right are Joe Gordon, who hit a solo homer in the sixth, Bob Lemon, who surrendered three runs in seven-and-one-third innings, Boudreau, and Gene Bearden, who saved it for Lemon.

Bob Feller and Satchel Paige (opposite page) compare grips at the Stadium. The Tribe lost its grip on the pennant in 1949, finishing in third place, eight games behind New York. Feller dropped to 15-14 with just 108 strikeouts while Paige slipped to 4-7.

Total attendance for the World Series was 358,362 with 238,491 fans attending the games in Cleveland. The whopping turnout resulted in a winning share of $6,772.07 for the victorious Indians.

Bearden had been on the mound for Cleveland's two biggest wins in 1948, but he would never again match his heroics. Nor would his teammates. In comparison to the 1948 Indians, little attention is paid to the 1949 Tribe. Bill Veeck had closed out 1948 with a trade that should have, and eventually would, make the team stronger. First baseman Eddie Robinson and pitchers Eddie Klieman and Joe Haynes went to the Senators for first baseman Mickey Vernon and pitcher Early Wynn. Under the guidance of Mel Harder, Wynn would blossom from a journeyman-caliber pitcher into a Hall of Famer.

Magic happens and the magic of 1948 could not be duplicated. Veterans Boudreau, Gordon and Keltner had crested. Bearden proved to be a one-year wonder, winning just eight of 16 decisions in 1949 and only 17 more in his big league career. Satchel Paige became mortal and Russ Christopher retired. Lemon won 22 games, but Feller dropped to 15. Mike Garcia, a 25-year-old right-hander, added 14 wins as a rookie.

The defending world champions finished third in 1949, eight games behind the New York Yankees and their new manager, Casey Stengel. Boston was again second, a game behind New York, in another crackling pennant race.

In addition to the typical distractions that come with a championship, an added burden was the filming of *The Kid From Cleveland*. Panned as a dreadful movie, the Republic Pictures production did capture some wonderful images of the Indians and Cleveland. Much of the filming took place in May and June, two sub-par months for the Indians who, when home, spent mornings filming on the set at League Park.

Another sideshow was the saga of Charlie Lupica. A passionate fan of the Indians, Lupica went up a flagpole early in the season and resolved to stay atop the pole until the Indians reclaimed first place. He ultimately had to give in and descend late in the season. Veeck took full advantage, staging an elaborate ceremony for the dismount.

Bill Veeck sheds a crocodile tear while coaches, players and officials stand in solemn silence (above) as team business manager Rudie Schaffer reads the service from the Bible of Baseball, *The Sporting News*, during a mock funeral at the Stadium in September 1949 after the Tribe dropped out of the pennant race. In one of Veeck's most bizarre stunts, the 1948 AL pennant and world championship banner (right) were both buried behind the center-field fence.

LEGENDS OF THE TRIBE

The Indians were officially dethroned on September 20 in Boston. When the club returned home, Veeck staged a mock burial of the American League champion and world champion banners that had flown over the Stadium during 1949. Veeck led the "funeral procession" driving a horse-drawn hearse to a grave dug behind center field. The flags were placed in a real casket and buried. The cardboard tombstone read "1948 Champs."

Financial considerations, including a pending divorce from his wife, Eleanor, and Veeck's never-ending desire for new challenges prompted him to arrange the sale of the Indians after the 1949 season. On November 21, the franchise was sold to a group led by 45-year-old Cleveland insurance executive Ellis Ryan. The flash that was the Bill Veeck ownership era was over. His great accomplishment, the 1948 world championship, may be the most cherished memory of modern Indians history. Whether he was shrewd, lucky, or both, Veeck's quick strike in Cleveland yielded an average home attendance of over two million per year for the three full seasons he owned the club. The Indians would not again reach such attendance heights until the 1990s. Veeck had also put in place the brain trust for the next era by bringing Hank Greenberg and Al Lopez into the fold.

Entering the new decade, general manager Hank Greenberg initiated a youth movement resulting in a 1950 team mixing the remaining heroes of 1948 with younger talent. There was stability in the outfield, the pitching staff and behind the plate. The Tribe infield, however, had an entirely new look. Lou Boudreau played just 81 games in 1950, his fewest since 1939, and became less a player and more a manager. A new left side featured 26-year-olds Ray Boone at shortstop and Al Rosen at third base. An exception to the youth movement was Luke Easter, a 35-year-old veteran of the Negro Leagues, who replaced the traded Mickey Vernon at first and provided added power.

Rosen's emergence meant the end of Ken Keltner's 12-year career in Cleveland. He signed on with the Red Sox, but played just 13 games for Boston (his only major league games out of a Tribe uniform) before calling it quits. In his 1,513 games with the Indians, Keltner became one of the club's all-time leaders in runs scored (735), home runs (163), doubles (306), RBI (850), hits (1,561), total bases (2,494) and extra base hits (538). He also set a Cleveland standard for defensive play at third base highlighted by the night in 1941 when he helped stop Joe DiMaggio's 56-game hitting streak.

Although the Indians posted the second-best record of Boudreau's tenure as manager—ranking behind only the 1948, 1920 and 1921 teams in team history—their mark of 92-62 was good only for fourth place, six games behind the Yankees.

The disappointing finish was sufficient cause for Greenberg to replace Boudreau at the helm with Al Lopez. Boudreau had managed the Indians for nine seasons with one first-place finish. Only the 1949 and 1950 clubs had finished within 10 games of first. But Lou Boudreau had defined Cleveland Indians baseball of the 1940s. As both manager and star player, he was the focal point through the war years and on to Cleveland's second world championship, joining another legendary player-manager, Tris Speaker, in leading the Tribe to ultimate victory.

Boudreau departed Cleveland third on the club's all-time games-played list (1,560). He is among the franchise's all-time leaders in runs scored (823), doubles (367), RBI (740), hits (1,706), total bases (2,392) and extra base hits (495).

Soon after being fired by Greenberg, Boudreau was quickly grabbed by Boston to play under former Indians manager Steve O'Neill. The next year, he succeeded O'Neill and also played his final four big league games.

Ray Boone was part of a youth movement as new general manager Hank Greenberg rebuilt three-fourths of the 1950 infield with 26-year-olds. Boone succeeded Lou Boudreau at shortstop, Bobby Avila took over at second for Joe Gordon and Al Rosen replaced Ken Keltner at third.

F irst baseman Luke Easter was known as the "Black Babe Ruth," when he was purchased from the Negro League's Homestead Grays in 1949. He hit 28 home runs with 107 RBI as a 35-year-old rookie in 1950.

Boudreau managed the Red Sox (1952-54) and Kansas City Athletics (1955-57) before returning to his native Illinois as a broadcaster for the Chicago Cubs, briefly leaving the broadcasting booth to manage the club in 1960. Boudreau ranks with Bob Feller as the greatest of Indians stars for a generation of Tribe fans. His accomplishments were extensively noted in 1970, both in Cleveland and nationally, when he was inducted into the National Baseball Hall of Fame. That same year, Boudreau's uniform number 5 became only the second ever retired by the Indians and the street alongside Cleveland Stadium was officially renamed Boudreau Boulevard.

LEGENDS OF THE TRIBE

To replace Boudreau, Greenberg promoted Al Lopez on November 10, 1950, from Cleveland's top farm club at Indianapolis. Born in Tampa, Florida, the 42-year-old Lopez had managed the Indianapolis Indians for three seasons, winning the American Association pennant in 1948, finishing second in 1949—but winning the AA playoffs and the Junior World Series—and finishing second again in 1950.

Nicknamed "El Senor," Lopez had been a catcher with the Dodgers, Braves, Pirates and Indians in a 19-year major league career that ended in 1947. He now began a Hall-of-Fame managerial career by outdistancing all teams outside of New York throughout his six-year Tribe tenure. His Indians finished second to the Yankees five times and, when they finished ahead of the Yankees in 1954, lost a four-game sweep to the New York Giants in the World Series.

The 1951 Indians combined young veterans with the experience of the 1948 World Series (Doby, Mitchell, Hegan and Lemon) with younger stars like Boone, Rosen and 27-year-old second baseman Bobby Avila. Lopez also had the best pitching staff in base-ball. Led by a rejuvenated Bob Feller, Cleveland had three 20-game winners in 1951: Feller (22), Garcia (20) and Wynn (20). Feller led the league in wins and Lemon added 17. One of Feller's wins, on July 1, was his third no-hitter, a 2-1 victory over the Tigers at the Stadium. At the time, Feller matched Cy Young for the most no-hitters in a big league career. The Big Four accounted for 130 starts, 159 games pitched and 1,041 of Cleveland's 1,391 total innings pitched.

Former catcher Al Lopez (left) was promoted to manager in November 1950 and guided the Tribe to the first of three consecutive second-place finishes in 1951. Bob Feller (above) is greeted by catcher Jim Hegan after pitching his third no-hitter, a 2-1 win over Detroit on July 1, 1951, at the Stadium.

The Best of Times for the Tribe

LARRY DOBY

OF • Indians • 1947-1955, 1958   National Baseball Hall of Fame, 1998

The great battle of 1951 (in fact, 1951-1956) was Cleveland's pitching and defense against the Yankees' powerful offense. In 1951, the Indians' offense was not enough of a match for New York. Cleveland finished fourth in the AL in runs scored and seventh in batting average. New York's pitching could not match the Tribe's, but it was close, led by 21-game-winners Ed Lopat and Vic Raschi and 17-game-winner Allie Reynolds, the former Indian.

The Yankees prevailed with 98 wins to the Indians' 93, winning their third straight AL pennant and beating the Giants in the World Series.

In conjunction with the 50th anniversary of the American League in 1951, the Indians established a team hall of fame. The initial inductees comprised an all-time Indians team for the club's first half-century, including two pitchers. The selections were pitchers Cy Young and Mel Harder, catcher Steve O'Neill, first baseman Hal Trosky, second baseman Napoleon Lajoie, shortstop Joe Sewell, third baseman Ken Keltner and outfielders Tris Speaker, Earl Averill and Joe Jackson, who was a controversial choice due to his role in the "Black Sox" scandal of 1919-1920.

There was a physical hall of fame inside the Stadium—on the concourse on the first-base side of the building—where old fans could relive memories and newer fans could learn about the Indians storied history. Inductions discontinued in the early 1970s, at which time the space in the Stadium was devoted to other use.

The Indians' offense blossomed to hold its own with, if not surpass, its pitching staff in 1952. Cleveland, not New York, led the AL in runs scored, home runs and slugging percentage. Al Rosen led the league with 105 RBI, one more than Larry Doby who led the league in runs scored (104), home runs (32) and slugging percentage (.541). Rosen, Dale Mitchell and Bobby Avila and all hit .300 or better.

Once again, the Big Four dominated the pitching achievements. Add fifth starter Steve Gromek and five pitchers accounted for 148 games started and 1,202 of 1,407 total innings pitched. Mike Garcia and Bob Lemon tied for the league lead with 36 starts. Lemon's 310 innings pitched was also a league high. Tribe pitchers turned in 80 complete games, led by Lemon's league-best 28.

Twenty-game winners became the norm for the Big Four starting rotation in the 1950s. Mike Garcia was 20-13 in 1951 (above). Garcia, Bob Lemon and Early Wynn (left photo, l-r) won 22, 22 and 23, respectively, in 1952.

Winning its first seven games and 25 of its first 42, Cleveland took the early lead in the 1952 AL race. One of the memorable early games of 1952 was a pitching duel between Feller and Bob Cain of Veeck's St. Louis Browns. (Veeck had purchased the St. Louis club in 1951). A year earlier when pitching for the Tigers, Cain had become best known for his part in Veeck's memorable 1951 stunt, pitching to midget Eddie Gaedel. On April 23, Cain was Feller's equal as both hurlers allowed just one hit apiece, setting an AL record for the fewest total hits in a game. Feller's was a lead-off triple to Bobby Young, who scored the only run of a 1-0 Browns win that actually gave them brief possession of first place.

In June, the Indians suffered a slump that would cost them the 1952 pennant. At the end of the month, slumping first baseman Luke Easter was farmed out to Indianapolis. The defense struggled and so did Bob Feller. Meanwhile, the Yankees won 21 of 30 decisions to move four games ahead of the Indians, who finished the season with a 93-61 record, just two games behind the champion Yankees.

A contending team was not good enough to keep the turnstiles clicking as they had been during the Veeck days. After drawing over 2.2 million fans in 1949 and over 1.7 million in 1950 and 1951, attendance fell to 1,444,607 in 1952. Still, only the Yankees had better home attendance in 1951 and 1952 as overall major league attendance slumped from its peak (over 20 million) in 1948 and 1949.

The ownership structure changed again following the 1952 season, establishing a pattern that would plague the franchise for decades. A majority of the owners voted out Ellis Ryan as club president. Ryan and his supporters sold their interest in the club, yielding a smaller ownership group with 65-year-old insurance executive Myron H. "Mike" Wilson, Jr., as president and including Donald Hornbeck, Harry Small, Nate Dolin, George Medinger and Charles M. Baxter. Hank Greenberg emerged in a stronger position as a result of the leadership changes.

A measure of apathy had set in by 1953 when the Indians ran second to New York (by 8.5 games) for the third straight season. Stengel's Yankees breezed to the pennant and interest in the Tribe suffered. Attendance plunged again by more than 25 percent.

With 43 homers, 145 RBI and a .336 batting average, Al Rosen almost won a triple crown while winning the AL MVP award in 1953.

There was, however, a dandy race, if not a pennant race, involving the 1953 Indians. Al Rosen made a valiant effort to capture batting's Triple Crown. The achievement of leading the league in batting average, home runs and runs batted in had been accomplished only twice since 1937, both times by Ted Williams of the Red Sox—1942 and 1947. Rosen edged out Philadelphia's Gus Zernial for the home run title, 43-42, and had no serious challenge to his AL-high 145 RBI. He also led the league in slugging percentage (.613) and runs scored (115). The race for the batting title matched Rosen

against former teammate Mickey Vernon of the Senators. On the final day of the season, Vernon held off Rosen to win the crown, .337 to .336. But Rosen's brilliant season earned him the American League's Most Valuable Player award.

Rosen's final bid for the Triple Crown coincided with Jack Graney's last broadcast as Indians radio announcer. Graney had been associated with the team since his playing days in the first decade of the century. Ed Edwards would take Graney's place in the radio booth for the 1954 and 1955 seasons.

The 1954 season promised to be special in Cleveland, if only for the return of the Major League Baseball All-Star Game, the first to be held in Cleveland since the third game of the series in 1935. As for the pennant race, the Yankees remained the team to beat for the Indians and every other AL club.

Cleveland's pitching staff, however, was better than ever. Art Houtteman, acquired from the Tigers in 1953, allowed Al Lopez to use Feller judiciously. At age 35, Rapid Robert was ready for one more quality season as a fifth starter behind a new Big Four of Bob Lemon, Early Wynn, Mike Garcia and Houtteman. A tandem of rookie relief pitchers—left-hander Don Mossi and right-hander Ray Narleski—would back-up the starters.

To further bolster the staff, Greenberg acquired his former teammate and two-time MVP Hal Newhouser from the Tigers. "Prince Hal" had won 200 games in his 15 seasons with Detroit as one of baseball's best starting pitchers. For the 1954 Indians, the 33-year-old left hander would start just once, but pitch 25 times in relief.

As the legendary Feller entered the twilight of his career, he was far from the dominant pitcher he had been in the 1940s, but still up to the challenge of most AL clubs. In 1954, Lopez restricted most of Feller's work to games against the second-division teams. The strategy paid off as Feller won all but three of his 16 decisions, the final winning season of his career.

If the 1954 Indians had one early weakness, it was at first base. Luke Easter got little opportunity to get on track and Bill Glynn provided minimal offense, though he did hit three homers in a game on July 5. Rosen saw considerable duty at first until June 1 when Chakales was traded to Baltimore for outfielder-first baseman Vic Wertz.

Left hander Don Mossi (left) and right hander Ray Narleski (center) were rookie relief pitchers who anchored the bullpen of the 1954 pennant winners. Art Houtteman (right) arrived from Detroit in 1953, then won 15 games as the fifth starter in 1954.

American Leaguers Al Rosen, Ted Williams, Mickey Vernon and Mickey Mantle (above, l-r) pose at Municipal Stadium prior to the 1954 All-Star Game, won by the AL, 11-9. Bobby Avila (right) was the Tribe's hitting star of 1954, winning the batting title with a .341 average.

After a slow start, the Indians climbed into first place in May. The White Sox briefly knocked them out of the top spot in June as the Yankees stayed close throughout the first half of the season.

The second All-Star Game at Cleveland Municipal Stadium provided several Indians with a chance to shine. Rosen hit a pair of home runs and drove in five. Avila had three hits in three at-bats. Cleveland set another record for All-Star Game attendance with a crowd of 68,751 who saw the AL prevail in a slugfest, 11-9.

On July 17, Feller pitched a two-hitter, with Don Bollweg collecting both hits, as Cleveland defeated Philadelphia for Feller's 256th career victory. On July 23, the Tribe kept a slim lead over New York by defeating the Yankees, 8-2, on two Larry Doby home runs and five RBI from Al Smith. Shortstop George Strickland, however, suffered a broken jaw and was lost until September. Doby's 10th inning home run the following day beat the Yankees again.

The Tribe continued to hold off New York. On August 21, Lemon started a triple play and Doby drove in his 100th run of the season to beat Baltimore, 4-1, and put the Indians 4.5 games ahead of the Yankees.

For the first time in franchise history, on September 9 at the Stadium, the Indians reached the century mark in victories. Rosen had three hits and Newhouser got the victory, a 5-4, 11-inning win against the Athletics.

After three straight seasons as second best, Cleveland finally put all the pieces in place to defeat New York. On September 12, a record crowd for a doubleheader of 84,587 fans crammed the Stadium to see the Indians battle the Yankees. In the opener, Rosen's two-run, seventh inning double broke a 1-1 tie and Lemon won his 22nd game with a six-hit, 4-1 victory. In the nightcap, fifth-inning singles by Wynn, Smith and Avila followed by Wally Westlake's double gave Cleveland three runs to overcome a two-run homer by Yogi Berra. Wynn won his 21st game with a three-hitter, 3-2. With a 104-40 record, the Indians opened an 8.5 game lead over the Yankees.

EARLY WYNN

Manager Al Lopez holds an Indians pennant while he and his Indians celebrate their clinching of the 1954 AL pennant following a 3-2 victory at Detroit on September 18.

Cleveland captured its third AL pennant on September 18 with a 3-2 victory in Detroit. In the seventh inning, a two-run, pinch-hit home run by Dale Mitchell followed by Jim Hegan's solo homer provided Wynn the support he needed. The next day, 2,000 fans greeted the champions when they returned home. Two days later, an 18-mile victory parade took place from Cleveland's East Side to the West Side.

To put icing on the regular season, Wynn flirted with a no-hitter on September 25 and settled for a two-hitter, his fourth of the season, to give Cleveland its 111th win. The Indians had broken the AL record for victories in a season, one more than the Yankees' 110 wins in 1927. The Tribe completed the best regular season in club history, and AL history, with a 111-43 record and hit the road for the World Series.

The five starting pitchers accounted for 147 starts and 93 victories. Lemon and Wynn tied for the league lead with 23 wins each. Garcia had 19 wins and led the AL with a 2.64 earned run average. Houtteman had 15 victories and Feller 13. Mossi (6), Narleski (3) and Newhouser (7) accounted for another 16 wins. The only other pitcher to enter the win column was Bob Chakales with a pair of victories. The Big Eight pitchers accounted for almost 95 percent (1,344) of 1,419 total innings pitched.

Cleveland led the AL in home runs for the fifth consecutive year, topped by league-leader Larry Doby's 32. He also led the league with 126 RBI. Bobby Avila won the batting title with a .341 average. Among AL clubs, only the Yankees outscored the Tribe.

Having finally dethroned the Yankees, the Indians were now faced with the New York Giants in the World Series. The Giants featured future Hall of Famers in outfielders Willie Mays and Monte Irvin, manager Leo Durocher and relief pitcher Hoyt Wil-

helm. New York had the best pitching staff in the National League led by 21-game winner Johnny Antonelli and relief aces Wilhelm and Marv Grissom. The Giants, winners of just 70 games under Durocher in 1953, won 97 in 1954, beating Brooklyn by five games in the standings. New York also held the home-field advantage, with the best-of-seven match-up starting on September 29 at the Polo Grounds.

Bob Lemon was Cleveland's first-game starter, opposed by veteran Sal "The Barber" Maglie. The Indians struck first in the first inning when Vic Wertz tripled off the right field wall to score Bobby Avila and Al Smith. The Giants tied the game in the third. Cleveland put runners in scoring position in the fourth, fifth and sixth innings, but could not score. Meanwhile, Lemon retired 12 of the 15 batters he faced from the fourth through the seventh inning.

The Indians drove Maglie from the box in the eighth when Larry Doby walked and Al Rosen singled. Relief pitcher Don Liddle came on to face Wertz who already had three hits. The slugging first baseman hit a mighty blow toward the deepest part of the Polo Grounds's expansive center field. Willie Mays turned at the crack of the bat, ran full speed with his back to the plate and made a spectacular catch 460 feet from home. Even better was his instantaneous whirling throw back to the infield. Doby and Rosen had anticipated the drive falling safely. Doby advanced to third as Rosen barely scrambled back to first. Liddle, having done his job, was relieved by Marv Grissom when Hank Majeski was announced to bat for Dave Philley. Lopez recalled Philley and sent Dale Mitchell to the plate. He walked to load the bases. Another pinch hitter, Dave Pope, was called out on strikes. Jim Hegan flied to left field to end the rally.

Willie Mays (left) makes his over-the-shoulder catch of Vic Wertz's eighth-inning drive in Game 1 of the 1954 World Series at the Polo Grounds. In the 10th, the Tribe's Dave Pope (right) leaps to no avail as a three-run game-winning homer by Dusty Rhodes sails into the right-field stands.

The starters for Game 1 of the 1954 World Series line up with manager Al Lopez at the Polo Grounds. From left to right are Lopez, Al Smith (LF), Bobby Avila (2B), Larry Doby (CF), Al Rosen (3B), Vic Wertz (1B), Dave Philley (RF), George Strickland (SS), Jim Hegan (C) and Bob Lemon (P).

Cleveland threatened to score again in the ninth and tenth innings, but was turned away by Grissom both times. In the New York tenth, Mays walked and stole second. Hank Thompson was intentionally walked. Durocher then called on outfielder James "Dusty" Rhodes to pinch hit for Irvin. On Lemon's first pitch, Rhodes hit a lazy fly down the right field line. Pope backed up to the wall and made a futile leap, but the ball landed in the front row of the stands, 260 feet from home plate, for a three-run game-winning homer.

For many fans and followers, the entire history of the Indians was forever altered by Mays's catch and Rhodes's home run. The difference of a Cleveland out that would have been a homer in any other park and a New York homer that would have been an out in any other park gave the Giants the lead—and the momentum—in the Series.

The Tribe took another early lead in the second game against Johnny Antonelli when Al Smith hit the first pitch of the game over the left field roof. With two out, Cleveland loaded the bases, but Antonelli escaped when George Strickland popped out. The Tribe threatened, but did not score, in the second and third innings. Willie Mays started another New York rally in the fifth with a walk.

Hank Thompson singled Mays to third. Again Durocher called on Dusty Rhodes to bat for Monte Irvin. The amazing pinch hitter delivered again with a game-tying single. Early Wynn struck out Davey Williams, but walked Wes Westrum to load the bases. Antonelli hit a grounder to Bobby Avila at second. He forced Westrum at second, but Strickland's relay throw to first was late and Thompson scored the go-ahead run. Rhodes delivered again in the seventh with a home run off the facade in right field. Antonelli scattered eight hits and the Giants won, 3-1, in the last World Series game ever played in the Polo Grounds.

The enthusiasm from Cleveland's pennant triumph over the Yankees had been clearly dampened by the two losses to the Giants in New York. A somewhat disappointing crowd of 71,555 was on hand for the third game pitting Ruben Gomez against Mike Garcia. The "Big Bear" struggled as New York scored once in the first and three times in the third when Rhodes delivered still another clutch pinch hit. Gomez did not allow a hit until the fourth inning and just four in the game, one a home run by Vic Wertz. Hoyt Wilhelm closed out a decisive 6-2 New York win that gave the Giants a virtually insurmountable three-games-to-none lead.

Rather than use Art Houtteman or Bob Feller, Lopez returned to Bob Lemon on just two days rest. The gamble backfired when the Giants opened to a 7-0 lead, scor-

LEGENDS OF THE TRIBE

ing four times in the fifth to drive Lemon from the game. Hank Majeski, batting for Ray Narleski, smashed a three-run homer off Don Liddle in the fifth to put Cleveland on the board. In the seventh, pinch-hitter Rudy Regalado drove in the Indians' fourth run, but Hoyt Wilhelm prevented any further damage.

When the Tribe rallied in the eighth, Durocher brought Johnny Antonelli out of the bullpen to strike out Vic Wertz and Wally Westlake. In the ninth, Dale Mitchell, batting for Dave Pope, became the last Indian to bat in a World Series game for 41 seasons when he fouled out to Hank Thompson. The Giants had won the final World Series contest ever played at Cleveland Municipal Stadium, 7-4, and accomplished the unthinkable, sweeping the Tribe and its vaunted pitching staff in four games. For Indians fans, the defeat overshadowed one of the greatest seasons in baseball history.

The defending AL champions and the mighty Yankees dominated the AL again in 1955. Unable to repeat the record setting performance of 1954, the Indians still battled New York into the final days of the season to try to defend the pennant.

Joining the battle was a 22-year-old left-handed rookie from Rosedale, New York, named Herb Score. Poised to follow in Feller's footsteps as the baseball's strikeout king, Score possessed a blazing fastball and set a rookie record with a league-leading 245 strikeouts in just 227 innings pitched. Score joined a revamped Big Four that included Lemon, Wynn and Garcia. Lemon tied for the AL lead with 18 wins.

Offensive output decreased throughout the lineup. Bobby Avila, the 1954 batting champion, fell from .341 to .272. Larry Doby's league-leading 32 homers and 126 RBI dropped to 26 and 75. Al Rosen, playing most of the season with a broken right index finger, fell from .300 to .244. A major setback occurred when Vic Wertz was stricken with polio and sidelined on August 26 for the remainder of the season.

Chicago Cubs slugger Ralph Kiner, a teammate of Hank Greenberg's in Pittsburgh in 1947, had been acquired to play left field, but the 32-year-old future Hall of Famer was past his prime. He had hit 351 home runs over a nine-year career, but contributed just 18 for the Tribe and 54 RBI in 1955. It was his final major league season.

On September 14, when Score broke the rookie strikeout record set by the Phillies' Grover Cleveland Alexander, the Indians held a one-game lead over the Yankees despite a 3-2 loss to the Senators—Ray Narleski's first defeat after nine straight wins. By week's end, Cleveland had lost four straight games and fell two games behind New York with

Attempting to reverse the Tribe's fortunes in Game 4, Al Lopez started Bob Lemon (left) on just two days rest. But Lemon was knocked from the box in the fifth inning as the Giants completed their four-game sweep of the 1954 World Series, 7-4. Additions to the 1955 roster included future Hall-of-Fame outfielder Ralph Kiner (right) who contributed 18 homers in what became his final major league season.

just five games remaining. The Indians (93-61) finished in second place, three games behind the Yankees, for the fourth time in five seasons.

The Cleveland Indians had become the baseball bridesmaids of the 1950s. Even the Brooklyn Dodgers, the chief competitor for such a title, finally nabbed a World Series triumph by beating the Yankees in the 1955 Fall Classic. With a slow start in 1956, the bottom fell out of the Cleveland baseball scene. Attendance crashed down to 865,467, the worst since 1945. The second-place finish, nine games behind the Yankees, was the club's most distant since 1947.

A changing of the guard was on display in 1955 and 1956. At age 36, Rapid Robert Feller was reaching the end of his career. He won just four games in 1955, the last being the 266th and final win of his major league career, still an Indians record.

By the start of the 1956 season, Larry Doby had been traded to the White Sox for shortstop Chico Carrasquel and outfielder Jim Busby. In just eight full seasons, Doby had become one of Cleveland's all-time leaders in runs scored, home runs, RBI, total bases, extra base hits and slugging percentage. By the end of 1956, Dale Mitchell was gone after being sold to the Dodgers. Mitchell's contact-hitting style was an exception for the Greenberg-Lopez Indians, but he batted .312 in 1,108 games to rank with the Tribe's all-time leaders. Though not a home run threat, Mitchell averaged more than 23 doubles per season from 1947 through 1953. With the departures of Doby and Mitchell, only Jim Hegan remained from the day-to-day position players of 1948.

Ownership also reorganized again in 1956. Purchasing control of the club were a threesome of William Daley, Ignatius O'Shaughnessy and Hank Greenberg. Daley and company spent $3,961,800 for the purchase, providing a handsome profit to the outgoing shareholders. The three owners acquired 55 percent of the team. Daley became chairman of the board and Greenberg remained general manager.

Daley and Greenberg were faced with an aging club in 1956. Seven of the eight day-to-day starters were 28-years-old or older. Despite an amazing comeback by Wertz, who overcame his bout with polio to lead the Indians with 32 homers and 106 RBI, the offense tied for last in the league with a .244 team batting average. The only regular under the age of age 28 was outfielder Rocky Colavito, 22, who finished second on the club with 21 homers and third with 65 RBI in just 322 at-bats.

The new Big Four almost matched the effort of 1954. Wynn, Score and Lemon each won 20 games, but Garcia had just 11 for the second straight season. There was no dependable fifth starter.

Although the outcome of the 1956 season became yet another disappointing second-place finish, nine games behind the Yankees, Score and Colavito looked ready and able to lead the next generation of Indians pennant contenders.

The 1956 season marked the end of an era in Indians baseball. Al Lopez would not be leading the next pennant-contending club. He resigned following the season and took the helm of the White Sox. Greenberg preferred controversial Leo Durocher to be the next manager, but could not come to terms with the leader of the Giants' 1954 World Series victory. Instead, Greenberg hired Kerby Farrell, the manager at Indianapolis.

In six seasons under Lopez, the Indians never finished lower that second. Although 1954 was clearly the pinnacle season, the Tribe also won more than 60 percent of its games under Lopez in 1951, 1952 and 1955 and Lopez's overall winning percentage of .617 is a team record. Only Lou Boudreau, Mike Hargrove and Tris Speaker had more victories.

Lopez resumed his chase of the Yankees in Chicago and overtook them again in 1959, but again could not capture the World

Herb Score warms up under the guidance of Al Lopez during spring training of 1956. The season became Score's greatest as he finished with a 20-9 record, a league-leading 263 strikeouts and a 2.53 ERA.

LEGENDS OF THE TRIBE

Series, losing to the Dodgers in six games. He was the only manager to dethrone Casey Stengel during the 12 seasons that Stengel managed the Yankees (1949-1960). Lopez also managed five more second-place teams with the White Sox. In all, he managed 2,425 games with 1,410 major league victories, earning a spot in the National Baseball Hall of Fame.

Al Rosen also departed, the result of a contentious salary dispute with Greenberg. Rosen turned his competitive fires to the investment business and ended his playing career at the tender age of 32. In seven full seasons with the Indians, he averaged over 101 RBI and hit 192 home runs.

Most notably, the 1956 season marked the end of the career of Bob Feller, the greatest legend in Cleveland Indians history. He concluded his major league career, spent entirely with the Indians, as the club's all-time leader in wins (266), strikeouts (2,581) and innings pitched (3,827). His exceptional winning percentage of .621 (266-162) ranked just behind Addie Joss (.623) and Wes Ferrell (.622) in Indians history. Perhaps, if not for World War II, Feller would have topped 300 wins and 3,500 strikeouts. Instead, he added to his legend by serving with honor in the United States Navy.

In 1957, Feller's uniform number 19 was the first ever retired by the Indians. In 1962, his first year of eligibility, Feller was inducted into the National Baseball Hall of Fame by receiving 150 of 160 possible votes (93.75 percent). With three no-hitters, 12 one-hitters, six seasons with 20 or more victories and eight selections to the All-Star Game, he was understandably voted the greatest living right-handed pitcher when the centennial of professional baseball was celebrated in 1969.

Bob Feller (left) completed his Hall-of-Fame career in 1956 at age 37, finishing with 266 victories, 2,581 strikeouts and a 3.25 ERA. That same season, Vic Wertz (right) made a comeback from a bout with polio to hit 32 homers and drive in 106 runs.

Frantic Frank and Rocky's Road

1957–1967

From 1947 through 1956, only the New York Yankees and Brooklyn Dodgers had won more games than the Indians' 928 victories. An era of success that started with stars like Boudreau, Keltner and Feller and continued with new stars like Rosen, Avila and Wynn seemed poised for a rebirth led by its two young stars, Rocky Colavito and Herb Score. Like Score, Colavito was also from New York and also cut his teeth in Cleveland's farm system, leading Reading (Eastern League) in home runs in 1953 and Indianapolis (American Association) in 1954. In addition to his powerful bat, Colavito's strong arm was another asset, ranking with the best of all major league outfielders.

Score had followed up his Rookie-of-the-Year season with 20 wins and led the major leagues again with 263 strikeouts in 1956. Only one other pitcher in 1955 or 1956 (Bob Turley of the Yankees in 1955) surpassed 200 strikeouts. With his big leg kick, Score had all the makings of a left-handed Bob Feller. The Boston Red Sox offered a million dollars (a staggering amount at the time) for Score, but the Indians refused. Baseball talent aside, Colavito and Score had the charisma that could make Cleveland a winner at the gate and on the field. Score's arm and Colavito's bat could keep the Indians right with the Yankees and Dodgers atop major league baseball's ladder of success.

Cleveland's future changed at Cleveland Municipal Stadium on May 7, 1957, when Score faced the first-place Yankees. In the first inning, Gil McDougald batted second for New York. On a 2-2 pitch, he hit a line drive back at Score. The pitcher was struck in the face, suffering a broken nose, a cut right eyelid, and swelling—then hemorrhaging—of the right eye. Good fortune, however, was on Score's side. He would recover. But, he was done for the 1957 season. Score and Bob Lemon, who had combined for 40 wins in 1956, had just eight in 1957.

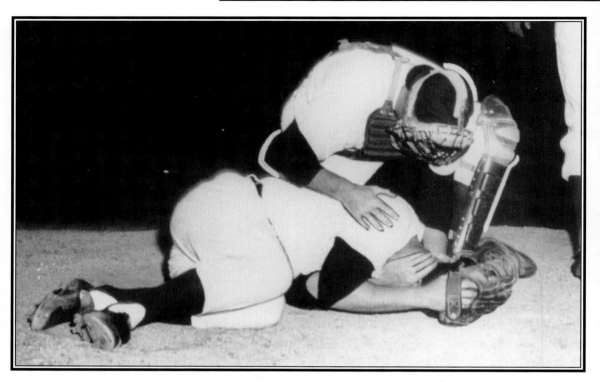

Herb Score lies bleeding on the mound as Jim Hegan checks on his condition after a sharp drive off the bat of New York's Gil McDougald smashed into Score's right cheekbone on May 7, 1957, at the Stadium.

Add even 20 of those wins and Cleveland would have been neck and neck with the Yankees again. Instead, the Tribe limped home in sixth place with a 76-77 record. Attendance dropped again to 722,256.

From 1949 through 1956, Bob Lemon, Early Wynn and Mike Garcia dominated the pitching staff. They accounted for 12 20-win seasons, 441 of the Indians' 751 victories and had a combined average of more than 55 wins per year. Wynn and Lemon established credentials that would earn them induction into the National Baseball Hall of Fame. This remarkable run of excellence ended in 1957 as Wynn fell off to 14 wins, still best on the staff ahead of 12 from Garcia and six from Lemon.

Cleveland's poor showing at the gate in 1956 and 1957 stood in serious contrast to other, less successful clubs that had found greener pastures in new markets. The Boston Braves, St. Louis Browns and Philadelphia Athletics had escaped apathetic fans (albeit in two-team cities) and found substantially-increased support in Milwaukee, Baltimore and Kansas City, respectively. The state of Minnesota and its twin cities of Minneapolis and St. Paul were in the market for a major league club.

According to Hank Greenberg's autobiography, published after his death, Greenberg thought Minnesota an ideal location for the Indians. But *Endless Summers, The Fall and Rise of the Cleveland Indians* (1995), Jack Torry's fine history emphasizing the business side of the Tribe from 1954 to 1994, disputes the notion that Greenberg was looking to have the club move in 1957.

Greenberg dismissed Kerby Farrell following the 1957 season and replaced him with 41-year-old Bobby Bragan on September 29. Greenberg was fired as general manager on October 16. His success as the top baseball man in the organization had always been balanced by an antagonistic relationship with the local media. When the Indians fell out of pennant contention, such a relationship became intolerable.

Greenberg's departure ended a run of top-quality baseball that was unmatched in Cleveland baseball history. Dating back to his arrival in 1948, the Tribe had won two of its first three American League pennants, its second World Series and had finished second five times, twice in races that went down to the wire. The Indians won a distinguished 60 percent of their games (737-493) while Greenberg was general manager.

At the outset of the 1957 season, the last three members of the 1948 champions still with the team—catcher Jim Hegan and pitchers Bob Lemon and Mike Garcia—were nearing the end of their memorable careers.

The 36-year-old Hegan, with pitcher Hank Aguirre, was traded to the Tigers for catcher J.W. Porter and pitcher Hal Woodeshick. Hegan had caught in more than 105 games each season for the Indians from 1947 through 1956. His highest batting average in a full, single season was .249, but his ability as a handler of pitchers was unquestioned. The Tribe's championship-caliber pitching was a testament to Hegan's talents.

Indians gather around Herb Score as trainer Wally Bock and coach Eddie Stanky prepare him to leave the field on a stretcher. Score recovered from his injuries, but did not return to the mound until 1958.

Hegan also made a significant off-field contribution to the franchise. His son, Mike, born in Cleveland and a 12-year major league veteran, became a color commentator on Indians telecasts in 1989. His tenure calling games on TV and, later, radio became one of the longest in club history.

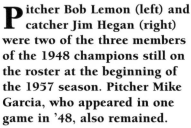

Pitcher Bob Lemon (left) and catcher Jim Hegan (right) were two of the three members of the 1948 champions still on the roster at the beginning of the 1957 season. Pitcher Mike Garcia, who appeared in one game in '48, also remained.

Bob Lemon won his final big league game in 1957 and made his final appearance with the Indians in 1958, retiring at age 38. In 460 major league appearances, all with Cleveland, he had 207 wins and a .618 winning percentage. He led the AL in wins three times, complete games five times and innings pitched four times. He is one of just three pitchers—with Bob Feller and Mel Harder—to win more than 200 games for the Tribe. He retired among the club's top five all-time leaders in shutouts (31), games pitched, wins, innings pitched (2,850), winning percentage and strikeouts (1,277).

From the mound, Lemon turned to managing and guided the expansion Kansas City Royals, Chicago White Sox and New York Yankees between 1970 and 1982, leading the Yankees to a World Series win in 1978. He was inducted into the National Baseball Hall of Fame in 1976 and his uniform number 21 was retired by the Indians in 1998.

Mike Garcia, who made his major league debut with the Tribe on October 3, 1948, hurt his back early in 1958 and, after nine straight seasons of pitching no fewer than 175 innings, had just eight innings pitched in six appearances. He attempted a comeback in 1959 followed by brief relief work for the White Sox in 1960 and the expansion Washington Senators in 1961 before retiring at age 37. "The Big Bear" started 272 games and made 125 relief appearances from 1949 through 1957. His 142 wins, 27 shutouts, 397 games pitched, 2,138 innings pitched, .597 winning percentage and 1,095 strikeouts are among the all-time leaders in Tribe history.

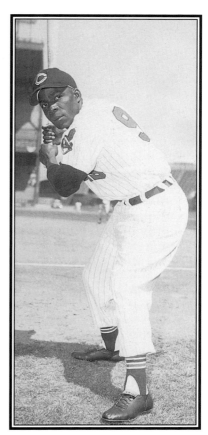

To replace Greenberg, ownership sought a dynamic leader who would make news and excite potential ticket buyers. Frank Lane was their man and became the new general manager on November 12. As general manager of the White Sox from 1949 through 1955 and the Cardinals from 1955 through 1957, Lane had developed a reputation for generating improvement on the field and at the gate. But his successes were often short lived. In Cleveland, Lane would set out to retool the Indians as a team more reflective of him and less of Hank Greenberg.

Greenberg's teams were reflective of himself—long on power and short on speed and defense. Lane seemed to prefer more speed, defense and daring. The first significant move came on December 4 when he traded Early Wynn and infielder-outfielder Al Smith to the White Sox for outfielder Minnie Minoso and infielder Fred Hatfield. Minoso was just the type of player Lane wanted. A line-drive hitter who began his major league career with the Indians in 1949, the Cuban-born Minoso brought speed and excitement. Ever so briefly, the starting outfield consisted of the 35-year-old Minoso, the 24-year-old Rocky Colavito and the 23-year-old Roger Maris.

Wynn had won 163 games in a Tribe uniform with four 20-win seasons. "Gus" led the team in innings pitched five times—including four straight seasons from 1954 through 1957—and ranked among Cleveland's all-time leaders in shutouts, games pitched, innings pitched, wins, winning percentage (.621) and strikeouts. A major contributor to the success of the Indians, Wynn was far from finished and would become a major obstacle to Cleveland's last pennant bid for decades in 1959.

The Minoso deal was the first of an almost non-stop barrage of transactions made by Lane. Many simply appeared to be trades for the sake of trades. Throughout 1958, he reacquired veterans like Larry Doby and Mickey Vernon and traded mainstays like pitchers Don Mossi and Ray Narleski, first baseman Vic Wertz and second baseman

Early Wynn (left) delivers to Ted Williams at the Stadium in 1957. At age 37, Wynn's record dropped to 14-17 and he was traded in the off season to the White Sox in the deal that brought aging, but still speedy, outfielder Minnie Minoso (right) to the Tribe.

Vic Power (above) ties a major league record by stealing home for the second time in a game against the Tigers on August 14, 1958, at the Stadium. The flashy first baseman had been acquired in June from Kansas City in a trade that sent outfielder Roger Maris (right) to the Athletics.

Bobby Avila. Future Hall-of-Fame reliever Hoyt Wilhelm, acquired by Greenberg just before he was fired in 1957, was sold to the Orioles. In particular, Lane set his sights on second baseman Billy Martin and first baseman-third baseman Vic Power. Maris was deemed expendable by Lane to get Power from the A's. On June 15, 1958, Lane traded Maris, first baseman Preston Ward and pitcher Dick Tomanek for Power and shortstop Woodie Held. Initially, Power and Held strengthened the Indians at first and short. Down the road, however, Maris won two MVP awards for the Yankees, played on seven pennant-winning teams and three world champions and set one of baseball's most legendary records by hitting 61 home runs in 1961.

Bobby Bragan's days as manager were numbered from the moment Lane was hired. He lasted just 67 games, still the shortest tenure of any manager to start a season at the Tribe's helm. According to legend, which Bragan emphatically disputes, the outgoing manager put a curse on the Indians. If he did try any magic, it was undoubtedly less effective than the erratic actions of "Frantic" Frank Lane.

To replace Bragan, Lane turned to another of Cleveland's 1948 champions, Joe Gordon, who had been out of baseball in 1958 after having managed San Francisco's Pacific Coast League club for part of 1956 and in 1957. "Flash" took the Cleveland helm with the team in sixth place (31-36), 12 games behind the first place Yankees. The Tribe went 46-40 under Gordon and moved up to fourth.

Attendance fell once again to 663,805, declining for the fourth consecutive season. Only the Senators had a lower home attendance in 1958 than the Indians, who had not fared so poorly at the gate, in comparison with other big league clubs, since finishing last in major league in attendance in 1901.

The 1958 Indians showed some slight offensive improvement and made significant strides in transition from the days of the Big Four to a competitive, if less dominant, pitching staff. Cal McLish, a 32-year-old right-hander, led the club with 16 wins. Ray Narleski, continuing the transition from reliever to starter made in 1957, won 13 games. Two other products of the farm system, 21-year-old right-hander Gary Bell and 22-year-old Jim "Mudcat" Grant, pitched in with 12 and 10 wins, respectively.

At the outset of the season, Herb Score appeared to have made a miraculous recovery from his 1957 injury. An impressive spring training camp made him the choice to pitch the regular-season opener. He lost the opener, but followed up with two straight wins, the second a 13-strikeout performance against the White Sox. After two rainouts, Score's next appearance came against Washington. During the game, the left-hander felt pain in his pitching elbow. With so much missed time in 1957, he decided to keep pitching. In fact, he had suffered a serious elbow injury and would again spend the bulk of the season on the disabled list.

Lane made two more deals in 1958 that would shape the type of team he wanted. On November 20, Mossi, Narleski and infielder Ossie Alvarez were sent to the Tigers for Billy Martin and pitcher Al Cicotte. On December 2, Vic Wertz and outfielder Gary Geiger were sent to the Red Sox for outfielder Jimmy Piersall. Within weeks, Lane had acquired two of the most tempestuous players of the time.

The 1959 lineup reflected Lane's wheeling and dealing. First baseman Power, second baseman Martin, shortstop Held and outfielders Minoso and Piersall were Lane acquisitions. Along with slugging star Colavito, young catcher Russ Nixon and veteran third baseman George Strickland, the Indians again had a formidable offense that could battle the contenders. Leading a balanced pitching staff was McLish followed by Bell, Grant and another product of the farm system, 23-year-old right-hander Jim Perry. At age 26, Herb Score would again try to recapture the magic of 1955 and 1956.

After years of chasing the Yankees, the Indians would return to pennant contention by fighting the White Sox of owner Bill Veeck, general manager Hank Greenberg and manager Al Lopez. Veeck became the majority owner of the White Sox on March 10, 1959, bringing along Greenberg just in time to make a run at the pennant.

Herb Score brushes back Luis Aparicio of the White Sox at the Stadium in April 1958. Score had recovered from his eye injury, but a torn elbow tendon limited his effectiveness. He made just 12 appearances with a 2-3 record.

Two of major league baseball's most tempestuous talents were coveted by general manager Frank Lane. Outfielder Jim Piersall (left) and second baseman Billy Martin (right) arrived for the 1959 season.

For the first time with Casey Stengel as manager, the Yankees would not be a challenger, falling all the way to last place in May before moving up to third. Chicago and Cleveland were the class of the AL. The Indians opened with six straight victories and stayed in, or near, first place for the first half of the season.

McLish won 11 of his first 14 decisions. Twenty-five-year-old outfielder-first baseman Tito Francona, acquired in March from Detroit for Doby, was batting at a .400 clip. Only a stretch beginning in late May of 11 losses in 13 games kept the race close.

Colavito put an end to the slump with an historic performance on June 10 in Baltimore's Memorial Stadium, a ballpark then notorious as a difficult place to hit home runs. It could not contain "The Rock" as he became the eighth player in major league history to hit four home runs in one game and just the third, following Bobby Lowe and Lou Gehrig, to hit four consecutive homers in a game.

The first was a two-run homer off Jerry Walker in the third inning. He next hit a pair off Arnold Portocarrero, a solo shot in the fifth and a two-run blow in the sixth. Lastly, Colavito cleared the fence with a solo homer off Ernie Johnson in the ninth. The Indians won the slugfest, 11-8. The Tribe stumbled again in July as the White Sox took the lead, setting the stage for a four-game first-place showdown in Cleveland at the end of August.

The largest AL crowd of 1959, 70,398, attended the first game, a 7-3 Chicago win as Bob Shaw defeated Mudcat Grant. Dick Donovan beat Jim Perry in the second game,

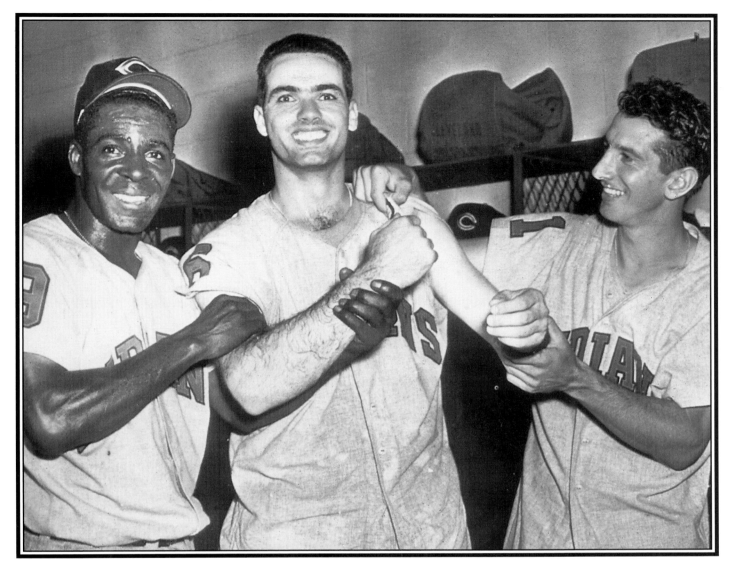

2-0. For the weekend finale, 66,586 fans massed at the lakefront stadium for a Sunday doubleheader featuring another familiar face, the rejuvenated Early Wynn. On his way to winning the Cy Young Award as best pitcher in baseball, Wynn beat Cal McLish and Barry Latman outlasted Gary Bell for a devastating sweep that pushed the Indians four games out of first.

As time ran out on the Indians, so did Joe Gordon's patience with Frank Lane. Gordon was platooning Jim Piersall and Billy Martin to Lane's dismay. On September 18, Gordon announced he would resign as manager at the end of the season, regardless of the outcome of the pennant race. Lane, in turn, said he would replace Gordon as soon as the Tribe was mathematically eliminated.

Cleveland's last real pennant bid for 33 years ended on September 22 against the White Sox. Wynn and relief pitcher Gerry Staley pitched Chicago to a 4-2 win and the first—and last—pennant for the White Sox since 1919.

Lane held a press conference the day after his club was eliminated to present the new Tribe manager. Leo Durocher was expected to finally take the helm, but, again, his contract demands had been too much for the Indians' brass. Instead, Lane amazingly introduced the same Joe Gordon who had announced his resignation only days earlier. Gordon was rewarded with a new two-year contract and a pay raise. In trying to explain the about-face, Lane said he had made a mistake in letting Gordon leave and decided to attempt to correct the mistake. The absurd managerial happenings provid-

Rocky Colavito displays his mighty muscles to Minnie Minoso (left) and Billy Martin (right) after becoming only the eighth player in major league history to hit four home runs in one game, on June 10, 1959, at Baltimore's Memorial Stadium.

ed an unfortunate forecast for the Indians under the Frank Lane regime.

The second-place Indians finished at 89-65 in 1959 with a home attendance (1,497,976) more than double that of 1957 or '58. Colavito tied third baseman Harmon Killebrew of the Senators for the American League lead with 42 home runs and drove in 111 runs, one behind league leader Jackie Jensen of the Red Sox. Vic Power and Minnie Minoso tied for the club lead with 172 hits, fourth best in the AL. Minoso's .302 batting average was fifth best. The Tribe led the AL with 745 runs scored and 167 home runs. Cal McLish was second in the league with 19 wins and Herb Score was fourth in strikeouts (147).

In just three years, Frank Lane had orchestrated an impressive turnaround in Cleveland's baseball fortunes. When he arrived, attendance was in decline and an aging team was in need of reinforcements. By 1959, the Indians had rebounded to have the second-best home attendance in the AL (behind the Yankees) and the fourth best in the majors (behind New York, Los Angeles and Milwaukee). He had assembled an exciting, competitive team expected to be a strong contender in 1960.

Within months, however, Lane would unravel all he had accomplished. Between December 1, 1959, and April 15, 1960, Lane was busily trading. On December 6, he sent Minoso, catcher Dick Brown and two pitchers to the White Sox for catcher John Romano, third baseman Bubba Phillips and first baseman Norm Cash. Nine days later, he traded his best pitcher, McLish, Billy Martin, and first baseman Gordy Coleman to Cincinnati for aging second baseman Johnny Temple. Before Cash ever played a game for the Indians, Lane shipped him off to the Tigers for third baseman Steve Demeter.

The biggest bombshell of the Frank Lane era in Cleveland—one of the biggest in Cleveland history and one of the biggest in major league baseball history—exploded on April 17, 1960, when Lane dealt Rocky Colavito, the American League's co-leader in home runs in 1959, to the Tigers for outfielder and 1959 AL batting champion Harvey Kuenn.

Kuenn was no slouch, having led the AL in hits four times, doubles three times and batting .306 or better in six of seven full seasons in Detroit. He had been American League Rookie of the Year in 1953 with a .308 average. But Colavito was Cleveland's own matinee idol—a fan favorite like no other since Lou Boudreau. Whatever minimal merits the deal may have had on paper or in Frank Lane's mind, the deal was a disaster for the Indians and, as much as anything, sent them reeling into a decades-long tailspin.

Lane's mind-numbing purge of the 1959 Indians concluded a day later when Colavito's friend, Herb Score was traded to the White Sox for Barry Latman, a young right hander and a key contributor to Chicago's AL pennant with eight wins as a starter and reliever. Score had won just 49 games for the Indians, leaving fans to forever wonder what he might have done had he avoided injury. Ultimately, the change of scenery to the Windy City did not reverse Score's pitching fortunes.

In the days before free agency, ownership's control of player movement provided greater continuity for each major league franchise. In Cleveland, Rocky Colavito was linked in a succession that dated back to Nap Lajoie's arrival in 1902. From Lajoie and Addie Joss, to Tris Speaker and Stan Coveleski, to Mel Harder and Earl Averill, to Bob Feller and Lou Boudreau, to Rocky Colavito and Herb Score, Cleveland had built tradition upon tradi-

Third baseman Steve Demeter (below) appeared in only four games in 1960 after being acquired from Detroit for first baseman Norm Cash in April. Cash played 15 seasons with the Tigers, finishing with 377 career homers and 1,103 RBI.

LEGENDS OF THE TRIBE

ito Francona provided consistent production after being acquired from Detroit in 1959. Platooning at both first base and center field, he sparked the offense that season with a .363 average, 20 home runs and 79 RBI. Francona hit 85 homers and drove in 378 in six seasons before being sold to St. Louis in 1964.

LEGENDS OF THE TRIBE

tion. The great crime of Frank Lane was to break the link and rip the guts out of the Indians franchise.

Fittingly, the 1960 regular season began against the Tigers in Cleveland. On opening day, 52,756 fans turned out at the Stadium, most of them to cheer for Rocky Colavito and against Frank Lane. Colavito was shut out in six at-bats, four of them strikeouts, but Detroit won the game, 4-2.

With the Tribe floundering in early August, Lane executed the last in a series of "Can You Top This?" moves by trading manager Joe Gordon to the Tigers for their manager, Jimmy Dykes—the first and only time in major league history that a manager was traded for a manager. The deal helped neither team. The Indians, 49-46 under Gordon, went just 26-32 under Dykes after one win with coach Jo-Jo White serving as interim manager. Cleveland finished fourth while Detroit, 44-52 under Dykes, went 26-31 under Gordon to finish sixth.

Without Colavito, the Indians' power and run production fell dramatically. Kuenn led the Indians with a .308 batting average, but 45 points below his 1959 mark. Vic Power led the club with 84 RBI and Woodie Held provided the most home runs, 21. Jim Perry tied for the AL lead with 18 wins, but no other Tribe pitcher reached double figures. Attendance dropped back below one million to 950,985.

Lane's three-year contract ended in 1960. His trading frenzy after the 1959 season and Cleveland's poor showing in 1960 ensured his departure. Before leaving, "Trader Lane" made one more deal, sending Kuenn to the San Francisco Giants for power-hitting outfielder Willie Kirkland and veteran pitcher Johnny Antonelli, one of the chief contributors to Cleveland's 1954 World Series defeat. Kuenn had spent just one season in Cleveland. Rocky Colavito spent four years in Detroit, hitting 139 home runs and helping the Tigers challenge for the 1961 American League pennant before finishing second.

On January 3, 1961, Lane departed to become general manager of the Kansas City Athletics. Ownership took its time in replacing him, entering the 1961 season without a full-time general manager. For a brief time, farm system director Walter "Hoot" Evers and his assistant, Bob Kennedy, ran the club while ownership looked for a general manager. Detroit's GM, William O. DeWitt was a possible choice.

Gabe Paul had become vice president and general manager of the expansion Houston Colt 45s, due to start play in the National League in 1962. He had taken the job late in 1960 after spending 25 years with the Cincinnati Reds, the last 10 as general manager. His new, primary boss would be Judge Roy Hofheinz, a majority stockholder in the new club. Paul soon saw that working with the flamboyant Hofheinz would be rough going. When Nate Dolin approached Paul about running the Indians as general manager and a part owner, he jumped at the chance. Gabe Paul would play a huge role in defining baseball in Cleveland for the next quarter century.

Paul inherited a team positioned for decline thanks to Frank Lane's trades, shaky ownership finances, an aging ballpark and "small market" disadvantages such as minimal revenue from radio and television broadcasts.

Frank Lane gives pointers to new manager Jimmy Dykes in 1960. Lane had acquired Dykes from Detroit for Indians skipper Joe Gordon in what remains the only trade of managers in baseball history.

Dick Donovan became the Indians' first 20-game winner since 1956 by finishing at 20-10 in 1962. The 34-year-old veteran was selected to the AL All-Star team and received the Tribe's Man of the Year award.

Cleveland was in decline as well. Only recently the sixth-largest city in the United States, it was losing population and the downtown was showing its age. Also aging far from gracefully was Municipal Stadium. The advantage of a giant seating capacity was a disadvantage without a gate attraction. The Indians' greatest drawing card, Rocky Colavito, was now in Detroit hitting 45 home runs in 1961.

The 1961 team was reflective of many squads over the next three decades. It had bits and pieces necessary for pennant contention, but lacked the key leaders and star players with championship backgrounds required to put it over the top. Newcomer Willie Kirkland led the club in home runs (27) and RBI (95). Woodie Held (23) and John Romano (21) also surpassed 20 as homers reigned supreme in the expanded AL with new teams in Washington (replacing the old Senators who departed to Minnesota) and Los Angeles, plus a schedule increased by eight games from 154 to 162. Ex-Indian Roger Maris's 61 homers for the pennant-winning Yankees (one better than Babe Ruth's single-season record of 60 in 1927) and Rocky Colavito's 45 for the second-place Tigers, emphasized the about-face the Indians had taken as a competitive and entertaining club. Home attendance dropped by almost 25 percent to 725,547.

Mudcat Grant led the team with 15 victories and Barry Latman added 13 as a starter-reliever, but the rest of the staff struggled. After a promising start of 38 wins in 60 games, good for first place on June 14, the Tribe lost 61 of its final 101 to finish fifth at 78-83, 30.5 games behind a streamlined Yankees club under new manager Ralph Houk. Jimmy Dykes did not last until the season finale. He was fired on October 1, ending his 21-year major league managerial career. Pitching coach Mel Harder managed the final game, an 8-5 victory in Los Angeles.

The second-half swoon of 1961 was indicative of too many Cleveland teams of the decade. Especially in 1961, 1962, 1965 and 1966, the Indians raised the hopes of their fans by staying in pennant contention until June or July, only to fall to the middle of the AL standings by season's end.

To replace Dykes following the 1961 season, Paul promoted 35-year-old first-base coach Mel McGaha. Although lacking managerial experience in the major leagues, McGaha had managed several years in the minor leagues and led two teams (Shreveport in 1954 and Toronto in 1960) to pennants. His success in the latter location earned the Louisiana native a spot on Dykes's 1961 coaching staff. He was expected to be not only a tougher manager than his predecessor, but to field a more disciplined club.

Days after the change, Jimmy Piersall was traded to the new Senators for pitcher Dick Donovan, catcher Gene Green and shortstop Jim Mahoney. Just prior to the start of the 1962 season, Vic Power and pitcher Dick Stigman were dealt to the Minnesota Twins for pitcher Pedro Ramos.

Donovan, a 34-year-old right hander, became the mainstay of the 1962 Indians pitching staff, winning 20 games for the only time in his career. Gary Bell responded to a move to the bullpen with 10 wins and 12 saves. Jim Perry had 12 wins and Ramos 10, but Grant and Latman fell to seven and eight wins, respectively. The pitchers, however, received minimal offensive support.

Only Romano topped the 80-RBI mark, leading the club with 25 homers and driving in 81. Only the Orioles and the expansion Senators scored fewer runs in the AL.

Whatever new chemistry existed in 1962, a familiar pattern resulted in another lackluster season of 80-82 and a sixth-place finish. The Indians started strong again by staying at, or near, the top of the standings into July. The highlight of the first half of the season was a four-game mid-June sweep of the Yankees at the Stadium. A crowd of 70,918, the largest since 1954, saw Donovan and Ramos win a doubleheader to conclude the series.

McGaha was dismissed on September 29 with two games left to play. Mel Harder once again was given the interim assignment and increased his managerial record to a perfect 3-0 when the Tribe won its final two games against the Angels.

The departure of McGaha was certainly hastened by the availability of Birdie Tebbetts who was finishing the season at the helm of the Milwaukee Braves. Tebbetts had managed for Paul in Cincinnati from 1954 until August of 1958 when he was fired and replaced by Jimmy Dykes. From Cincinnati, he had gone to Milwaukee, serving as executive vice president until Chuck Dressen was fired late in the 1961 season.

Team ownership underwent another change after the 1962 season. On November 20, Ignatius O'Shaughnessy, Nate Dolin, George Medinger and Harry Small sold their portion of stock. The ownership was reorganized with Gabe Paul emerging as the largest single stockholder, owning 20 percent. Daley, who briefly became club president with the death of Mike Wilson, Jr., on August 19, returned to his position as chairman of the board of directors, retaining 18 percent. Paul became president and treasurer while retaining his duties as general manager. The board included 19 directors.

The new owners took on a franchise that saw another attendance decline in 1962. Only two major league clubs, the Chicago Cubs and the Kansas City Athletics had less home attendance in 1962 than Cleveland's 716,076. Daley said the major goals of the new group were to keep the Indians in Cleveland and to have a winning team.

Another new group also sprang into action to help save the Indians. Al Rosen and other concerned businessmen-baseball fans created the Wahoo Club as a booster organization. Over the years, the Wahoo Club would lend consistent grass roots support to a franchise in need of any help it could get. The club also established the Golden Tomahawk award, with the first award going to Indians infielder Jerry Kindall. The award was renamed after noted Cleveland sportswriter Gordon Cobbledick in 1966.

Major league attendance had bottomed out in the mid 1950s and average home attendance of one million or better per season was again the norm. Thanks to expansion, Major League Baseball had set a new attendance record of 21,375,216 in 1962. In a decade, the major league landscape had changed dramatically after some 50 years of stability. Fertile ground had been found in California, Wisconsin and Texas. Concerns that the Indians might look for greener pastures, real enough even when the team was in contention, increased as success on the field and at the gate declined.

One effort to help the struggling franchise was to bring the All-Star Game back to Municipal Stadium. For the previous four years (1959-1962), two All-Star games had been held, in two different cities each year, with the goal of increasing the financial benefits. If anything, interest in the game suffered. The additional contest was discontinued after 1962. With its large seating capacity, Cleveland Municipal Stadium offered the best opportunity for a big All-Star Game payday.

Catcher John Romano provided power at the plate after joining the Tribe in 1960 following an off-season trade that sent Norm Cash to Cleveland and Minnie Minoso back to the White Sox. Romano was an All-Star in 1961-62, averaging 23 homers and over 80 RBI.

The Tribe's new brain trust gathers at Tucson, Arizona, for the start of spring training, 1963. From left to right are coach Mel Harder, manager Birdie Tebbetts and coaches George Strickland and Elmer Valo. The Indians failed to improve, finishing in a fifth-place tie with Detroit.

Bringing in National League stars like Willie Mays, Hank Aaron, Roberto Clemente and others was hoped to bring some baseball excitement back to Cleveland. Instead, just 44,160 fans turned out on July 9—by far the lowest All-Star Game crowd in Cleveland during the Cleveland Stadium era. The NL began a long mid-summer winning streak with a 5-3 win. Mays earned the Arch Ward Trophy as most valuable player by stealing two bases, scoring two runs, and making a great catch in the outfield.

If the All-Star Game did not excite Cleveland baseball fans, neither did the 1963 Indians. A team in transition, the farm system produced talented prospects like outfielder Vic Davalillo and third baseman Max Alvis, young players not yet ready to play championship-caliber ball in the major leagues. Likewise, 20-year-old left-handers Sam McDowell and Tommy John were in need of further grooming.

Two struggling pitchers, Cleveland's Jim Perry and Minnesota's lefty, Jack Kralick, were swapped on May 2. Both responded to new surroundings and Kralick, who had pitched a no-hitter against the Athletics in 1962, led the Tribe with 13 victories.

The 1963 season was almost a carbon copy of 1962 and home attendance sank to 562,507 for the fifth-place club. Only one other club (Washington) failed to draw at least 700,000 fans to home games. At the All-Star Game break, rumors began to circulate that the Indians might be moving to Atlanta.

One historic bright spot during the season was Early Wynn's final victory with the Indians. He had returned to the Tribe in June as a 43-year-old free agent, bringing with him 299 wins. "Gus" made five unsuccessful attempts to reach the charmed 300-win circle, then finally, on July 13, he struggled through five innings against the Athletics before handing the lead to reliever Jerry Walker, who protected the 7-4 victory.

LEGENDS OF THE TRIBE

Wynn's 300th became the last in a major league career that had spanned four decades beginning in 1939 with the Washington Senators. Following the 1963 season, he was hired as pitching coach for Tebbetts's 1964 staff. In 1972, he was inducted into the National Baseball Hall of Fame.

Ironically, Wynn succeeded Mel Harder, the pitching coach who had helped make him a success and integral part of the Big Four. Harder's phenomenal run of 36 years in Cleveland dating back to 1928, concluded in 1963. He remained a pitching coach for another six years, working for Casey Stengel's New York Mets in 1964, the Chicago Cubs in 1965, the Cincinnati Reds from 1966 through 1968 and finally for Joe Gordon and the expansion Kansas City Royals in 1969. After retiring from baseball, Harder returned to the Cleveland area. He received the ultimate recognition possible from the Indians in 1990 when the organization retired his uniform number 18.

As the long tenure of Mel Harder concluded with the Indians, another long-term relationship blossomed between the Tribe and one of his protégés, Herb Score. Barely 30 years old, Score had valiantly, but unsuccessfully toiled for three seasons in Chicago (1960-62) with six wins and 12 losses for the White Sox. Score even went down to the minors, but could not return to winning form. Turning his career toward broadcasting, he landed a job as the color commentator on Indians telecasts on WJW-TV starting in 1964. Score replaced Ken Coleman who returned to his native Massachusetts to call Red Sox games after covering the Tribe on television since 1954 on WXEL, WEWS, and WJW. Bob Neal would be Score's partner. Jimmy Dudley continued on the radio side along with former sportswriter Harry Jones.

Cleveland's financial woes cut deep at the foundation of the franchise. The productive farm system was slashed to four teams from as many as nine in 1956. Scouting was curtailed. Promotion and marketing was kept to a minimum. Little bonus money was paid to prospective young talent. Daley, Paul and company wanted a winner, but revenues were not sufficient to accommodate needed expenses and ownership was unwilling and/or unable to foot the bill.

The Indians were further derailed by health problems in 1964. Manager Birdie Tebbetts suffered a heart attack on April 1 as spring training was concluding. Coach George Strickland took over and led the team into the second half of the season. Third baseman Max Alvis, winner of the 1963 Man of the Year Award presented by the Cleveland Baseball Writers, suffered spinal meningitis and was lost from June 26 to August 5.

By the time Tebbetts and Alvis were back in action, the Indians had again fallen to the middle of the standings and out of pennant contention. In the fourth season of the 10-team American League, the Tribe again finished just below the break-even level with 79 wins and 83 losses and in sixth place.

Providing reason for optimism, however, were Sam McDowell and 23-year-old right hander Luis Tiant. "Sudden Sam" won 11 games, second to Jack Kralick, and registered 177 strikeouts in 173 innings. Tiant, called up from Portland in July, finished third with 10 victories in just 19 appearances. Another prospect, 27-year-old right hander Sonny Siebert, won seven of 16 decisions. A capable bullpen featured Gary Bell, Don McMahon and Ted Abernathy. Tribe pitchers set an AL record in 1964 with 1,162 strikeouts.

There was also some new energy in the batting order. Colorful slugger Leon "Daddy Wags" Wagner led the Indians with 31 homers and 100 RBI. Shortstop Dick Howser scored 101 runs, only the second Indian since 1955 to reach the century mark.

Center fielder Vic Davalillo was one of several rookies expected to pay dividends in 1963. But the 22-year-old Venezuela native missed two months with a broken forearm after being hit by a pitch from Detroit's Hank Aguirre in June. Davalillo returned to finish with a .292 batting average.

A new wrinkle became part of the Cleveland revenue picture in 1964. To keep the team afloat, Paul looked to make deals that would bring much-needed cash to the club. At the trading deadline, June 15, he dealt Mudcat Grant to the Twins for pitcher Lee Stange, third baseman-outfielder George Banks and cash. On September 5, he sold pitcher Pedro Ramos to the Yankees for $75,000 and two players to be named later (who turned out to be pitchers Ralph Terry and Bud Daley). Ramos became the ace fireman for New York and played a large role in bringing one last pennant to the Bronx before a long dry spell. In 1965, Grant was the best pitcher in the AL, leading the Twins to the World Series against the Dodgers.

Outfielder Leon Wagner (left) and third baseman Max Alvis (right) were two mainstays of the mid 1960s. Wagner arrived in a trade with the Angels in December 1963 and then hit 82 homers from 1964-66. Alvis was the second rookie to be selected Indians Man of the Year after batting .274 with 22 homers and 67 RBI in 1963. Spinal meningitis threatened his career in 1964, but he recovered to remain through the 1969 season.

The term "cash call" entered Cleveland's baseball vocabulary in 1964. Stockholders were called on to make additional cash investments so that the franchise could meet its financial obligations. Despite an improved attendance (653,293), the Indians' status in Cleveland was very much in jeopardy. The team's lease at Cleveland Municipal Stadium expired in 1964, making the ball club something of a free agent. In August, distinguished sportswriter Hal Lebovitz wrote of the danger that the club might move.

On September 17, 1964, Seattle, Washington, mayor Dorm Braman admitted that his city was trying to lure the Indians. Oakland, California, was also reportedly seeking the Tribe. On October 6, the directors met to determine the fate of the club, but deferred action and sent Paul and Daley on a fact-finding trip. They visited Seattle, Oakland and Dallas, Texas. The directors also set a goal of selling 4,500 season tickets to measure fan support in Cleveland.

Seattle, Oakland and the Dallas-Fort Worth metroplex would all, ultimately, get major league franchises. In 1964, however, none of the cities had a major league ballpark ready for occupancy in 1965 and could not guarantee one right away. The threat these cities represented to major league baseball in Cleveland, and, by extension, to Cleveland as a "major league" city prompted support that may not have otherwise developed. On October 16, the directors voted to sign a new, 10-year lease at Cleveland Municipal Stadium that would include $4 million in improvements to the park and a reduction in rent. The lease also included an escape clause that would allow the Indians or the City of Cleveland to terminate the deal at the end of any calendar year by giving 90-days notice.

The situation became the most significant threat to major league baseball in Cleveland since Frank Robison sent his best players from the Spiders to St. Louis in 1899. It ended with a reprieve for the only home city the Indians had ever known. The fear of losing the club generated new support. To keep that support, the franchise would now need to take steps to create an exciting, winning team.

To capitalize on the support gained following the 1964 season, Gabe Paul made a bold move to undo the mistake of April 17, 1960, and to put the Indians back on track with the fans. On January 20, 1965, he reacquired Rocky Colavito in a three-way deal with the White Sox and Athletics. Traded from the Tigers to the A's after the 1963 season, "The Rock" had finished fourth in the AL with 34 home runs and fifth with 102 RBI for the last-place Kansas City club in 1964. To make the deal, the Indians parted with two of their best young prospects, left-handed pitcher Tommy John and outfielder Tommy Agee, plus veteran catcher John Romano.

The trade actually sent Colavito to Chicago for outfielders Jim Landis and Mike Hershberger and a pitcher to be named later. The White Sox then sent Colavito with catcher Camilo Carreon to Cleveland for Agee, John and Romano. Pitcher Fred Talbot later went from the White Sox to the Athletics to complete the deal.

The Tribe paid a steep price to reacquire the popular Colavito. Romano had been a two-time all-star and a source of stability behind the plate, but John and Agee were two prizes of the Cleveland farm system. John became a big winner with the Dodgers and the Yankees in the 1970s and early 1980s, especially after drastic arm surgery in 1974, a ligament transplant operation now known as "Tommy John surgery." The late-blooming lefty won 288 major league games, plus another six in post-season (Championship Series and World Series) play. After two solid seasons with the White Sox in 1966 and '67, Agee was traded to the New York Mets where he became the lead-off hitter and center fielder for the world champions of 1969. John and Agee played in a total of four World Series and six Championship Series during a time (1965 through 1982) when the Indians rose as high as third place just once.

In 1965, however, the present was more important to Gabe Paul than the future. Colavito's return gave the Tribe its most charismatic star since his departure in 1960. Colavito could save the franchise and, if not bring a championship, at least provide a bridge to new young talent that could make the Indians a champion again.

With Colavito, Wagner, Alvis and slugging first baseman Fred Whitfield, the Indians again had some respectable offensive punch. Only the Red Sox and the Tigers hit more home runs in 1965. Vic Davalillo finished third in the AL batting race with a .301 average and tied for fourth place with 26 stolen bases. A solid starting rotation featured McDowell, Siebert, Tiant and veteran Ralph Terry who was acquired in the Pedro Ramos deal.

The Indians fashioned another competitive start in 1965, moving into first place in late June. With 15 wins in 17 games, including 10 straight from June 13 to June 22, they tied for the AL lead on June 28 when Tiant defeated the Red Sox. Four players (Colavito, Alvis, McDowell and Davalillo) were selected for the All-Star Game. At the All-Star Game break, the Tribe was in second place with a 48-34 record.

On July 25, the Indians' largest home crowd since 1962 (56,634) saw them split a twin bill with the Yankees, winning the nightcap on Whitfield's home run. The Tribe remained in the hunt, 4.5 games behind first-place Minnesota. As late as mid August, after taking three of four games from the Twins, Cleveland was second, but eight games off the pace.

Pitcher Tommy John (below) and outfielder Tommie Agee were two of the Indians' top prospects sacrificed to the White Sox in the three-team trade that returned Rocky Colavito to Cleveland for the 1965 season. John continued a long, productive career that included 288 victories.

Larry Brown (left) and Leon Wagner (right) lie on opposite sides of the left-field line (top photo) after colliding while chasing Roger Maris's pop fly on May 4, 1966, against New York at Yankee Stadium. The injured Brown then receives immediate medical attention (lower photo). He would miss six weeks with a fractured skull, cheekbone and nose.

The Indians continued to slide in the standings. On September 16, Boston's Dave Morehead pitched a no-hitter and defeated the Tribe, 2-0, at Fenway Park for the first no-hit defeat suffered by the Indians since Allie Reynolds no-hit the club in 1951.

Colavito finished the season with an AL-leading 108 RBI, 26 home runs and a .287 batting average. In the final game, he tied a major league record by playing in his 162nd consecutive game—the entire 1965 season—without committing an error. He also set a record by leading the league's outfielders in games played for the fifth time. McDowell pitched the final game and finished as the AL leader with 325 strikeouts and a 2.18 earned run average. Indicative of the 1965 campaign, the Tribe lost its final game, 2-1, and finished fifth, 15 games behind the first-place Twins. Still, with 87 wins, Cleveland had its most victories in a season, and its first winning season, since 1959. Home attendance (934,786) increased by some 43 percent and ranked fifth in the AL.

Rocky Colavito's return to Cleveland bore a large responsibility for the increased attendance and, for a time, decreased talk about the possible relocation of the Indians. Better yet, the Tribe appeared to be capable of becoming a contender again. The Indians certainly had the look of a contender at the outset of the 1966 season. They jumped to another fast start, setting an AL record and tying the major league record of 10 straight wins to open the season.

Seven different pitchers earned victories over the span—Siebert, McDowell, Kralick, Bell, Tiant, Bob Allen and John O'Donoghue. Included was a one-hitter by McDowell on April 25 in a 2-0 win over Kansas City. The great start, however, was only good for a one-game lead over the also-hot Baltimore Orioles.

"Sudden Sam" opened May with a second consecutive one hitter for his fourth victory of the young season, defeating Tommy John and the White Sox 1-0. Two days later, Tiant pitched his third straight shutout to give the Tribe a 12-1 record.

The next day, disaster struck at Yankee Stadium. With two out in the fourth inning, Roger Maris hit a pop fly to shallow left field. Left fielder Leon Wagner and shortstop Larry Brown converged on the ball and crashed into each other. Brown suffered a fractured skull and might have died had Don McMahon not kept him from swallowing his tongue. Wagner suffered a broken nose and a concussion. Wagner was able to play again within days, but Brown was lost for six weeks. The Indians won the game, 2-1.

McDowell became sidelined for 16 days, starting on May 25, with a shoulder injury. By the All-Star Game break, the Tribe had fallen from first place by 4.5 games to third place, 10 games behind the Orioles.

A trade for relief ace Dick Radatz did not improve matters. The top fireman in the AL from 1962 through 1964, the 29-year-old Radatz struggled in Cleveland with three losses and a 4.61 ERA to go with 10 saves.

As hopes of contention slipped away, the financial picture seemed to improve on August 13 when Vernon Stouffer paid $8 million to buy controlling interest in the ball club. Stouffer bought out William Daley and other associates of Daley's, and took Daley's position as chairman of the board. One of Stouffer's first moves was to lock up Gabe Paul as general manager on a long-term basis.

L uis Tiant was one of an outstanding group of promising pitchers to emerge in the mid 1960s. Tiant, along with Sonny Siebert, Sam McDowell, and Steve Hargan, gave the Tribe one of the best young starting staffs in baseball. Tiant won in double figures in each of his first four seasons (1964-67), then won 21 games in 1968 with an AL-best 1.60 ERA.

Frantic Frank and Rocky's Road

Stouffer had built the Stouffer Foods empire of restaurants, frozen foods and hotels. A successful, innovative businessman, Stouffer seemed to have the wherewithal that had been missing from the Indians for years. With Paul as general manager and the experienced Hank Peters in charge of the farm system, the days of quick-fix plans and penny pinching appeared ready to yield to a financially-stable ownership with a talented front office that would have the tools to return the Indians to contention.

The dramatic turnaround on the field and in the ownership prompted Birdie Tebbetts to resign on August 19. George Strickland took the helm again. The Indians completely collapsed under Strickland, losing 24 of 39 games. A season that had started brilliantly ended once again in mediocrity. The fifth-place 81-81 record marked the eighth time in 10 seasons (1957-1966) that the Indians' winning percentage was no lower than .484, but no higher than .503.

Like the club itself, Sam McDowell's campaign unraveled after a brilliant start. The shoulder injury held him to just nine wins with eight losses. He had a dazzling 225 strikeouts, good enough to lead the AL again, in just 194 innings. Sonny Siebert led the staff with 16 victories, including a no-hitter in June versus Washington—the first by an Indians pitcher since Bob Feller's third in 1951. Gary Bell, back in the rotation, won 14 games, but lost 15. Steve Hargan, a 23-year-old right hander, won 13 and Luis Tiant added 12.

Offensive output dropped dramatically from 1965 to 1966. Three players (Leon Wagner, Rocky Colavito and Max Alvis) scored 88 or more runs in 1965, but Wagner led the team in 1966 with just 70. Colavito led with 30 homers, but drove in just 72 runs, second to Fred Whitfield's 78.

Rocky Colavito continued to hit home runs in his first two seasons after returning to the Tribe. Platooned in left field by new manager Joe Adcock in 1967, Colavito asked for a trade and was dealt to the White Sox in July for outfielder Jim King, infielder Marv Staehle and cash.

The Indians of the 1960s had gone back and forth between laid-back managers and disciplinarians. The next disciplinarian would be Joe Adcock in 1967. An all-star first baseman who hit 336 homers as a player from 1950-66, he had never managed in the major leagues. The Louisiana native pledged to stress fundamentals and set strict rules. He also decided to platoon outfielders Wagner and Colavito. The entire package promised to cause unrest and it did. The Tribe slumped to just 75 wins in 1967 with a .463 winning percentage that was the club's worst since 1946 and an eighth-place finish that matched the worst (1914) in franchise history. Home attendance (662,980) fell to dead last among the 20 major league clubs. The only other team to draw fewer than 750,000, the Kansas City Athletics, would be playing in a new city—Oakland—the following year.

The Indians' talented pitching was wasted because of poor offensive support. Hargan led the club with 14 wins. McDowell was a disappointing 13-15 and finished second to Boston's Jim Lonborg in strikeouts with 236. Tiant won 12 games and finished fourth in the AL with 219 strikeouts. Siebert won 10 games.

Colavito's unhappiness led to a trade demand. On July 29 he was dealt to the White Sox for outfielder Jim King, infielder Marv Staehle and cash. Also dealt was Gary Bell to Boston for outfielder Don Demeter and first baseman Tony Horton, who finished

with 44 RBI, third behind Alvis (70) and Wagner (54). Colavito and Bell went to pennant contenders. Boston won the AL pennant on the final day of the regular season. Bell was a major contributor with 12 wins for the Red Sox. Chicago stayed in the hunt until the final weekend of the season, finishing three games behind Boston. Colavito drove in 29 runs for the light-hitting Pale Hose.

The Rocky Colavito era of Cleveland Indians baseball concluded in 1967. The Rock had hit 190 home runs for the Tribe—fifth best in club history at the time. Add the 173 he hit during his five-year exile from Cleveland (1960-1964) and he would have been, by far, Cleveland's all-time home run leader. "What might have been" is the overriding sentiment that accompanies thoughts of Cleveland baseball from the Rock's rookie season in 1956 until 1967. Perhaps, if not for the Colavito-Kuenn trade, the Indians would have remained in contention throughout the 1960s rather than slip to the middle of the American League standings.

Colavito returned to Cleveland several more times. He was a color commentator on Indians telecasts in 1972, 1975 and 1976. He also served the Indians as a coach in 1973 and from 1976 through 1978. In 1976, Tribe fans voted him the Most Memorable Personality in Cleveland Indians history.

Sonny Siebert was a converted minor league first baseman-outfielder who finally made it to the Indians at age 27 in 1964. He won seven games his rookie season, then went 16-8 the next two campaigns. Siebert pitched a no-hitter at the Stadium on June 10, 1966, a 2-0 win over the Washington Senators.

Many Changes, but Few Solutions

1968-1979

Gabe Paul's fourth managerial hiring for the Indians brought a man familiar to Tribe fans to the helm. The new manager for 1968 would be Alvin Dark, the opposing shortstop for the Boston Braves in the 1948 World Series and the New York Giants in the 1954 series. Dark would be the franchise's third opening-day manager in three years.

Dark had distinguished himself as a tough player with the Braves and Giants. He had helped both clubs turn from relying on power to speed and defense and, in the process, helped them become champions. As a manager, Dark led the San Francisco Giants to the 1962 World Series during his four seasons (1961-1964) there. Dismissed after the 1964 campaign, he was hired by Charlie Finley and the Kansas City Athletics in 1966. When controversy erupted in 1967, Dark was again out of a job. When he took the Cleveland position, Alvin Dark became the first manager ever hired by the Indians who had managed a team into the World Series.

The 1968 season was known as "The Year of the Pitcher." With an outstanding pitching staff, the Indians were well positioned to be competitive in such a season. Sam McDowell, Luis Tiant, Sonny Siebert and Steve Hargan were all back to lead the staff. Knuckleball-throwing Eddie Fisher, acquired from the Orioles, bolstered the bullpen.

Between 1967 and 1968, the outfield underwent a substantial transformation. Trades following the 1967 season brought speedsters Tommy Harper from Cincinnati and Jose Cardenal from California. The 27-year-old Harper was a decent hitter and capable base stealer. The 24-year-old Cardenal had shown similar ability. The Indians would be reflective of their new manager, well suited to compete in an era emphasizing speed, defense, smart play and low-scoring games rather than raw power.

Following their ongoing pattern of the 1960s, the Indians' 1968 season opened with promise, especially in the pitching department. On opening day, Sonny Siebert pitched a two-hitter, catcher Duke Sims hit two home runs and Max Alvis added one as the Indians defeated the White Sox, 9-0. Hargan pitched a one-hitter on April 24 as the Tribe beat Detroit, 2-0. Sam McDowell launched a six-game winning streak on May 1 when he struck out 16 and out pitched Blue Moon Odom and the Oakland Athletics. In his next start, McDowell struck out 14 more, setting a new AL record with 30 strike-outs over two games. He beat the Yankees in spite of a home run by Mickey Mantle.

While McDowell piled up strikeouts, Luis Tiant was on a shutout streak, pitching his fourth straight shutout on May 12 as the second-place Indians beat the Orioles. Tiant's streak reached 41 innings before Baltimore broke through and defeated the Cleveland right hander on May 17. The Indians remained on the heels of the first place Tigers into late June.

Tiant's record setting continued on July 3 against the Twins, striking out 19 batters in 10 innings, pitching his seventh shutout and winning his 13th game, 1-0. "El Tiante's" brilliant efforts earned him the starting assignment in the 1968 All-Star Game. The only other Tribe pitcher to have started an All-Star Game was Bob Feller in 1941 and 1946. Tiant allowed just one run, a first inning tally by Willie Mays, but that was the difference as the NL blanked the AL, 1-0. McDowell pitched a scoreless seventh. Tiant and McDowell's battery mate, Joe Azcue, was on the team as well.

After 22 years without a pennant and having missed the AL title by just one game in 1967, the Tigers were a team with a purpose in 1968. Cleveland's last best chance to make a race for the 1968 AL pennant came in early August when the Indians and Tigers met seven times in nine days. Detroit won six of the seven contests and essentially decided the race.

The Indians' third-place finish at 86-75 was their best since 1959, but 16.5 games behind the Tigers in the final season before the leagues were divided into two divisions each. Tiant's dazzling 1.60 ERA led the AL and his 21 wins were the most for an Indians pitcher since 1954. McDowell was almost as great with a 1.81 ERA, reclaiming the league strikeout crown (283), but winning only 15 games against 14 losses. Veteran Stan Williams won 13 games, Siebert added 12 and Hargan struggled to an 8-15 record.

Offensively, the 1968 Indians finished second in the AL with 115 stolen bases, the most since 1918. Their 75 team home runs, however, was the lowest total since 1945.

Luis Tiant (left) is congratu-lated by Lou Johnson after his 19-strikeout performance in a 10-inning complete-game win over the Minnesota Twins on July 3, 1968, at the Stadium.

Tony Horton (14) and Duke Sims (11) were the only Indians with more than 10. All but two AL clubs outscored the Indians. The need for another slugger in 1969 was readily apparent.

Finishing third was a shot in the arm for Indians baseball. Attendance rose back to 857,994. But the Tribe had finished closer to first in 1962 and 1965, just a half game further back than in 1966 and even with the eighth-place finish of 1967. Seasons to come would make Tribe fans long to finish that well.

Major changes for the Indians and Major League Baseball came in 1969. Baseball marked the 100th anniversary of "professional" baseball, as defined by the debut of the 1869 Cincinnati Red Stockings as a team of paid professionals, with a year-long celebration, another expansion and divisional play. Now, the team with the most wins would not be guaranteed a spot in the World Series. Instead, two division winners in each league would battle for a trip to the annual Fall Classic.

The Indians would compete in the AL Eastern Division with the Yankees, Orioles, Tigers, Red Sox and Senators. Cleveland was stuck in a division with "big market" clubs from New York and Boston, the defending world champions from Detroit and a Baltimore team ready to dominate the league. Worse, the Tribe lost Tommy Harper and prized prospect outfielder Lou Piniella in the expansion draft.

Big changes were also brewing in the Cleveland leadership as Alvin Dark made a grab for increased power in the organization. Vernon Stouffer agreed with Dark's proposal to take on the duties of general manager as well as field manager. Gabe Paul was "moved up" with the title of president.

Dark saw the missing piece that would make the Indians contenders in Boston outfielder-first baseman Ken Harrelson. In six major league seasons, including two under Dark for the Athletics (1966-67), "Hawk" had never driven in more than 66 runs in a season until 1968. Still, Harrelson became a valuable commodity after he was suddenly released by the A's eccentric owner, Charlie Finley, after criticizing Finley for firing Dark. Harrelson's timing was perfect. Boston, which had lost star slugger Tony Conigliaro to a severe beaning, signed the free agent outfielder to fill the void.

Harrelson helped Boston win the AL pennant in 1967, then led the league in RBI (109) in 1968 along with career highs in home runs (35) and batting average (.275). With Conigliaro's expected return in 1969, Harrelson was expendable in Beantown. Dark sent pitchers Sonny Siebert and Vicente Romo and catcher Joe Azcue to Boston

Alvin Dark argues with umpire Larry Barnett in a game against Minnesota in 1969. After finishing in third place in Dark's first season as manager in 1968, the bottom dropped out for the Indians in 1969 as they fell to 62-99, last in the AL East in the first season of divisional play.

Tony Horton was an intense and highly-competitive player who arrived from Boston in 1967. The power-hitting first baseman produced his best numbers in baseball's centennial season of 1969 (right) with 27 home runs, 93 RBI and a .278 batting average. But Horton's drive to excel came with a price as he suffered a nervous breakdown during a game in August 1970 and never played again.

LEGENDS OF THE TRIBE

for Harrelson and two veteran left-handed pitchers, 29-year-old Dick Ellsworth and 32-year-old Juan Pizarro. The trade nearly imploded when Harrelson refused to report and threatened to retire. A hefty pay raise convinced the "Hawk" to land in Cleveland.

Harrelson, a walking definition of the "mod" look of the time with his love beads and Nehru jackets, did, indeed, bring more power and run production to the Indians, hitting 27 home runs and driving in 84 runs. With one weakness addressed, a new one arose, however, as Luis Tiant suffered an about-face from his amazing 1968 season, leading the AL with 20 losses. No pitcher had lost 20 games in a season for Cleveland's AL club since Pete Dowling came over from Milwaukee in 1901.

The about-face applied to the Indians as well. With 99 losses, the Tribe fell just short of the 1914 team record of 102 and, with just 62 wins, finished dead last (sixth in the AL East) for the first time since 1914. Even the expansion Kansas City Royals (managed by Joe Gordon) and Seattle Pilots lost fewer games. Sam McDowell (18-14 record and league-leading 279 strikeouts) was one of the few bright spots in one of the most dismal seasons in Cleveland Indians' history.

If the Indians were not as close to a pennant as they may have seemed in 1968, neither was the club as terrible as its 1969 record indicated. Following the season, Cleveland made three trades that changed the look of the club. In a swap of outfielders, Jose Cardenal went to the St. Louis Cardinals for 31-year-old Vada Pinson. Pitchers Tiant and Stan Williams were sent to Minnesota for veteran pitchers Dean Chance and Bob Miller, outfielder Ted Uhlaender and highly-touted third base prospect Graig Nettles. Then, just before the 1970 season opened, Max Alvis and outfielder Russ Snyder were traded to the new Milwaukee team (relocated from Seattle) for outfielder Roy Foster and infielder Frank Coggins. Nettles, Pinson and Uhlaender moved into the line up.

While the 1960s were a decade of much change and turmoil for the Indians, Max Alvis was a source of stability. In his eight seasons with the Tribe, he hit 108 home runs and topped 20 three times (1963, 1965 and 1967). Twice (1963 and 1967) he was honored with the Man of the Year award as selected by local members of the Baseball Writers' Association of America. The Jasper, Texas, native played his final season in 1970— 62 games for the Milwaukee Brewers.

Ray Fosse, the Tribe's first draft choice in Major League Baseball's first amateur draft (1965), became the full-time catcher. The Indians had a new, youthful keystone combination in 23-year-old second baseman Eddie Leon and 20-year-old shortstop Jack Heidemann (Cleveland's first choice in the 1967 June draft).

Fosse became the Tribe's leader on the field, earning a spot in the 1970 All-Star Game along with his battery mate Sam McDowell. The game, at Cincinnati's new Riverfront Stadium, would forever change the course of the 1970s Indians.

McDowell followed starter Jim Palmer to the mound in the fourth inning and pitched three scoreless innings. Fosse entered to catch his teammate, replacing Bill Freehan. Fosse singled and scored the first run of the game in the sixth. His sacrifice fly in the seventh gave the AL a 2-0 lead. The visitors took a 4-1 lead into the ninth, but the NL rallied for three runs to force

Ken "the Hawk" Harrelson makes his maiden flight with the Tribe in April 1969 at the Stadium. He hit a single and a triple as the Yankees defeated the Indians, 11-3.

extra innings. With two out in the 12th inning and lefty Clyde Wright pitching for the AL, hometown favorite Pete Rose of the Reds singled and took second on a hit by the Dodgers' Billy Grabarkewitz. The Cubs' Jim Hickman followed with a single to center. As Rose raced for home, Fosse blocked the plate in anticipation of the throw from center fielder Amos Otis. As the throw approached, Rose slammed into Fosse, driving the catcher head over heels and scoring the game-winning run. One of baseball's most memorable games ended with both Fosse and Rose being helped off the field.

Pete Rose barrels into Ray Fosse to score the winning run on Jim Hickman's single in the 12th inning of the 1970 All-Star Game at Cincinnati's Riverfront Stadium. Fosse, who was blocking the plate in anticipation of a throw from center fielder Amos Otis, received a severe shoulder injury.

Fosse, nicknamed "Mule," lived up to his reputation by returning to action immediately, but he did so with a severely injured shoulder. Although a serious power threat in the first half of the season, Fosse was reduced to a singles hitter after the injury, finishing the season with what became a career-high 18 home runs. He was never again the same player.

The two players Al Dark counted on to power the 1970 Tribe, Tony Horton and Ken Harrelson, would both be gone for parts of the season.

Dissatisfied with the contract offered by Dark, Horton threatened to not report to camp. Finally, on March 18, the young first baseman agreed to terms. The next day, Harrelson suffered a badly broken right ankle. The injury brought a premature end to the 28-year-old slugger's career. He returned to play in 17 games near the end of the season, then retired after batting just .199 in 52 games in 1971.

Horton, an intense young man, succumbed to the pressures of major league baseball 115 games into the 1970 season. He was having another solid year, with 17 homers, 59 RBI and a .269 batting average. That was not good enough for Horton. During a double-header on August 28 against the Angels, he departed the field and never returned, the victim of an emotional breakdown. His seven-year career was over at age 25.

Harrelson's injury opened an outfield spot for the newly-acquired, 25-year-old outfielder, Roy Foster. The rookie provided some of the power expected from Harrelson with 23 home runs and 60 RBI. He was selected by *The Sporting News* as its American League Rookie Player of the Year. Graig Nettles led the team with 26 homers. Vada Pinson led the way with 82 RBI. In addition to Foster and Nettles, Pinson and Duke Sims reached the 20-homer plateau with 24 and 23, respectively.

Cleveland's first choice in the 1970 June Draft was right-handed pitcher Steve Dunning of Stanford University. Quickly dubbed "Stunning Steve," he was less than two weeks out of Stanford when he started against the Brewers on June 14 at the Stadium before 25,380 fans (a large crowd in 1970). Dunning got the win, but lost nine of his remaining 12 decisions and won just 18 games in a Cleveland uniform.

At age 27, Sam McDowell had his best season ever, finally cracking the hallowed 20-win circle with a 20-12 record. He also topped the 300-strikeout level for the second time with a major-league-best 304 strikeouts and an AL-high 305 innings pitched.

Steve Hargan enjoyed a comeback season with 11 wins. Dean Chance won nine games before he was sold to the New York Mets in September. The Indians improved to 76 wins and fifth place in the American League East. Attendance increased from 619,970 in 1969 to 729,752 in 1970.

Adding to the problems of injury and illness was a financial crisis that proved to devastate the franchise. Vernon Stouffer saw the future boom of microwave technology and acquired ownership in Litton Technologies. When the value of its stock took a dive, Stouffer's finances also plunged. Like Charles Somers decades before, Vern Stouffer was suddenly unable to compete financially to build a winner in Cleveland.

When a downturn in fortune forced Charlie Somers to sell the Indians, financially-stable ownership was found to rebuild the franchise. A well-heeled ownership group awaited Stouffer's Indians, but a drastic miscalculation would result in more hard times for the Tribe. Stouffer thought he had an answer that would solve the financial woes of the Indians and himself. The novel concept involved playing a portion of the Indians' home games in New Orleans, a city looking to build a new giant domed stadium. Major league baseball would energize the project. Stouffer envisioned sellouts in a new city and increased attendance at fewer games in Cleveland, a win-win situation that would put the Tribe back in the black.

The split-city concept revived memories of the Indians bouncing between League Park and Cleveland Municipal Stadium, or, worse, the days when Frank Robison moved his best players from Cleveland to St. Louis. Cleveland fans and media felt sure that the idea of playing some home games in New Orleans was the first step toward playing all home games there. The idea was thoroughly trashed in the Cleveland newspapers.

Cleveland's owner turned his sights toward two groups wishing to purchase the club. One group, featuring former Tribe star Al Rosen, was led by Clevelander George Steinbrenner III. Leading the other group of potential owners was 41-year-old Nick Mileti, a rising mover and shaker on the Cleveland scene who had brought the National Basketball Association to town with the expansion Cleveland Cavaliers. As owner of the Cavaliers, the famed Cleveland Barons of the American Hockey League and the Cleveland Arena, Mileti had become a major sports figure in the city. Steinbrenner had owned the Cleveland Pipers of the short-lived American Basketball League of the early 1960s. The Pipers won the league championship and Steinbrenner earned a measure of notoriety by hiring John McClendon as head coach, the first African-American to coach a pro basketball team. Steinbrenner also signed Ohio State University star Jerry Lucas, but the ABL folded beforehand.

The Steinbrenner group reportedly offered $8.6 million for the Indians franchise. The Mileti group offered $9.75 million. Stouffer accepted the larger offer, though it was laden with much more non-cash value than the lower offer.

Sudden Sam McDowell was a 20-game winner in 1970 (right) for the only time in his career, finishing at 20-12 with a league-leading 304 strikeouts. McDowell was an AL All-Star for the fifth time and was co-recipient with Ray Fosse of the Indians Man of the Year award.

Roy Foster avoids a pickoff attempt in a game against Minnesota in July 1970. The 25-year-old left fielder hit 23 home runs that season to earn AL Rookie Player of the Year honors from *The Sporting News*.

LEGENDS OF THE TRIBE

Gomer Hodge receives a hero's escort from manager Alvin Dark (left) and trainer Jim Warfield (right) after a game-winning hit in May 1971. The 27-year-old rookie's nickname resulted from a resemblance in speech to the title character played by Jim Nabors in the television series "Gomer Pyle U.S.M.C." He delivered four pinch hits in his first four at-bats and 16 in what became his only major league season.

Steinbrenner's group found another team for sale, the New York Yankees. For $10 million, Steinbrenner and his partners purchased the Yankees and rebuilt the great baseball dynasty back into a world championship club, leaving Indians fans to wonder what might have happened if Steinbrenner and company had gotten the Indians instead. The Yankees had fallen on hard times since last winning the AL pennant in 1964. Under Steinbrenner, the Yanks would return to being a major thorn in the side of the Indians throughout the remainder of the 1900s.

Mileti's ownership group formally purchased the Indians on March 22, 1972. Vernon Stouffer died on July 26, 1974.

What Mileti purchased was an Indians team that had collapsed again in 1971. Roy Foster proved to be a one-year wonder. At age 32, Vada Pinson could not match his last outstanding season and Jack Heidemann suffered a knee injury that ruined his career. McDowell's production fell off dramatically with a 13-17 record and 192 strikeouts in 215 innings. Hargan won just once and lost 13 games. Young pitchers like Steve Dunning, Rich Hand and Alan Foster were rushed to the majors and suffered accordingly.

An exception to the failings of 1971 was a 27-year-old rookie from Rutherfordton, North Carolina. Harold "Gomer" Hodge made the 1971 club as a pinch-hitter and utility player. He immediately became something of a folk legend with a pinch-hit single on opening day followed by a ninth-inning single to give the Tribe a thrilling 3-2 win.

Nicknamed "Gomer" because of a resemblance (especially in speech) to the title character played by Jim Nabors on the television show "Gomer Pyle, U.S.M.C.," Hodge appeared in 80 games, 74 as a pinch hitter. His 16 pinch hits were the most in the majors. But despite his success, Hodge never played another major league game.

Another highlight was the play of 22-year-old first baseman Chris Chambliss, the Tribe's first-round choice in the 1970 amateur draft. Chambliss batted .275 to earn the Rookie of the Year award, the first Indian so honored since Herb Score in 1955.

Vernon Stouffer realized the mistake he had made in granting Alvin Dark sweeping powers and on July 30, 1971, Dark was fired and replaced by coach John Lipon. Gabe Paul resumed his duties as general manager. Bad under Dark (42-61), the club went into a free fall under Lipon with just 18 more wins in 59 games. The Indians tied the club record with 102 losses and tumbled back into the basement of the AL East, 43 games behind the division-winning Orioles.

An oft-repeated story portrays the status of the club Nick Mileti purchased in 1972. As the story goes, Stouffer asked Hank Peters what would result if the budget for the Tribe's farm system was drastically reduced. Peters said that if Stouffer planned to sell the Indians soon, he should not worry. If, however, Stouffer intended to keep the team, cutting back on the farm system would be a drastic mistake. Indeed, Stouffer cut the

Chris Chambliss is mobbed by teammates after hitting a game-winning homer against Texas in 1972. A first-round draft choice of the Tribe in 1970, Chambliss became the starting first baseman in 1971 and won the AL Rookie of the Year award with a .275 average.

S hortstop Frank Duffy tags out Bernie Allen on a steal attempt in a game against the Yankees at the Stadium in 1972. Duffy, who had been acquired in the off-season trade that sent Sam McDowell to the Giants and Gaylord Perry to the Tribe, provided quality defense for six seasons (1972-77).

budget and Peters left the club to become president of the National Association (the governing body of minor league baseball). As the Indians headed into the 1972 season, the club would struggle to generate the revenue and the talent needed to compete.

As the Stouffer era ended in Cleveland, so did the Sam McDowell era. Unlike Stouffer's sale of the club, the deal that sent McDowell away ranks as one of the most successful in Indians history. On November 29, 1971, McDowell was traded to the San Francisco Giants for pitcher Gaylord Perry and shortstop Frank Duffy.

Unlike the 28-year-old McDowell, who had a sub-par 1971 season, the 32-year-old right-handed Perry was 16-12 for the National League's Western Division champions. The Giants envisioned McDowell returning to his strikeout form. The Indians saw in Perry a dependable hurler capable of leading a young staff featuring three young right handers: Dick Tidrow (25), Milt Wilcox (22) and Steve Dunning (23).

McDowell did not regain his form in San Francisco and won just 19 more games in four seasons with three teams—the Giants, Yankees and Pittsburgh Pirates. Loaded with talent, McDowell became the winningest left-handed pitcher in Indians history. Only Bob Feller had more strikeouts than McDowell's 2,159. With five strikeout titles and 122 wins, McDowell was one of Cleveland few legitimate stars of the 1960s.

Like Indians players before and after him, McDowell battled with alcohol dependency. Little of his problem was reported in the media of the 1960s and 1970s, but he eventually admitted his problem and gained control of his life. Better yet, McDowell became a successful counselor about alcohol and drug addiction, working for several major league teams and helping other players avoid his demons.

Hank Peters's farm system produced another gem for the starting lineup in 1972, Buddy Bell, just 20 years old and the son of former major league outfielder Gus Bell. The rookie earned a spot in the Tribe's opening-day outfield along with center fielder Del Unser and the truculent Alex Johnson.

GAYLORD PERRY

P • Indians • 1972-1975   National Baseball Hall of Fame, 1991

The 1970 American League batting champion, Johnson had come to Cleveland in a deal that sent Vada Pinson and Alan Foster to the Angels. Unser was obtained in an eight-player trade with the new Texas Rangers, formerly the Washington Senators.

The new manager for 1972 was former Indians infielder Ken Aspromonte whose managerial debut would have to wait, however, as Major League Baseball suffered its first-ever regular-season disruption due to unrest between the players and the ownership.

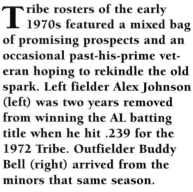

Tribe rosters of the early 1970s featured a mixed bag of promising prospects and an occasional past-his-prime veteran hoping to rekindle the old spark. Left fielder Alex Johnson (left) was two years removed from winning the AL batting title when he hit .239 for the 1972 Tribe. Outfielder Buddy Bell (right) arrived from the minors that same season.

Guided by union leader Marvin Miller, major league players, unhappy with their existing pension plan, walked out of training camp and remained on strike until an agreement was struck in early April. The 86 games lost to the strike would not be played.

The measure of success enjoyed by the 1972 Indians is largely thanks to Gaylord Perry. The big right hander had one of the best seasons ever, leading the AL with 24 wins, one third of the Tribe's 72 total victories. His 1.92 ERA was second best in the league. In a remarkable comeback, Luis Tiant returned from baseball oblivion to edge Perry with a league-leading 1.91 ERA and help pitch the Red Sox within one half game of the AL Eastern Division title won by the Tigers.

Perry's outstanding work made him the first Indians hurler to receive the ultimate pitching honor, the Cy Young Award, named for Cleveland's past pitching legend. Dick Tidrow, meanwhile, won 14 games and earned the Rookie Pitcher of the Year award from *The Sporting News*. After Perry and Tidrow, the rest of the staff was 34-53.

Buddy Bell had a successful debut in 1972, finishing third behind Graig Nettles and Chris Chambliss as a run producer. Groomed as a third baseman, Bell had been moved to the outfield as Nettles held down the hot corner. With Bell in hand to play third, the Indians dealt Nettles and catcher Gerry Moses to the Yankees for outfielders Rusty Torres and Charlie Spikes, catcher-first baseman John Ellis and infielder Jerry Kenney. The key to the deal was Spikes who was projected to become a slugging star.

Within weeks, Gabe Paul followed Nettles out the door and off to the Big Apple. Paul and minority investor F.J. "Steve" O'Neill sold their stock in the Tribe and joined the Yankees. Paul became Steinbrenner's general manager.

On January 10, 1973, the Indians' new general manager became baseball veteran Phil Seghi, who had joined the organization in November 1971 as vice president and director of player personnel. Before coming to the Tribe, he had been farm director of the Oakland Athletics, responsible for a department that helped fuel a dynasty featuring three consecutive world championships (1972-74).

With a fading farm system and limited financial resources, Seghi chose to wheel and deal to improve the team and wasted little time in remaking the Indians. By June 1, he had traded Alex Johnson, Ray Fosse, Jack Heidemann, Tom McCraw and Steve Dunning. From Oakland, Seghi obtained a hot prospect in outfielder George Hendrick and catcher Dave Duncan in exchange for Fosse and Heidemann. For Dunning, he acquired pitcher Dick Bosman and outfielder Ted Ford from the Rangers.

The American League introduced a new twist in 1973 by creating a designated hitter. The new rule, which was not adopted by the National League, would allow the pitcher to be replaced in the batting order by a player whose only job would be to hit. The concept extended the careers of hitting greats Orlando Cepeda, Tony Oliva, Frank Robinson, Tommy Davis and later Al Kaline, Harmon Killebrew and Hank Aaron.

Dick Tidrow finished with a 14-15 record and a 2.77 ERA in 1972 to win the AL Rookie Pitcher of the Year award. But after a 14-16 mark the following season, he was included in the seven-player trade with the Yankees in April 1974 that brought four pitchers to Cleveland, including starter Fritz Peterson.

The Indians' first designated hitters were newly-acquired Oscar Gamble, John Ellis, Walt Williams and Charlie Spikes.

An opening-day record crowd of 74,420 at the Stadium greeted the start of the 1973 season as Gaylord Perry dueled Mickey Lolich of the Tigers. Chris Chambliss's two-run home run and a great defensive play by shortstop Leo Cardenas highlighted a 2-1 victory. Perry had a more mortal 19-19 record in 1973 and the Indians could not improve on 1972's record. Again, there was little pitching support after Perry and Tidrow (14-16). Spikes delivered by leading the Tribe with 23 homers and 73 RBI. The 24-year-old Hendrick hit 21 home runs and Gamble added 20 as the Tribe led the AL with 158 homers.

As the Indians dropped to sixth place in 1973, financial problems mounted once again. Attendance at the Stadium fell to an AL low 605,073. Nick Mileti turned over leadership of the franchise to Alva "Ted" Bonda, a respected Cleveland businessman. Mileti retained the title of club president. Bonda became executive vice president and would be able to concentrate on the Indians while Mileti dealt with his other ventures, including a grand, modern arena (to be called the Coliseum) located between Cleveland, Akron and Canton.

On-field improvement in 1974—which hopefully would translate into improved attendance—would require the Tribe to improve its pitching. In March, Seghi traded for Gaylord Perry's brother and former Indian Jim Perry. On April 3, Seghi traded outfield-first base prospect Pedro Guerrero to the Dodgers for pitcher Bruce Ellingsen, a deal that became a disaster. The 25-year-old lefty won one game for the Indians. Guerrero became one of the NL's top power hitters.

The Bogalusa Bomber, outfielder Charlie Spikes, arrived in November 1972 as part of a six-player trade with the Yankees. Expected to add power to the Tribe's young offense, Spikes delivered with 23 and 22 home runs in 1973 and 1974, respectively.

Jim Perry, winner of the Cy Young Award with the Twins in 1970, struggled for the Tigers in 1973. Back in Cleveland and pitching alongside his 35-year-old brother, the older Perry (37) rebounded to finish second on the club with 17 wins.

Another familiar face returned to the Tribe. Larry Doby joined the coaching staff along with Clay Bryant and Tony Pacheco. Rocky Colavito, Warren Spahn and Joe Lutz were dismissed as coaches.

Still short of pitching, Seghi gambled on a big deal with his former boss, Gabe Paul. Seghi sent Chambliss, Tidrow and pitcher Cecil Upshaw to the Yankees for four pitchers—Fritz Peterson, Steve Kline, Fred Beene and Tom Buskey. In one swoop, Cleveland had a pitching staff, but paid a great price. Along with the previously-traded Graig Nettles, Chambliss and Tidrow would become champions in New York. Peterson had been involved in another trade, one that literally rewrote the definition of a "New York tabloid story." In 1973, it was reported that he and fellow Yankees pitcher Mike Kekich had swapped wives, children and houses. Kekich was traded to the Tribe in June 1973, but after going 1-4, he was released the next spring. Peterson finished 9-14 in 1974 and 14-8 in 1975. He was 0-3 in '76 when he was traded to Texas.

Enthusiasm for the Tribe increased in 1974 and, coupled with the novel promotion of offering beer at 10 cents a cup, brought 25,134 fans to the Stadium for the game on

Gaylord Perry's Hall-of-Fame career made a stop in Cleveland from 1972 until he was traded to Texas in June 1975. Perry won the Cy Young award with a 24-16 record in 1972, later becoming the only pitcher to win it in both leagues when he received the award as a San Diego Padre in 1978. In 1974 (left), Perry won 15 straight to tie Johnny Allen's 1937 club record, finishing at 21-13.

Many Changes, but Few Solutions

With baseball bats in hand for protection, fellow Rangers escort Jeff Burroughs (center) to the dugout after he was attacked by fans in left field during the ninth inning of "Beer Night" at the Stadium on June 4, 1974.

June 4 against the Texas Rangers. With no limit on the beer sales, many fans became increasingly unruly as the game went on. Play was delayed in the sixth and seventh innings when fans ran onto the field. In the ninth inning, when Cleveland rallied from a 5-3 deficit to tie the game, hundreds of fans spilled out of the stands and began to start a riot on the field. At one point, the Rangers charged from the dugout to left field, bats in hand, to rescue Jeff Burroughs and escort him to safety. Rangers manager Billy Martin refused to put his team back onto the field. Umpire Nestor Chylak tried in vain to restore order, but was finally forced to declare the game a forfeit.

In the short-term, the big trade with the Yankees paid off. The Indians won 40 of their next 64 games. After losing on opening day, Gaylord Perry became unbeatable, winning 15 straight. On July 7, Jim Perry pushed the Indians into first place by beating the Angels, 6-2. With eight wins in nine games, Cleveland's record was 45-35. The following day, Perry's winning streak was broken when rookie Claudell Washington's 10th-inning single gave Oakland a 4-3 win.

The end of Perry's winning streak seemed to take the steam out of the Indians and out of Gaylord himself. Perry returned to the 20-win circle, but lost 12 of his last 18 decisions. Dick Bosman provided one memorable highlight with a no-hitter against the world-champion Athletics on July 19 at the Stadium. Only one runner reached base on Bosman's own throwing error. The win was one of 16 against 28 losses that dropped the Tribe into fourth place with a 61-63 record.

Acquisition of two aging sluggers bolstered the Indians' offense in anticipation of a stretch run for the pennant. In August, Rico Carty (34) was purchased from Cordoba

of the Mexican League. A former NL batting champ, the "Big Mon" hit .363 in 33 games. On September 12, the Indians acquired Frank Robinson (39) from the Angels. Robinson hit .200 in 15 games as the Tribe slipped to a fourth-place finish, 14 games behind the first-place Orioles, with a 77-85 record. Responding to the best finish in a full season in the games-behind column since 1959, Indians fans boosted home attendance over the one-million mark for the first time since 1959.

Charlie Spikes improved on his 1973 performance. The "Bogalusa Bomber" hit .271 with 22 home runs and 80 RBI. Oscar Gamble led the regulars with a .291 batting average and tied George Hendrick for second on the club with 19 homers.

By 1974, 27 years after Jackie Robinson broke the color barrier in major league baseball, no major league club had yet hired an African-American manager. Cleveland

Tribe pitcher Tom Hilgendorf receives police protection as he leaves the field after being struck in the head by a flying object during "Beer Night." The ninth-inning incident between fans and players resulted in the game being forfeited to Texas.

Dick Bosman is greeted by catcher John Ellis following his no-hitter, a 4-0 victory over the A's at the Stadium on July 19, 1974. It was the 13th no-hitter in franchise history.

had one candidate to become the first in coach Larry Doby, also the first black player in the American League when he made his Tribe debut in 1947. After Frank Robinson arrived in Cleveland, the Indians had a managerial candidate who was mentioned every time the subject of a black manager came up.

If Robinson's acquisition was meant to invigorate the Indians, it backfired. His arrival seemed to polarize the club. Robinson and Gaylord Perry were immediately at odds. Perry expected to be the highest-paid player on the Indians and objected when Robinson's more favorable contract terms for 1975 were publicized. When the Tribe faded down the stretch in 1974, it seemed certain that Ken Aspromonte, in the final year of a three-year contract, would not return to manage the club in 1975.

Fresh off their most successful season in years, the Cleveland Indians brought new national attention to the franchise on October 3, 1974, with a press conference introducing Frank Robinson as their new manager. To signify the importance of the event, Commissioner of Baseball Bowie Kuhn and American League President Lee MacPhail were both in attendance.

Robinson not only became the first African-American manager in the history of Major League Baseball, he also also followed Cleveland legends such as Nap Lajoie, Tris Speaker and Lou Boudreau by becoming a player-manager. Robinson's leadership ability as a player was notable. The future Hall of Famer had become the first player to win the Most Valuable Player award in both leagues, with the Reds in 1961 and with the Orioles in 1966. He led by example. His determination and talent helped earn five pennants—Cincinnati in 1961 and Baltimore in 1966, 1969, 1970 and 1971—and two world championships with the Orioles in 1966 and 1970. Robinson was also preparing himself to become a manager, gaining valuable experience with several years of managing in the winter leagues in Puerto Rico.

Robinson down played the significance of his hiring, saying, "I'm the first black manager only because I was born black." Ted Bonda, who would formally become president of the Indians on March 20, 1975, and general manager Seghi were lauded for making the historic appointment.

Frank Robinson's regular-season debut as manager of the Indians, April 8, 1975, made for one of the most memorable moments in Tribe history. With 56,715 fans at Cleveland Stadium, the Indians opened the season against the New York Yankees and pitcher George "Doc" Medich. Robinson placed himself second in the batting order as the designated hitter. In the first inning, in his first at-bat as player-manger, he drove a home run into the left-field stands. Fans later selected Robinson's home run as the most memorable moment in club history. The Indians won, 5-3, with Gaylord Perry earning the victory. Opening day was one of the lone bright spots for Robinson and the Indians in 1975. With 10 losses in 13 games in early May, they fell to last place.

The future looked a little brighter when the Tribe won 27 of its final 42 games to complete the campaign with a 79-80 record, good for fourth place. Robinson played just 49 games, but oversaw extensive lineup changes. His old Baltimore teammate, John "Boog" Powell, acquired to play first base, earned Comeback Player of the Year honors at age 34 by hitting .297 with 27 homers and 86 RBI.

Duane Kuiper became the starter at second base. Rookie fly chaser Rick Manning became the center fielder, allowing George Hendrick to move to left. Another rookie, Alan Ashby, gradually took over the starting catching duties. Veteran Rico Carty, signed out of the Mexican League in 1974 by Phil Seghi, settled in at designated hitter and led the club with a .308 batting average.

The biggest transaction of the season came on June 13 when Gaylord Perry was traded to the Texas Rangers for pitchers Jim Bibby, Jackie Brown, Rick Waits and cash. Perry, whose record was 6-9 at the time, and Robinson were simply incompatible. The 36-year-old hurler furthered his Hall-of-Fame credentials with 42 wins for the Rangers (1975-77). He won his second Cy Young Award with the San Diego Padres in 1978, becoming the first to win the award in both leagues. He won his 300th game in 1982 with Seattle, finishing with 314 in 1983.

Right handers Bibby and Brown and left hander Waits would all have a significant impact on the Indians for the next several years. In 1975, the trio combined for 12 wins in both starting and relief roles. Fritz Peterson pulled his weight with a club-high 14 victories. Dennis Eckersley, a 20-year-old rookie right hander won 13 and was named the American League Rookie Pitcher of the Year by *The Sporting News*.

The 1976 Tribe continued to spin its wheels, posting its first winning record (81-78) since 1968, but still finishing fourth, 16 games out of first. Boog Powell could not repeat his comeback season. Charlie Spikes, who slumped dramatically in 1975, slid further with just three home runs and never achieved anything near his 1973 or 1974 numbers again, much less the heights predicted for him. The Indians did have four pitchers win 10 or more games for the first time since 1968. Newly-acquired veteran Pat Dobson led the way with 16 victories. Eckersley and Bibby had 13 apiece. Lanky right hander Jim Kern became a relief specialist and emerged as one of the best firemen in the game. Paired with veteran left-handed reliever Dave LaRoche, Cleveland had one of the best lefty-righty relief combinations in baseball.

Also on the bright side, Ray Fosse, reacquired from Oakland, batted .301 in 90 games, second best to Rico Carty's .310 average. Carty also led the club with 83 RBI and was named the Indians Man of the Year for 1976.

Frank Robinson arrives home to a handshake from John Lowenstein after hitting a first-inning homer on opening day, April 8, 1975, at the Stadium. Robinson's debut as baseball's first black manager found the Tribe beating the Yankees, 5-3.

Many Changes, but Few Solutions

Major League Baseball was forever changed by the advent of free agency in the 1970s. After decades of a system in which ownership controlled player movement, players now had a large degree of control over where they would play. For many fans, the sign of having a competitive team was being competitive in the free agent market. And so, following the 1976 season, on November 19, the Indians took their first plunge into free agency and signed 25-year-old right-handed pitcher Wayne Garland to a then seemingly-outrageous 10-year contract for $2.3 million.

In his third full season with the Orioles and first as a starter, Garland was 20-7 with a 2.67 ERA, 14 complete games and four shutouts. With Garland, Eckersley, Bibby and Waits as starters and Kern and LaRoche in the bullpen, the Tribe expected to have the foundation for extended pitching success.

Along with free agency, the Indians faced another expansion draft after the 1976 season. Among the players left unprotected was Carty. The new Toronto Blue Jays organization called Cleveland's bluff and took him in the draft. Popular stars were in short supply in Cleveland and sufficient outrage was expressed at the loss of "The Big Mon" that Seghi dealt with Toronto to reacquire Carty. Highly-regarded catching prospect Rick Cerone and enigmatic outfielder John Lowenstein, then best known for hitting .242 on a consistent basis, were traded to get Carty back.

Seghi ended 1976 with a flurry of trades. In addition to the Carty deal on December 6, Trader Phil sent George Hendrick to the Padres on December 8 for outfielder John Grubb, catcher Fred Kendall and infielder Hector Torres. Then, in one of his most

Duane Kuiper throws over the top of a sliding Rich Bladt to complete a double play against the Yankees in 1975. A rookie that season, Kuiper batted a career-high .292. on his way to a lifetime average of .271. He led the AL in fielding percentage twice during his eight seasons in Cleveland.

memorable steals, Seghi sent Jackie Brown to the Montreal Expos for a first baseman-outfielder named Andre Thornton who had shown glimpses of power and promise in four big league seasons. In Cleveland, Andre Thornton became an all-star slugger and brought a new measure of dignity to the roster. His autobiography, *Triumph Born of Tragedy,* is a compelling account of Thornton's life, his ability to overcome the death of his wife and daughter in a tragic auto accident, and the quiet strength of his personality. "Thunder" led the 1977 Indians with 28 home runs and finished second to Rico Carty with 70 RBI. Garland also showed his mettle by pitching almost 300 innings with a sore shoulder, but won just 13 of 32 decisions.

Fans were again growing restless and Robinson continued to cause a large share of friction. When Carty accepted his Man of the Year award, he criticized the manager's lack of leadership and was suspended for 15 days and fined $1,000. With another mediocre start in 1977, the Frank Robinson experiment came to an end and coach Jeff Torborg took over. Like Robinson, Torborg was respected for his baseball knowledge and was expected to become a successful manager. He had little success in Cleveland.

Of managers who guided the Tribe for at least 325 games, Torborg compiled the lowest winning percentage of them all (.439). In 1977, Cleveland lost 59 of its final 97 games under the new manager to finish the year at 71-90, a distant fifth in the AL East. One of the victories was a no-hitter by Dennis Eckersley on May 30 against the Angels. Cleveland's fewest wins in a season since 1971 resulted in the lowest home

attendance since 1973 (900,365). The 1978 team fared no better with another 90 losses, just 69 wins and a fifth-place finish.

The Indians continued to suffer from a lack of sufficient financing that began with the reversal of Vernon Stouffer's fortunes, worsened with the choice of Nick Mileti's group over George Steinbrenner's and continued to deteriorate despite the determined efforts of Ted Bonda and his partners. For all their shortcomings, Stouffer, Mileti and Bonda all had deep roots in Cleveland and refused to allow the Indians to relocate. By 1977, the need for an owner with deep pockets was ever more apparent. On March 31, 1977, IBC Corporation was created to serve as the new general partner of the ball club. As the 1977 season progressed, Bonda sought a new owner for the Indians. One deal to sell the club to Youngstown developer Edward J. DeBartolo fell apart when the Major League Baseball leadership refused to approve the transaction due to DeBartolo's ownership of several racetracks.

Fortunately for baseball in Cleveland, a familiar face was prepared to be next in the line of owners that would refuse to let the Indians leave Cleveland. F. J. "Steve" O'Neill was one of the many investors in the Indians in the 1960s. O'Neill later joined George Steinbrenner's group that bought the New York Yankees in 1973.

In agreeing to purchase the Indians, O'Neill stipulated that Gabe Paul would return to Cleveland. O'Neill became the majority owner on February 3, 1978. Paul was installed as president and chief executive officer. Seghi remained as vice president and

Frank Robinson brought the same combative, competitive style to his managerial role as he exemplified in his 21-year Hall-of-Fame playing career. The Indians, however, failed to improve in the standings, finishing fourth in 1975 and '76. With the Tribe stuck in fifth in June 1977, Robinson was fired and replaced by Jeff Torborg.

general manager. Bonda continued as a minority stockholder and director.

Another director became the majority owner of the Cleveland Browns, Art Modell. The purchase price was reportedly $11 million, including an assumption of debt amounting to more than $5 million.

Indicative of Cleveland's problems in the late 1970s was a clerical snafu that cost the Indians pitcher Jim Bibby, who was due a $10,000 bonus for starting 30 games in 1977. When the bonus was not paid on time, an arbitrator ruled that Bibby's contract had been breached and declared him a free agent. The big right hander signed with Pittsburgh and helped the Pirates win a World Series in 1979.

A move to strengthen the pitching staff and the offense backfired when Dennis Eckersley and catcher Fred Kendall were sent to the Red Sox for pitchers Rick Wise, Mike Paxton, catcher Bo Diaz and infielder Ted Cox. While Eckersley won 20 games for the Red Sox, the veteran Wise led the AL with 19 losses and just nine wins. Diaz missed most of the season with a broken ankle. Cox, a prized prospect, did not live up to expectations and spent just two seasons as an Indian. Paxton won 12 games, second to Rick Waits's 13. Jim Kern won 10 in relief and David Clyde, a former phenom with the Rangers, won eight of 19 decisions.

Minus Bibby and Eckersley, the 1978 Indians also lost Wayne Garland when he was diagnosed with a torn rotator cuff and underwent surgery in May. During the 1970s, pitchers did not rebound from torn rotator cuffs. Garland tried gallantly, but won just 13 more games in three seasons following the shoulder surgery.

A saving grace of the season was Andre Thornton's breakout as one of baseball's top sluggers. His 33 home runs were the most by a Tribesman since Rocky Colavito hit 42 in 1959. His 105 RBI were the most since Colavito's 108 in 1965. John Grubb rebounded from an injury-riddled 1977 season to hit 14 homers and drive in 61 runs before an August 31 trade sent him to Texas. New catcher Gary Alexander finished second to Thornton with 17 homers and tied Buddy Bell for second with 62 RBI. Kuiper and Manning had solid seasons.

With few other options at his disposal, Seghi kept wheeling and dealing. Kern and infielder Larvell Blanks were sent to the Rangers for veteran outfielder Bobby Bonds and pitcher Len Barker. Two prized prospects, shortstop Alfredo Griffin and third baseman Phil Langford, were traded to Toronto for relief pitcher Victor Cruz. Pitcher Cardell Camper brought outfielder Joe Charboneau from the Phillies. To cap another wave of December deals, fan favorite Buddy Bell went to Texas for Toby Harrah in an exchange of third basemen.

Bell had been steady, if not spectacular, during seven seasons with the Indians. He led the club in hits three times (1973, 1975 and 1978) with a total of 1,016 hits and a lifetime .274 batting average. In Texas, however, Bell really blossomed, winning six consecutive Gold Glove awards for stellar defense at third base and batting .294 or better in five of his six full seasons with the Rangers. He also had two fine seasons for the Reds before end-

Dennis Eckersley delivers a pitch during his no-hitter on May 30, 1977, a 1-0 win over the Angels at the Stadium. Eckersley won 40 games as a starter from 1975-77 before being traded to the Red Sox. He became a reliever with the A's in the 1980s, won a Cy Young award in 1992 and retired in 1998 as the AL's all-time saves leader.

ing his 18-year playing career back with Texas in 1989. Wins were somewhat scarce when Bell played for the Indians, but he was part of the Tribe's return to glory as a coach for the 1995 American League champions before moving on to manage the Tigers. In 2000, he became manager of the Colorado Rockies.

Another slow start in 1979 signaled the end of Jeff Torborg's duty as manager of the Indians. Amid rumors that Gabe Paul might replace him with Bob Lemon, Torborg announced he would resign at the end of the season. Paul acted even sooner, replacing Torborg with coach Dave Garcia on July 22. The Indians, 43-52 under Torborg, immediately responded to the leadership of Garcia with a 10-game winning streak. The Tribe won 38 of its final 66 games under the new manager to finish one game over .500 at 81-80, though still sixth in the American League East.

Offensive leaders Thornton, Harrah, Bonds, Manning and early-season addition Mike Hargrove (acquired from Texas in exchange for outfielder Paul Dade) brought a new zest to the Indians. Harrah (20), Bonds (34) and Manning (30) ran Cleveland to the third highest stolen base total (142) in the league, the most for the Tribe in a single season since 1918.

Hargrove, a 27-year-old left-handed hitting outfielder-first baseman-designated hitter led the 1979 Indians with a .325 batting average. Known as "The Human Rain Delay" for a deliberate routine of hitches and twitches before each pitch, he became one of the most adept players in baseball at getting on base.

The Indians' second half surge in 1979 was also attributable to designated hitter Cliff Johnson. Acquired from the Yankees for pitcher Don Hood at the June 15 trading deadline, Johnson caught fire in Cleveland and hit 18 home runs with 61 RBI in just 72 games.

Rick Waits, who pitched a one-hitter against Boston in the home opener, again led the team in victories with a 16-13 record. Rick Wise rebounded for a 15-10 mark. Relief pitcher Sid Monge added 12 wins. Fans responded to the second-half success and pushed attendance over a million (1,011,644) for only the second time since 1959.

As the 1970s closed, the Indians had gone 25 years without a pennant. With the exception of 1974, they had not come close to one since 1959. The Tribe had not finished higher than fourth since divisional play began in 1969. But, hope springs eternal and a good finish in 1979, increased attendance, and Steve O'Neill's finances gave faithful fans reasons for optimism.

Third baseman Toby Harrah (left) provided veteran leadership offensively and defensively from 1979-83 after being acquired from Texas for Buddy Bell. In the 1979 home opener, Rick Waits (right) threw a one-hitter, then finished with a team-high 16 victories.

INNING 8

Super Joe and Other False Hopes

1980–1993

Cleveland Indians baseball in the 1980s began with the phenomenon of "Super Joe" Charboneau, who had been acquired in a small deal with the Philadelphia Phillies in 1978. For a fleeting moment, the kid from Belvidere, Illinois, was the subject of a book, (Super Joe), and a song, ("Go, Joe Charboneau") and was the biggest thing in Cleveland baseball. By the time Charboneau became all the rage, the Tribe, and its 1980 hopes, had been decimated. Andre Thornton suffered a severe right knee injury and missed the entire season.

Right-handed pitcher John Denny, acquired in a trade with St. Louis for Bobby Bonds and expected to fortify the pitching staff, took ill and missed the start of the campaign. When Denny returned, he pitched well until suffering a season-ending heel injury in July. Injuries provided opportunities for Len Barker and Dan Spillner who became the big winners. Barker reached his potential with 19 wins and led the AL with 187 strikeouts in 246-and-one-third innings pitched. Spillner moved into the starting rotation and won 16 games.

In place of a pennant race, Charboneau was the Cleveland baseball story of 1980. Super Joe was as entertaining a character as the Indians had ever employed. The 25-year-old right-handed hitting outfielder and designated hitter opened beer bottles with his eye sockets and drank beer through his nose. And, he hit. In 1980, Charboneau led the Indians with 23 home runs and 87 RBI and became the third player in Indians history to win the American League Rookie of the Year award.

Left fielder Miguel Dilone, acquired from the Cubs in early May, set a team record with 61 stolen bases and led the club with a .341 batting average. Mike Hargrove played first base and hit .304 with 85 RBI and set a club record by drawing 111 walks that stood until Jim Thome drew 127 in 1999.

The Indians' popular second baseman Duane Kuiper was traded to the Giants for pitcher Ed Whitson following the 1981 season. His steady play was punctuated by two memorable moments. On August 29, 1977, after 1,381 official plate appearances for the Indians, Kuiper hit a home run off Baltimore's Steve Stone in a 9-2 Tribe victory at Cleveland Stadium. Kuiper never hit another home run in 3,379 total major-league at-bats over 10 seasons. On July 27, 1978, he tied a major league record by hitting two bases-loaded triples in the same game.

The return of the All-Star Game promised to make 1981 a special season in Cleveland. But any optimism for 1981 was tempered by player-owner unrest that threatened to disrupt the season. The addition of curveball artist Bert Blyleven from the Pirates gave the Indians the makings of an outstanding pitching staff. With a starting rotation of Blyleven, John Denny, Rick Waits, Len Barker and Wayne Garland, the Tribe charged into first place.

With a 15-8 record, the Indians opened a home stand with the Toronto Blue Jays on May 15. Large Len Barker opened the home stand against Luis Leal. The 7,290 hearty fans on hand quickly took note that Barker was especially sharp. Relying on a devastating curve, he retired the Jays inning after inning. By the ninth, Barker was bidding for a perfect game. He quickly dispatched Rick Bosetti and pinch-hitter Al Woods. Pinch hitter Ernie Whitt followed and lofted a fly to center field. Rick Manning charged in to grab the 27th out. Len Barker had a perfect game.

Less than a month later, Major League Baseball was halted by a players' strike. As June turned into July, the All-Star Game was postponed. Finally, a measure of compromise was reached and the strike ended. The All-Star Game was rescheduled for August 9 as the big opening number to launch baseball's return.

Barker and catcher Bo Diaz, along with Dave Garcia who served as a coach, were Cleveland's representatives in the 1981 All-Star Game. Any fears, or hopes, that the rescheduled game would attract a small crowd, sending a message that fans were fed up with players and owners, were dispelled when Cleveland fans set another All-Star Game attendance record, the third in four games played at Cleveland Stadium.

Miguel Dilone steals second against Seattle in 1980. After being purchased from the Cubs in May, the 25-year-old center fielder stole a then-club-record 61 bases (now held by Kenny Lofton's 75 in 1996) and batted a career-high .341.

LEGENDS OF THE TRIBE

Indeed, Cleveland fans sent the message that the city itself was on the comeback trail. After a long downturn culminated when the city of Cleveland fell into default in 1978, politicians and businessmen were working to improve Cleveland. The downtown was a major development target and the national attention gained from the All-Star Game brought positive attention to "The Comeback City." The 72,086 fans packed into the Stadium gave Dave Garcia the largest ovation. Barker, in relief of starting pitcher Jack Morris, pitched two perfect innings. Catcher Gary Carter's two home runs powered the National League to a 5-4 victory.

To compensate for the 50-day long players' strike, Major League Baseball adopted a split-season format. The division leaders when the strike began would face the team in their division with the best second-half record to determine the League Championship Series participants. Cleveland's tepid play after Barker's perfect game had dropped the club to sixth place, five games behind the first-place Yankees, for the first half. The Tribe's reprieve, granted by the split-season format, was short lived. With just 4,773 fans on hand at the Stadium for the start of the second half, the Indians lost to Milwaukee and began stumbling to seven losses in eight games.

A spurt of 14 victories in 20 games helped, but the Tribe could not sustain that pace and finished fifth in the second half, five games behind the Brewers, with a 26-27 record.

The Indians' effective pitching was undermined by devastating injuries to Andre Thornton and Joe Charboneau. Thornton was again sidelined in spring training with a broken hand. Later, he suffered a badly sprained thumb. Charboneau, playing in pain, had a terrible first half and was demoted to Cleveland's Triple-A farm club. In October, Super Joe underwent back surgery. Like Louis Sockalexis almost a century earlier, Joe Charboneau was a shooting star on the Cleveland baseball landscape. He played the final 22 of his 201-game major league career—all with the Indians—in 1982.

Mike Hargrove led the 1981 Tribe with a .317 batting average and Bo Diaz batted .313. Miguel Dilone (29) and Rick Manning (25) paced the Indians to the AL lead in team stolen bases with 119. After having five home crowds (in just 22 home dates) of over 30,000 fans in the first half of the 1981 season, the biggest home crowd in the second half was just 12,790.

Andre Thornton's courageous comeback in 1982 and the emergence of Von Hayes were bright spots in a lackluster season that marked the conclusion of Dave Garica's tenure as skipper. "Thunder" Thornton led the club with 32 homers and 116 RBI. The 23-year-old, left-handed hitting Hayes drove in 82 runs. Toby Harrah hit .304 with 25 homers and 78 RBI. Bake McBride, a successful hitter acquired from Philadelphia to play right field, was sidelined in May with an eye infection. Batting .365 in 27 games, he was done for the season. Bert Blyleven underwent elbow surgery and pitched in just four games. Rick Waits struggled with a knee injury and lost 13 of 15 decisions. Len Barker won 15 games and newcomer Rick Sutcliffe added 14.

Ron Hassey (left) played seven seasons in Cleveland (1978-84), the best being 1980, when he batted .318 with 65 RBI. Hassey caught the perfect games by Len Barker (right) in 1981 and by Montreal's Dennis Martinez in 1991. Barker's best season out of five in Cleveland (1979-83) was also 1980 when he finished at 19-12 with 187 strikeouts. He pitched his perfect game against Toronto at the Stadium on May 15, 1981.

Andre Thornton was acquired from Montreal in December 1976 and proceeded to average 29 homers and 89 RBI his first three years. A first baseman and designated hitter, he overcame injury and personal tragedy to play 10 seasons with the Tribe, earning two All-Star selections and two Man of the Year awards. Entering the 2000 season, his 214 homers and 749 RBI were fifth and ninth, respectively on the club's all-time career lists.

LEGENDS OF THE TRIBE

Cleveland's 1982 season ended on a humbling note when the Indians fell into a tie for last place in the AL East with the Toronto Blue Jays. The Jays, in business for less than a decade, had caught, and would soon surpass, the established Indians.

As the Indians went from bad to worse on the playing field, fundamental changes in the leadership of the franchise again raised concerns about the future of the club. To replace Dave Garcia, who was not rehired after the 1982 season, Gabe Paul turned to an upcoming field leader he had hired to manage in the New York Yankees' farm system. Mike Ferraro, 38-year-old first base coach of the Yankees, became the new manager of the Indians on November 4, 1982.

Paul and Phil Seghi followed Ferraro's hiring with a blockbuster trade. The Philadelphia Phillies had set their sights on Von Hayes as a key to remaining a contender in the National League East. They would trade quantity, including a young and flashy hitting prospect, shortstop Julio Franco. On December 9, the Tribe traded Hayes to the Phillies for the 21-year-old Franco, Gold Glove Award-winning second baseman Manny Trillo, outfielder George Vukovich, pitcher Jay Baller and catcher Gerry Willard.

Before Ferraro could take charge of the club in spring training, he was diagnosed with cancer. On February 9, he underwent surgery to have a cancerous kidney removed. The surgery was gauged a success. Whether or not the new manager changed and lost his intensity, as was conjectured, the Indians showed no spark for Ferraro. After just 100 games (of which 60 were losses), Paul fired him. Only Bobby Bragan was given a more abrupt dismissal as manager of the Indians.

Among the managerial candidates available in July 1983 was Pat Corrales, recently fired by the Phillies. His dismissal on July 18 was historic because Philadelphia was in first place, albeit with a pedestrian 43-42 record, in the NL East. He was the first major league manager to be fired during a season with his team in first place. The Los Angeles native, a big league catcher from 1964 through 1973 and back-up to Hall of Famer Johnny Bench for the Reds from 1968-1972, was expected to bring the intensity that Ferraro seemed to lack.

Paul and Seghi were busily changing players along with the manager. In June, Rick Manning and Rick Waits had been traded to Milwaukee for slugging outfielder Gorman Thomas and pitchers Ernie Camacho and Jamie Easterly. In August, Trillo went to the Montreal Expos for outfielder Don Carter and cash while Miguel Dilone was traded to the White Sox. As the NL pennant race heated up, Paul and Seghi found another opportunity to acquire young talent from the Atlanta Braves. In exchange for Len Barker, the Indians would acquire outfielder Brett Butler and third baseman Brook Jacoby to accompany pitcher Rick Behenna and cash.

Manning had spent nine seasons in the outfield, entertaining fans with defensive play that earned him a Gold Glove as a rookie in 1975. After a solid 1976, he suffered a serious back injury in 1977, recovering to become one of Cleveland's all-time leaders in stolen bases. After 1,063 games with the Indians, Manning played another 492 games with the Brewers before retiring after the 1987 season. In 1990, he began a new career as a color commentator for the cable-television broadcasts of Indians games on SportsChannel-Fox Sports Ohio. Manning and broadcaster John Sanders established a partnership on the cable telecasts that continued into the new century.

Mike Hargrove's time-consuming routines at the plate earned him the nickname, "The Human Rain Delay." But Hargrove stopped delaying long enough to play seven seasons at first base for the Tribe (1979-85) before embarking on his long managerial career.

Within a month after Pat Corrales was hired on July 31, the franchise was dealt another blow with the death of 83-year-old club owner Steve O'Neill. With his death, control of the club passed to his nephew, Patrick O'Neill, who expressed no interest in owning the club and set forth to honor his uncle's wishes and find a new owner who would be committed to keeping the Indians in Cleveland. He did not rule out the possibility that the club could be sold to owners that might want to move the team elsewhere.

The Indians improved some under Corrales, winning 30 of 62 games to finish at 70-92 and alone in

Bert Blyleven delivers a pitch in September 1984 when he won his 19th game of the season against Minnesota at the Stadium. At age 33, Blyleven added veteran stability to a shaky pitching staff. He missed five starts with a fractured foot, but finished at 19-7 with 170 strikeouts and a 2.87 ERA.

last place in the AL East for the first time since 1973. Julio Franco led the team with 80 RBI and 32 stolen bases. Gorman Thomas hit 17 homers, but struck out 98 times in his only season in Cleveland. Rick Sutcliffe led the pitchers with 17 wins.

Another less-than-successful trade, following the season, sent Toby Harrah and pitcher Rick Browne to the Yankees for outfielder Otis Nixon and pitchers George Frazier and Guy Elston. Harrah was a consistent performer in his five seasons with the Indians, topping the 70-RBI mark three times and the 20-homer mark twice. With Brook Jacoby ready to step in at third base, however, the Indians looked to benefit from Nixon's speed at the plate and in the outfield. In fact, the trade provided little benefit to Cleveland or New York.

With the financial limitations of an ownership focused on selling the franchise, players that wanted to play for more money on contending teams, and unable to compete for star-quality free agents, the Indians continued to try to retool in 1984. In the midst of another lost season—75 wins and a distant sixth-place finish—Paul and Seghi made one last score in the trade market. With the trading deadline approaching on June 13, they sent pitchers Sutcliffe, George Frazier and catcher Ron Hassey to the Chicago Cubs for outfielders Joe Carter and Mel Hall, and pitchers Don Schulze and Darryl Banks. Sutcliffe caught fire, winning 16 of 17 decisions, leading the Cubs to post-season play for the first time since 1945 and earning the Cy Young Award. Carter, however, would more than balance the trade by becoming one of baseball's best run-producers.

Two surviving veterans in 1984 had stellar seasons. Andre Thornton drove in 99 runs and hit 33 homers. Bert Blyleven finally returned to form and won 19 games with a 2.87 earned run average. Leading the newcomers was Brett Butler who stole 52 bases and scored 108 runs—the most for a Cleveland player since Al Smith's 123 in 1955.

Concerns raised by Pat O'Neill that the Indians might move were heightened dramatically on November 29 when Peter Bavasi was hired as president and chief operating officer. Bavasi, son of longtime baseball executive Buzzy Bavasi, had previously been working as a consultant with the goal of attracting a major league team to Indianapolis and/or Tampa-St. Petersburg. Earlier, the 42-year-old Bavasi had helped to build two expansion teams, the San Diego Padres and the Toronto Blue Jays. He would be entering a similar situation in Cleveland.

Bavasi's arrival marked the end of Gabe Paul's long tenure at the top of the organization. He retired, remaining on the board of directors and as a consultant. Phil Seghi was reassigned (demoted) to senior player personnel advisor. Bob Quinn, vice president of player development and scouting, left the position he had held since 1973.

To handle baseball operations, Bavasi hired Joe Klein and Dan O'Brien. Klein took the role of general manager, a position he had held with the Texas Rangers from 1982

J oe Carter came from the Cubs in 1984 and became a premier power hitter two years later. From 1986-89, he averaged nearly 31 homers and 108 RBI before being traded to San Diego in the deal that brought Sandy Alomar Jr. and Carlos Baerga to Cleveland.

to 1984. O'Brien initially became an advisor to Bavasi before becoming senior vice president-baseball administration and player relations.

Charged with a franchise now 30 years removed from its last post-season appearance, in a stadium increasingly seen as part of the problem and attendance that crashed to 768,941 in 1983 and 734,269 in 1984, Bavasi set forth making dramatic changes. He raised ticket prices, restricted fan-made banners and closed the bleachers for night games.

Even for those fan-unfriendly moves, the most alarming change came with a redesign of Indians caps following the 1985 season. The "C" representing Cleveland would be replaced with Chief Wahoo. Home and road uniform shirts said "Indians" across the front. With no reference to Cleveland anywhere on the uniforms, the Indians would be that much easier to relocate to another city.

The impending doom expected by many fans manifested itself on the field in 1985 as the Indians suffered through a club-record-tying 102 losses and finished seventh in the seven-team AL East for the second time in three years. The Indians were a dismal 39.5 games behind the division-champion Blue Jays. Home attendance of 655,181 was the worst since 1973. Cleveland was the only AL team to draw fewer than one million fans and last in major league attendance for the third consecutive season.

No Tribe pitcher won as many as 10 games. A disgruntled Bert Blyleven, like so many other Cleveland players looking to land with a contending team, got his wish when he was traded to the Minnesota Twins for four players including infield prospect Jay Bell. Blyleven and left-handed pitcher Neal Heaton had nine wins each to lead the staff. Brett Butler led the team with 106 runs scored, 47 steals and a .311 batting average. Julio Franco led with 90 RBI.

The 1985 season became the last as a player for Mike Hargrove, who retired as one of baseball's all-time leaders in on-base percentage, compiling a .290 career batting average (.292 with the Indians).

Hargrove was chosen the Indians Man of the Year in 1980 and 1981, and received the Frank Gibbons Good Guy Award in 1985. The award, established in honor of the Cleveland sportswriter in 1968, was selected by Cleveland-area members of the Baseball Writers Association of America. In 1986, Hargrove began a new career as a coach for Cleveland's farm club at Batavia, New York. "Grover" would rise quickly through the Tribe system, return to Cleveland as first base coach in 1990 and in 1991 became the manager to lead the Indians to heights that were only dreamed of during the 1980s.

Only the Red Sox, Blue Jays and Yankees had a higher team batting average than the Indians in 1985 and only the Blue Jays and Yankees had more stolen bases. But Cleveland's team earned run average of 4.91 was the worst in club history and the worst by any major league club since the 1962 New York Mets.

The complexion of the pitching staff was dramatically improved as spring training concluded in 1986. Phil Niekro, a future Hall of Famer who won 16 games— number 16 being the 300th of his major league career for the 1985 Yankees—was released by New York and snapped up by Cleveland on April 3. The 47-year-old knuckleball pitcher not only gave the Tribe a credible starter, he became a mentor for 28-year-old Tom Candiotti. Under Niekro's wing, Candiotti's knuckleball would flourish. With another off-season acquisition, Ken Schrom, the Indians had a much-improved rotation.

Cleveland's lineup of young veterans became the best offensive squad in the major leagues in 1986, leading the majors in runs scored (831), hits (1,620) and batting average (.284). Not since the 1948 world champions had a Cleveland team scored so many runs and not since 1936 had the club had a higher batting average.

With a 10-game winning streak, the Indians surged into first place in early May and revitalized local interest. The offense got stronger on June 12 when 24-year-old outfielder Cory Snyder was called up from Cleveland's Maine AAA farm club. The Tribe's first choice (fourth overall) in the June 1984 draft and a star in the 1984 Summer Olympics, Snyder was considered a "can't miss" prospect. Pat Corrales used the versatile Snyder at shortstop, third base and in the outfield. His strong arm drew comparisons to Rocky Colavito. His bat delivered 24 home runs and 69 RBI in just 103 games.

By the end of July, the Indians had fallen to fifth place, but just six games out of first. Five home crowds had topped 40,000 led by 73,303 for a Fourth-of-July victory over the world champion Royals. Opening August, 65,934 fans saw a doubleheader split with the Yankees. In total, 153,491 fans attended the four-game series. Only one other three-date series (August 1-3, 1948, against the Yankees) had attracted more fans.

A poor August ended any pennant chances, but 19 wins in the final 31 games gave the Tribe its best record (84-78) since 1968, a fifth-place finish, and an increase of 24 victories from 1985, the best single-season improvement in franchise history. Attendance (1,471,805) was, by far, the most improved in the majors and the best at Cleveland Stadium since 1959.

Joe Carter led the attack with a league-high 121 RBI, the first Tribe player to lead the league in RBI since Rocky Colavito in 1965. Playing outfield and first base, Carter narrowly missed the elite 30-home-run/30-stolen-base club with 29 homers and 29 steals. He also had 200 hits and 108 runs scored, leading the team in both departments. Carter, second baseman Tony Bernazard, shortstop Franco and first baseman/designated hitter Pat Tabler all batted over .300, led by Tabler's .326 average.

Candiotti led the pitchers with 16 wins and a league-leading 17 complete games. Schrom added 14 victories. Niekro had 11 wins and 24-year-old lefty Scott Bailes had 10 as a starter and reliever. Reliever Ernie Camacho rebounded from arm trouble to lead the club with 20 saves.

Pitching looked to get even stronger with the debut of 21-year-old left hander Greg Swindell on August 21. His debut was an embarrassing 24-5 loss to the Red Sox, but the Texan, the Tribe's first choice (second overall) in the June 1986 draft, rebounded to win five of his remaining six decisions. Swindell and Snyder became shades of Herb Score and Rocky Colavito.

Even as the Indians were having their best season in decades, another sale of

Phil Niekro (left) and Tom Candiotti compare grips in 1986, the season in which the 47-year-old Niekro joined the Indians and helped Candiotti perfect his knuckleball style. Niekro won 18 of his 318 career victories in two seasons with the Tribe on his way to the Hall of Fame.

the team was being negotiated. A suitable buyer had come forward in the brothers Richard and David Jacobs. The pending sale, announced in the summer, was formally approved on December 9, 1986. The era of the Steve O'Neill ownership had ended on a positive note and the torch was passed to ownership capable of bringing championship baseball back to Cleveland.

At the time Richard Jacobs, with his brother David, became owner of the Indians, he was one of the most prominent businessmen in Cleveland. Accustomed to success and association with successful projects, Jacobs intended for the Indians to likewise be successful and was willing to build a winning organization from the bottom up rather than search for short-term, quick-fix options. Shortly after the ownership transition, Peter Bavasi resigned as club president. Joe Klein and Dan O'Brien remained to direct the baseball operation in 1987.

By 1987, every AL East team other than the Indians had taken a turn at the top during the previous six years—the Yankees (1981), Brewers (1982), Orioles (1983), Tigers (1984), Blue Jays (1985) and Red Sox (1986). With its surge in 1986 and the precedent of six different division champs in six seasons, a school of thought prevailed that it was the Tribe's turn. *Sports Illustrated* fed the idea by picturing Joe Carter and Cory Snyder on the cover of its 1987 baseball preview issue and predicting that the Tribe would win the East. Never was the "SI Jinx" more effective.

Steve Carlton's many attempts to salvage his Hall-of-Fame-bound career included a stop in Cleveland in 1987. At age 42, he appeared in 23 games with a record of 5-9 before being traded to Minnesota in late July.

The gap between the Indians and legitimate pennant contention became painfully apparent in 1987 when they crashed back to last place and lost 101 games. After losing 10 of their first 11, the Tribe never recovered.

The pitching staff that seemed adequate or better in 1986 fell apart with a team earned run average of 5.28, breaking the club record set in 1985. No pitcher managed more than seven wins. Greg Swindell suffered from arm trouble and Ernie Camacho was demoted to the minors in May with a 9.22 ERA.

Neither Phil Niekro nor fellow 300-game winner Steve Carlton, signed as a free agent at the start of the season, could get the Tribe on track. Two 300-game winners and future Hall of Famers did not buy time for the young pitchers to develop and both legends were gone, via trades, by mid-August. Carlton won just five of 14 decisions. Niekro won seven and provided one of the few bright spots of the season. On June 1, he defeated the Tigers, 9-6, for his 314th major league victory. Combined with his brother Joe's 216 wins, the total of 530 victories made the Niekros the winningest brothers in major league history.

The Indians set a club record with 187 home runs and tied an AL record by having three players (Carter, Snyder and Jacoby) hit more than 30 each. But offense exploded everywhere in 1987 and only two AL clubs (Baltimore and Kansas City) scored fewer runs than the Tribe.

Andre Thornton, who entered the season only 12 home runs short of Earl Averill's club record of 226, played just 36 games and hit no home runs in his final season in the majors. His departure was a disappointment to many. As legitimately talented players and pretenders came and left Cleveland from 1977 through 1987, Thornton was a constant source of pride for the fans, even during his injury-plagued 1980 and 1981 seasons.

Thornton was fourth on the Indians' all-time home run list (214) and among the all-time leaders in RBI (749) and extra base hits (419). Unfortunately, there was no position for him with the organization, on the field or in the front office, after the 1987 season, though he remained an active member of the Cleveland community.

Pat Corrales took the fall for the poor performance on July 16, 1987, when the club was 31-56. Coach and former Tribe catcher Doc Edwards took over. The Indians won 30 and lost 45 for Edwards to finish the season back in seventh place, 37 games behind the division-winning Tigers.

The methodical process of rebuilding the Indians, begun when Richard and David Jacobs bought the franchise, took its next big step on November 2 when Hank Peters returned after 12 successful years as general manager of the Baltimore Orioles. As president and chief operating officer, Peters was charged with building a baseball organization that could compete with the best. His efforts to build a great player-development system earlier in Cleveland (1966-71) were undercut by insufficient finances. Now Peters would have the money to do the job.

One of the pieces that Jacobs, Peters and others thought was vital to rebuilding the Indians was a new ballpark. In 1984, county voters had been asked to approve a property tax to finance a new domed stadium. Lacking key political support, the measure went down to a big defeat and, for a time, talk of a new ballpark died down.

When the Jacobs brothers bought the Indians, Richard Jacobs made clear that a new ballpark was mandatory. The Blue Jays, White Sox and Orioles were all developing new ballparks. With the passing of Chicago's Comiskey Park, only the hallowed grounds of Boston's Fenway Park, Detroit's Tiger Stadium and New York's Yankee Stadium in the American League and Chicago's Wrigley Field in the National League would be older than Cleveland Stadium. For all its history, glory and great moments, Cleveland Stadium was not thought of as a baseball shrine in the same way as Fenway, Tiger, Yankee and Wrigley. And, with its huge seating capacity, the Stadium made it virtually impossible for the Indians to pre-sell tickets in any quantity. A cornerstone of the Indians' rebuilding plan would be the creation of an outdoor, baseball-only ballpark with a grass field and a limited seating capacity.

In the wake of the 1984 dome issue defeat, a new entity, the Greater Cleveland Domed Stadium Corporation, was created to pick up the pieces and find the formula for a new ballpark. With public and private financial support, Dome Corp began to assemble the necessary parcels of land necessary for a new ballpark in an area known as the Central Market site, so named because it had been home to a thriving produce market for years. The site, at the southwest corner of Cleveland's downtown area, had fallen into disrepair and was marked by scattered businesses, empty buildings and surface parking lots. The area would be dubbed "Gateway" for its position as an entrance to the downtown. It would become ground zero for a new golden age of baseball.

Richard Jacobs was not much interested in a domed stadium. He and Major League Baseball, preferred a baseball-only, open-air ballpark more in the tradition of Fenway Park and Wrigley Field. As Dome Corp continued to assemble the necessary property, a new player, the Gateway Economic Development Corporation of Greater Cleveland, took the field. Led by executive director Tom Chema, Gateway took a new approach by presenting plans for dual facilities at the site, one for the Indians and one for the

Cory Snyder is congratulated in the dugout after hitting his second home run in a win over Minnesota in 1987, the season in which he hit a career-high 33 homers. The Tribe's top choice in the 1984 amateur draft and a member of the 1984 U.S. Olympic team, the right fielder's offensive production declined steadily through 1990 and he was traded in the off season to the White Sox.

Brook Jacoby produced solid seasons at third base and at the plate after being assigned to the Indians in October 1983, completing the trade that sent Len Barker to Atlanta. Jacoby played nine years in Cleveland, the best being 1987 when he batted an even .300 with 32 home runs, earning him the Man of the Year award.

NBA's Cleveland Cavaliers. The plan called for the Cavaliers to move from the Richfield Coliseum back into downtown Cleveland in a new arena. The combination of the Indians and Cavaliers would provide for year-round activity at Gateway and create an economic development package that would attract the required political support.

The 1988 Indians helped the cause with an exciting season, even if it did end up in another sixth-place finish. A healthy Greg Swindell, a winning Tom Candiotti, a productive new starter in 25-year-old right hander John Farrell, and a newfound relief ace in 30-year-old right hander Doug Jones made the Indians again relatively competitive on the mound.

With Joe Carter, Cory Snyder, Julio Franco and outfielder Mel Hall leading the offense, the Tribe bolted out to a surprising 36-21 start and second place in the AL East. Just as Tribe fans might have dared to dream that the *Sports Illustrated* prediction was just a year too soon, the Indians slid back with 22 losses in 31 games before the All-Star Game break.

Cleveland remained as high as fourth place until the end of July, had the two largest crowds in the majors (71,188 on June 10 and 56,485 on June 17), and improved by 17 wins to a 78-84 record. Attendance improved to 1,411,160 (third best since 1952) and surpassed one million before the All-Star Game break for the first time since 1948. Fans again established that, old stadium or new, they would come out to see a competitive baseball club.

The hiring of Hank Peters began a flow of front office talent from Baltimore to Cleveland. Tom Giordano came over as an assistant to the president as did Dan O'Dowd as director of player development. John Hart followed in 1989 as a special assignment scout. Peters expanded the farm system (from four to seven teams) and the scouting department while directing efforts to find young talent in Latin America.

Peters would try to keep the Indians competitive, but he would also slowly gut the major league club, reduce the player payroll and pave the way for his farm system to provide young, affordable talent. After the 1988 season, Julio Franco was traded to Texas for first baseman Pete O'Brien, second baseman Jerry Browne and outfielder Oddibe McDowell, who was traded by mid season to Atlanta for outfielder Dion James. Jay Bell went to the Pirates for shortstop Felix Fermin. Outfielder Mel Hall brought catcher Joel Skinner and outfielder Turner Ward from the Yankees.

Franco had provided the offense expected when he was acquired from Philadelphia. He batted .295 from 1983 through 1988 and led the club in batting average in 1987 and 1988. An erratic defensive shortstop, Franco had finally moved to second base in 1988. He continued to thrive at second for Texas and won the AL batting title with a .341 average in 1991. After five seasons with the Rangers, one with the White Sox and one in Japan, Franco returned to the Indians in 1996.

Cleveland was again a .500 kind of club in 1989, but so was most of the rest of the AL East. With a spurt of 15 wins in 22 games in early July, the Tribe charged into second place and climbed to within 1.5 games of first on August 4 with a 54-54 record. When 24 losses in 35 games followed, Doc Edwards was axed and replaced on an interim basis by John Hart. The Indians won eight of 19 games for Hart to finish sixth again with a record of 73-89, 16 games behind the division winning Blue Jays. By Cleveland's standards since 1959, the 1988 and 1989 seasons were reasonably successful, but they were not nearly the successes Hank Peters planned to achieve.

Peters was slowly building a powerhouse and two key figures moved up the ladder in 1990. Hart was promoted to the director of baseball operations. Becoming skipper was veteran manager John McNamara. First base coach would be former Indian Mike Hargrove. Peters would groom Hart to become general manager and McNamara would groom Hargrove to become field manager. Hart and Hargrove would lead the Indians out of the baseball wilderness and make the club a genuine championship threat.

During McNamara's 239-game tenure, Peters completed the housecleaning that sent discontented veterans out of Cleveland in exchange for younger talent. In one of the most successful trades in Tribe history, its best player, Joe Carter, determined to get out of Cleveland, was traded to the San Diego Padres for 23-year-old catcher Sandy Alomar, Jr., 21-year-old infielder Carlos Baerga and 27-year-old outfielder Chris James.

With 151 home runs and 530 RBI for the Indians in less than six full seasons, Carter could have been one of Cleveland's all-time greats. But he was also representative of an era in which the Indians were thought of as losers more often than as winners. Carter would go on to greater glory, not with the Padres, but with the Blue Jays. Alomar and Baerga would help change the prevailing image of baseball in Cleveland and lead the Indians to the Promised Land.

To provide some added leadership, the Indians signed former National League Most Valuable Player Keith Hernandez to play first base. The signing was a bust as Hernandez played just 43 games in an injury-plagued conclusion to his career.

The 1990 season brought another change of significance to the broadcast coverage. Joining Herb Score on the radio broadcasts was a 35-year-old Wisconsin native, Tom Hamilton, who soon became a fixture in the booth. Only Score, Jack Graney, Jimmy Dudley and Bob Neal have spent more time calling Tribe games on the radio than Hamilton. Efforts to create stability in the 1990s were evident in the broadcast booth.

Hamilton and Score were familiar voices on radio stations WKNR and later WTAM. Jack Corrigan, who began calling Tribe games on TV station WUAB in 1985, then teamed with Mike Hegan throughout the 1990s and with Rick Manning and John Sanders on the cable telecasts, provided a steady presence for the Indians on television.

The next effort to provide for a new baseball home in Cleveland also came in 1990. Instead of a property tax, Cuyahoga County voters would be asked to approve an excise tax on the sale of alcohol and tobacco to help fund the new ballpark and arena. The "sin tax" was envisioned to pay half the cost of the new facilities. The other half of the needed funding was to come from revenues contributed by the Indians and Cavaliers to be generated by luxury seating in the new facilities.

On May 8, 1990, voters narrowly approved the sin tax measure by a 51.7 to 48.3 percent margin. The Cleveland baseball renaissance had moved another step closer. It moved still closer in 1991 when the Indians signed a 20-year lease to play at the new Gateway ballpark.

The Indians won 77 games under John McNamara in 1990 to finish fourth while Alomar became the fourth Tribe player to win AL Rookie-of-the-Year honors. The angular young catcher batted

Sandy Alomar Jr. began his long career in Cleveland by winning the 1990 AL Rookie of the Year award. The 24-year-old catcher also made the first of six All-Star Game appearances (below) before finishing the season with a .290 average.

.290 with nine home runs and 66 RBI and was a unanimous choice for the rookie honor. Doug Jones broke his own club record by saving 43 games. Tom Candiotti led the club with 15 victories. Newly-acquired outfielder Candy Maldonado paced the team with 22 homers and 95 RBI. Cory Snyder had his second straight disappointing season, batting just .233 with 14 homers and 55 RBI and was traded after the season.

In the process of rebuilding, the 1991 Indians suffered through the worst season in franchise history, losing 105. With the worst record in the majors, home attendance barely surpassed one million (1,051,863) and was the lowest since 1985. Only the Montreal Expos had a lower home attendance in 1991.

The silver lining was the development of several young players who would become the stars of the Jacobs Field-era Indians.

Albert Belle (left) became an offensive force in 1991 with 28 homers and 95 RBI. He followed with 34 and 112 in 1992, the first of eight straight seasons he would break the 30-homer and 100-RBI plateaus. Greg Swindell (right) was a 1984 U.S. Olympian and the Tribe's top choice in the 1986 amateur draft. He overcame elbow trouble to win in double figures from 1988-90, but after falling to 9-16 in '91, he was traded to Cincinnati.

The lineup included Alomar, Baerga, and a 24-year-old outfielder-designated hitter named Albert Belle. The Indians had gambled on Belle in the 1987 June draft, taking the temperamental star of Louisiana State University's baseball program in the second round. Known as Joey Belle when he debuted with the Tribe in 1989, the right-handed hitting slugger struggled in 62 games with a .225 batting average, seven homers and 37 RBI. He played just 42 games (nine with the Indians) in 1990, missing most of the season after checking into the Cleveland Clinic to undergo treatment for alcoholism.

Afterward, as Albert Belle, he led the Indians in home runs (28), RBI (95), doubles (31) and slugging percentage (.540) in 123 games. His playing time was curtailed by a one-week suspension handed down by AL president Dr. Bobby Brown and a four-week trip to the minors. With his temper and attitude sufficiently under control, Belle would become one of the most feared hitters in baseball.

Right hander Charles Nagy was the Indians' top winner in 1991. The Tribe's second first-round choice (17th player chosen overall) in the 1988 June draft, Nagy was a pitching ace at the University of Connecticut and a star of the 1988 United States Olympic team that won the gold medal at Seoul, South Korea. Nagy won 10 games in 1991, one more than Greg Swindell, who was traded after the season, and three more than Tom Candiotti who was traded away in June. Steve Olin, a 25-year-old relief pitcher, led the team with 17 saves and reliever Eric Bell had the distinction of winning four games without a loss for a team that lost over 100.

Jim Thome completed his quick rise through the farm system on September 4. The 20 year old was a steal by the Indians in the 13th round of the 1989 June draft. Although he hit just 24 home runs in his first 274 professional games, the left-handed-hitting infielder from Peoria, Illinois, would mature into a premier major league power hitter.

Thome's development signaled the end of Brook Jacoby's Indians career. Due to be a free agent after the 1991 season, he was traded to Oakland for two minor-leaguers on July 26. As a free agent, Jacoby returned in 1992 for a final season. He was one of the few constants wearing an Indians uniform from 1984 through 1992, playing in 1,240 games.

Mike Hargrove's ascent to manager was accelerated by the Tribe's poor start in 1991. McNamara's band was 25-52 when Hargrove was installed on July 6. The club did not do much better for Hargrove, finishing with 32 wins in 85 games.

As he had planned, Hank Peters completed his work with the Indians in 1991. In September, John Hart was promoted to vice president and general manager of baseball operations. At the same time, former Ohio State University athletic director (and, for five months in 1988, chief operating officer of the Yankees) Rick Bay was hired as executive vice president. Bay succeeded Peters as president and chief operating officer on January 1, 1992. Bay, and the position of president and COO, seemed to prove unnecessary to the revamped front office.

Bay left the Tribe on November 20, 1992, to pursue other interests. Hart was promoted to executive vice president-general manager and Dennis Lehman, hired in 1988 to run the business side, was promoted to executive vice president-business. Dick Jacobs, as chairman of the board and chief executive officer, seemed to take a more active role as CEO, especially after the death of his brother, David, in September.

Significant development was seen at the Gateway site and at Cleveland Stadium in 1992. In January, the Sheriff Cold Storage building was imploded, thus clearing the way for excavation to begin for the new Tribe ballpark.

At the Stadium, the Indians improved by 19 games and tied for fourth place in the AL East. Charles Nagy led with 17 victories and Steve Olin had a team-leading 29 saves. Albert Belle hit 34 homers and drove in 112 runs to pace the offense.

Carlos Baerga finished with a season that ranked with the best ever by a second baseman. With 205 hits, 20 homers, 105 RBI and a .312 batting average, Baerga became the first AL second baseman ever to reach or surpass 200 hits, 20 homers, 100 RBI and a .300 average in the same season. Only Hall of Famer Rogers Hornsby had achieved the same numbers in the National League. Baerga was honored with the Indians' Man of the Year award for the second straight season.

Rookie Kenny Lofton gave the Tribe a needed sparkplug in the lead-off spot and in center field. The 25-year-old left-handed hitter, who was acquired with infielder Dave

Doug Jones overcame a forgettable career as a minor league starter in the Milwaukee system, joining the Indians in 1986, then becoming their ace reliever at age 31 two seasons later. Jones saved 112 games from 1988-90, including a then-club-record of 43 in 1990.

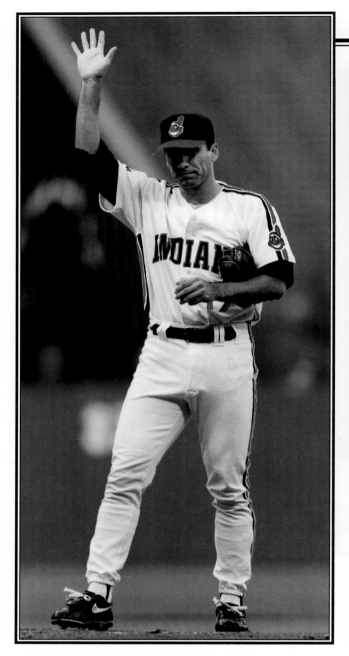

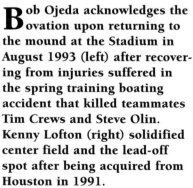

Bob Ojeda acknowledges the ovation upon returning to the mound at the Stadium in August 1993 (left) after recovering from injuries suffered in the spring training boating accident that killed teammates Tim Crews and Steve Olin. Kenny Lofton (right) solidified center field and the lead-off spot after being acquired from Houston in 1991.

Rohde from the Astros for pitcher Willie Blair and catcher Eddie Taubensee in December 1991, led the American League with 66 stolen bases—the first Tribe player to do so since George Case in 1946—and scored 96 runs.

If anything, the rebuilding effort started by Hank Peters and inherited by John Hart and Mike Hargrove was ahead of schedule. The progress was tangibly recognized when the periodical *Baseball America* bestowed its prestigious Organization of the Year award on the Indians franchise for the 1992 season.

With the opening of the new Gateway ballpark still a year away, the Indians took root in a new spring training site in 1993 after 46 straight seasons (1947-1992) of training in Tucson, Arizona. The new spring home was to have been in Homestead, Florida. Sadly, shortly before spring training, the city and the new training facility were the victim of Hurricane Andrew. The Indians then made arrangements to take over the vacant training site at Winter Haven, Florida.

Tragedy, however, struck again on March 22 when, on a rare spring training day off, pitchers Steve Olin, Tim Crews and Bob Ojeda, riding in a bass-fishing boat on Little Lake Nellie in Clermont, Florida, crashed into a dock extending into the lake. Olin died instantly and Crews died the following day. Ojeda survived the crash, but suffered severe injuries requiring a long recuperation. Ojeda pitched just nine games for the Indians and only two more games in his big league career after leaving Cleveland. Only the death of Ray Chapman ranks with the Little Lake Nellie tragedy. Olin had become one of the Indians' most popular players and was a rising relief star. Crews had been signed as a free agent after six quality seasons as a long reliever with the Dodgers. Ojeda, a free agent signee, was a 13-year veteran with post-season experience who had won 18 games for the world champion Mets of 1986. He was to have been the elder statesman of the starting staff. Tragedy would strike once again after the 1993 season. Pitching prospect Cliff Young, signed as a 28-year-old minor-league free agent in 1992, was killed in an automobile accident on November 4. Young had finished with a 3-3 record for the Indians in 1993.

For the final opening day at Cleveland Stadium, 73,290 fans paid tribute to Olin and Crews and reflected on the aging home of the Tribe. With stars like Belle, Baerga and Lofton, the nostalgia of the final season at the Stadium and the lure of getting seating priority at Jacobs Field in 1994 by buying seats at the Stadium in 1993, attendance was the best since the Bill Veeck days.

Jose Mesa, acquired in July 1992 from the Orioles for Kyle Washington, was Cleveland's number-one starter in 1993 and the only Tribe pitcher to start more than 16 games. Arm trouble restricted Charles Nagy to just seven starts. Pitchers Mike Bielecki, Mark Clark, Tommy Kramer and Jeff Mutis followed Mesa in the rotation.

After an understandably slow start, the Indians rose to the challenge with a 48-40 record between June 21 and September 26. Two losses in three games at Kansas City ruled out a .500 season and preceded the final three games at Cleveland Stadium.

October first, second, and third of 1993 became a celebration of Cleveland Indians history. Three consecutive crowds of more than 70,000 (72,454 on Friday, 72,060 on Saturday and 72,390 on Sunday) turned out at the "Gray Lady on the Lake." The final series gave the Indians a 1993 home attendance of 2,177,908, best for the club since 1949 and third best in franchise history. Somewhat fittingly, the Indians lost all three games to the Western Division champion Chicago White Sox. Since 1960, the Indians had done a good deal more losing than winning at the Stadium. The organization and many fans looked forward to building a new winning heritage at the new Gateway ballpark.

On Sunday, October 3, Charles Nagy got the losing decision as the White Sox shut out the Indians, 4-0. At the conclusion of the game, representatives of Indians teams from different eras took the field. Cleveland legend and former Tribe stockholder Bob Hope sang a special version of "Thanks for the Memories." Mel Harder threw the "final pitch." Home plate was dug out of the ground and flown by helicopter to the new ballpark.

In reality, even before Little Lake Nellie, the 1993 season seemed to be an afterthought for the Indians. The entire organization seemed to be focused on leaving Cleveland Stadium and beginning a brand new legacy in a new home in 1994.

Charles Nagy delivers the first pitch of the final game at Cleveland Municipal Stadium on October 3, 1993. The Tribe was defeated by the White Sox, 4-0, before a crowd of 72,390.

INNING 9

Indian Uprising at Jacobs Field

1994–2000

Rarely have plans worked out as well as those for the rebuilding of the Indians into a championship contender. Those plans called for the Indians to grow with young players and for a new ballpark to be the final catalyst to launch the club into contention. The Indians' "Blueprint for Success" was a thoughtful, practical approach to making the franchise competitive again. The blueprint focused on developing young players and, when warranted, offering them long-term contracts to keep them in Cleveland. When sufficient homegrown talent was in place, the blueprint called for augmenting those players by strategically reaching into the free agent market for players (especially those with championship experience) who would fundamentally help the Indians succeed.

Jacobs Field was the key to the blueprint, not only as a state-of-the-art ballpark that would increase attendance and revenue, but as a symbol that the Indians planned to rejoin baseball's elite teams. A talented management team, led by executive vice president and general manager John Hart in baseball operations, manager Mike Hargrove on the field, and executive vice president Dennis Lehman on the business side, was entrusted with bringing the blueprint to reality and making the Indians a baseball and a business success.

On December 2, 1993, the Tribe again mined the Baltimore connection and announced the signing of two free agents that would give the Indians the look of a champion. Cleveland added 39-year-old right-handed pitcher Dennis Martinez and 39-year-old first baseman-designated hitter Eddie Murray. Together, they brought 35 years of major league experience to the young Tribe. Both began playing professional baseball in the Baltimore system and both had been members of the Orioles teams that went to the World Series in 1979 and 1983, winning the latter over the Philadelphia Phillies.

A view from the stands in the left-field corner on opening day, April 4, 1994, at Jacobs Field. The Indians defeated the Seattle Mariners, 4-3, before a crowd of 41,459.

Martinez fell on hard times as he battled with alcoholism and arm trouble. After missing almost the entire 1986 season, his career was resurrected in Montreal where he won 100 games, including a perfect game in 1991. He came to the Indians as the seventh pitcher with 100 or more wins in both the AL and the NL.

Murray was one of the great run producers in modern baseball, closing in on the all-time leaders in RBI, hits and home runs. Traded to Los Angeles after the 1988 season, the switch-hitting slugger spent three seasons with the Dodgers and two with the Mets. He came to Cleveland with at least 75 RBI in each of his 17 major league seasons.

In the past, free agents like Martinez and Murray would have shown little or no interest in Cleveland, but new ownership, new management, a new ballpark, a young and aggressive team and competitive finances made the city attractive.

Two other new faces transformed the Indians of 1994. Hart traded Felix Fermin and Reggie Jefferson to Seattle for shortstop Omar Vizquel, a Gold Glove winner in 1993 who was emerging as a premier defensive shortstop. Manny Ramirez, who had risen quickly through the farm system after being chosen in the first round of the June 1991 draft, became the new right fielder. At 21, Ramirez was the best hitting prospect in the Tribe organization.

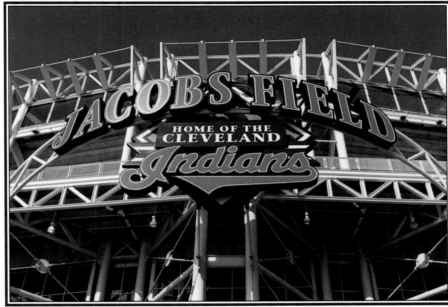

One more trick of the baseball gods stood in the way of the Tribe's return to glory—another dispute between the players and owners, the worst since the 1981 season. Like 1981, the 1994 campaign began with the possibility that it might not finish. It also began with a realignment of the American and National Leagues into three divisions. The Indians were placed in the AL Central with Kansas City, Minnesota, Milwaukee and Chicago.

The opener at Jacobs Field dawned on a cold, clear April 4, against the Seattle Mariners. The facility was an ideal example of the trend begun by Oriole Park at Camden Yards to build ballparks that would combine creature comforts with baseball-only touches. The asymmetrical playing field was a hitter-friendly 325 feet down the lines and 410 feet to center field. It was bounded by an eight-foot wall from right field to center field which then extended to 19 feet from center field to the left-field line. Home runs would now fly into places like the "home run porch" between the bleachers and the left-field foul pole or the "picnic plaza" beyond the center-field wall.

Like League Park, but unlike Cleveland Stadium, there was little foul territory and seating was more closely configured to the baseball diamond. Unlike League Park and Cleveland Stadium, there was not an obstructed-view seat. Some of the best seats were in the bleachers, flush against the left field wall. No home runs were ever hit into the distant bleachers at Cleveland Stadium, but the bleachers at Jacobs Field would become a target for Tribe players and opponents.

The opener was a nail-biter as Dennis Martinez dueled Seattle's big lefty, Randy Johnson. In storybook fashion, Wayne Kirby singled home Eddie Murray in the 11th inning to give the Indians a 4-3 win and send 41,459 fans home happy.

The season marked the start of a bright, new future, but with memories of past glory. New uniforms were reminiscent of those worn by the 1948 world champions.

Jacobs Field became the next in a series of old-style ballparks combining baseball-only touches with modern creature comforts. "The Jake" featured an asymmetrical playing field, a home run porch, a picnic plaza, old-fashioned bleachers and close-to-the-field seating.

Indian Uprising at Jacobs Field

Dennis Martinez came to Cleveland in 1994 as an 18-year major league veteran who was one of only seven pitchers to win 100 games in each league. He won 11 in the strike-shortened 1994 season, then went 12-5 in the pennant-winning 1995 campaign.

One of the stars of 1948, Larry Doby, was honored when his uniform number 14 was retired on July 3rd, 47 years to the day after he integrated the American League.

Jacobs Field provided a home field advantage like the club had never experienced. Cleveland led the American League in doubles (240), home runs (167) and runs scored (679). From May 13 to June 19, the Tribe rattled off a club-record 18-game home winning streak.

The Indians were tied for first place at the All-Star Game break. With the possibility that the 1994 regular season could end at any moment, and with no telling how a labor disruption might affect post-season play, every game after the All-Star Game was critical. Cleveland fell to second place with a loss at Chicago on July 14. The Indians and White Sox played eight times in July, each winning twice at home and twice on the road. The four games in Cleveland drew over 41,000 fans for each game as pennant-race excitement returned to the shores of Lake Erie. Unable to gain ground against Chicago, the Indians managed to play only .500 ball afterward.

On August 12, the players went on strike with the Tribe a game behind Chicago. On September 14, Major League Baseball announced the cancellation of the remainder of the season and the World Series. The bitter player-owner dispute made 1994 a season of "what might have been" for the Indians. With a 66-47 record, they were solidly in position to earn a wild-card birth—three games ahead of the next-best Royals—if not overtake the White Sox. The Indians' 35-16 (.686) record at Jacobs Field was the best at home since 1954. Attendance was on pace to top three million, but finished at 1,995,174 in 51 dates.

The Indians joined the White Sox as the only teams with four starters winning 10 or more games: Mark Clark (11), Dennis Martinez (11), Charles Nagy (10) and Jack Morris (10). Albert Belle drove in 101 runs in just 106 games while leading the team in home runs (36). Kenny Lofton won his third straight stolen base crown (60) and second straight Gold Glove award. Carlos Baerga had another spectacular season with a .314 average, 19 homers and 80 RBI. Eddie Murray extended his streak of consecutive seasons with at least 75 RBI with 76.

With a new baseball palace and a worthy club to play in it, the big question entering 1995 was whether Major League Baseball itself would survive or collapse under the animosity between the players and owners. Spring training was populated by unknown hopefuls known as replacement players or, less kindly, scabs. Some of them headed north as the club broke camp, went to Columbus for the Ohio Cup exhibition game on March 31 (a loss to the Reds) and an exhibition on April 1 (a win against the Mets) at Jacobs Field. By the time of the game in Cleveland, the striking players and owners had finally reached an agreement to end the 232-day strike. Another spring training would come before a new opening day on April 27 and a truncated regular season of 144 games.

The second training camp of 1995 welcomed one-time Cy Young Award-winning pitcher Orel Hershiser, signed on April 8 after spending his entire career (1983-1994) with the Dodgers. The 36-year-old right hander joined Dennis Martinez, Charles Nagy and Mark Clark to form the Tribe's starting rotation.

The bullpen, an Achilles heel in 1994, was solidified when Jose Mesa emerged as the closer. Once he became comfortable in his role, he was almost unbeatable, converting 46 of 48 save chances. The 46 saves set a club record and his 38 saves in 38 consecutive opportunities broke the major league record set by Dennis Eckersley in 1992.

With a full-time closer in Mesa, Mike Hargrove was able to further specialize with his relief pitchers. Young Julian Tavarez excelled as a set-up man for Mesa, winning 10 of 12 decisions. Left handers Paul Assenmacher, Alan Embree and Jim Poole and right hander Eric Plunk gave Hargrove maximum flexibility to match pitchers against left-handed or right-handed batters.

After a lackluster road trip of four wins in seven games to start the season, the Indians caught fire and ran away from the rest of the AL Central clubs. At the halfway point of the campaign, Cleveland had 50 wins and a 13.5 game lead in its division. While other teams were struggling to regain fan support after the strike, Tribe fans embraced a club that ranked with the best in team history. Starting on June 12, every game at Jacobs Field was sold out for the remainder of 1995. The home attendance record of 2,620,627 was eclipsed on September 15. The Indians' final home attendance in 1995 was a club-record 2,842,725.

Eddie Murray was one of modern baseball's greatest run producers, closing in on the all-time leaders in RBI, hits and home runs, when he signed with the Tribe as a free agent in December 1993. He hit his 450th homer in June 1994 and reached the 3,000-hit mark in July 1995 before returning to the Baltimore Orioles in 1996.

Indian Uprising at Jacobs Field

As fans watched the Indians climb toward a pennant, they also watched Eddie Murray move ever closer to the 3,000-hit milestone. Entering 1995 at 2,930, Murray stroked a single off Twins pitcher Mike Trombley for No. 3,000 on June 30 in the Metrodome. Murray joined Nap Lajoie and Tris Speaker as the third player to reach the plateau in a Cleveland uniform.

In place of a pennant race, the second half of the season became a countdown to a division-clinching celebration. The momentous game came on September 8 against Baltimore. Orel Hershiser pitched into the seventh inning and the Tribe scored all its runs in the second inning off Kevin Brown. With two out in the ninth, Jeff Huson hit a foul pop-up off Jose Mesa near third base. Jim Thome settled under the ball and, at 11:02 p.m., made the catch to end the game and start the festivities. The celebrating players walked to center field and jointly raised Cleveland's first baseball championship banner since 1954 in an emotional ceremony.

One regular-season team goal remained. With 86 wins on September 8, the Indians needed 14 in the final 21 games to reach the century mark. At the start of October, they hammered the Royals 17-7 for their fifth straight win and an even 100 in 144 games.

In Tribe history, only the 1954 Indians (.721) had posted a better winning percentage than the 1995 Indians' .694. They not only won often, but often in dramatic fashion. During the regular season, the Tribe won 27 games in its final at-bat, came from behind to win 48 times and was undefeated in 13 extra-inning games.

The big individual goal looming down the home stretch was 50 home runs for Albert Belle. He hit three homers against the White Sox on September 19, breaking Al Rosen's club record of 43 by one. He hit two homers against the Royals on September 23, then took a day off for the first time all season. On September 27, with two more homers against the Twins, Belle became only the eighth player in major league history with 100 extra-base hits in a season, the first since 1948. Finally, on September 30, Belle thrilled a capacity crowd at "the Jake" with a sixth-inning drive off Melvin Bunch of the Royals that cleared the fence for his 50th home run. Belle also became the first player in major league history to have 50 or more homers and 50 or more doubles in the same season.

Belle led the club with 126 RBI, followed by 107 from Manny Ramirez, 90 from Carlos Baerga and 82 from Eddie Murray. Ramirez (31), Thome (25), first baseman Paul Sorrento (25) and Murray (21) joined Belle with more than 20 home runs. As a team, the Indians' offense led the AL in runs scored (840), hits (1,461), home runs (207), steals (132), batting average (.291) and slugging percentage (.479).

The pitching staff led the AL in earned run average (3.83). Orel Hershiser and Charles Nagy tied for the team lead with 16 wins, followed by Dennis Martinez (12) and Julian Tavarez (10). Mark Clark, recovering from a broken wrist suffered in 1994, struggled to a 9-7 record. Bolstering the staff was right-hander Ken Hill, acquired in July from the Cardinals for three players, including Buddy Bell's son, David.

Cleveland's Central title earned the team a spot in the expanded playoffs against East-champion Boston in the first-ever Division Series. The opener, before a record 44,218 fans on a rainy night at Jacobs Field,

Jose Mesa emerged as one of baseball's dominant closers in the pennant-winning season of 1995. With 46 saves, he finished tied for the AL lead and also broke the club record of 43 set by Doug Jones in 1990.

matched Dennis Martinez against Boston ace Roger Clemens. The Indians took a 3-2 lead in the sixth, but Boston tied the score in the eighth and took a 4-3 lead in the 11th, setting the stage for two of the most dramatic home runs in Tribe history. Belle pulled Cleveland from the brink of defeat with a homer off Rick Aguilera in the 11th. In the 13th, with the game more than five hours old, Tony Pena, a frequent substitute for injured Sandy Alomar Jr. in 1995, worked a 3-0 count against Zane Smith. Pena then drove the next pitch into the left-field bleachers. The 38-year-old backstop jubilantly circled the bases. Cleveland had its first post-season win since 1948, 5-4.

Orel Hershiser was masterful the following day, allowing just three hits into the eighth inning. Omar Vizquel's two-run double in the fifth and Eddie Murray's two-run home run in the eighth provided all the offense. Three relievers, Julian Tavarez, Paul Assenmacher and Jose Mesa, wrapped up a 4-0 victory.

Charles Nagy was dominant in Game 3 at Fenway Park. Jim Thome hit a towering two-run homer off Tim Wakefield in the second inning and the Tribe drove the knuckleball pitcher from the mound in the sixth with five runs. Nagy pitched seven innings, Tavarez handled the eighth and Assenmacher finished an 8-2 win and a series sweep.

The Kingdome was the site of Cleveland's first AL Championship Series game. The Mariners had won a dramatic, five-game series against the Yankees, draining their pitching staff in the process. To open against the Indians, Seattle manager Lou Piniella started a rookie, Bob Wolcott. He survived a first-inning threat and pitched seven strong innings as the Mariners beat the Indians and Dennis Martinez, 3-2.

Manny Ramirez came alive in the second game with four hits and two homers. Orel Hershiser threw eight tough innings in a 5-2 victory. Back in Cleveland, Randy Johnson handcuffed the Tribe, but Charles Nagy matched him and the third game went into extra innings. Jay Buhner's three-run home run off Eric Plunk gave Seattle a 5-2 win and Cleveland its first extra-inning loss of 1995.

Pitching rallied the Indians again when Ken Hill, Jim Poole, Chad Ogea and Alan Embree combined on a six-hit shutout in the fourth game. Eddie Murray and Jim Thome hit home runs off loser Andy Benes to power a 7-0 Indians victory.

For the fifth game, Mike Hargrove brought back Hershiser on three days rest. "The Bulldog" responded with yet another six tough innings. Still, he trailed, 2-1, as the Indians batted in the sixth. Facing Chris Bosio, Thome turned the game around with a towering two-run homer. Julian Tavarez replaced Hershiser and was immediately plunged into trouble when Paul Sorrento made consecutive errors at first. After a fielder's choice put runners on first and third with one out, Hargrove called on lefty Paul Assenmacher to face Ken Griffey Jr. Assenmacher electrified Jacobs Field with back-to-back strikeouts of the left-handed Griffey and the right-handed Buhner. Plunk polished off the eighth thanks to a brilliant unassisted double play by Omar Vizquel. Jose Mesa slammed the door in the ninth, the final out coming when Kenny Lofton grabbed a long line drive by designated hitter Edgar Martinez.

Orel Hershiser returned to the mound on three days rest for Game 5 of the 1995 ALCS. He responded with six strong innings as the Indians beat Seattle, 3-2, at the Jake.

Jim Thome's two-run homer in the sixth inning overcame a one-run deficit and provided the margin of victory in the Tribe's 3-2 win over Seattle in Game 5 of the 1995 ALCS. The 440-foot blast into the right-field mezzanine was his second home run of the series.

The 3-2 victory gave the Tribe its first lead in the series. It also forced Johnson back to the mound on three days rest against a battered, but rested, Dennis Martinez in Seattle. Pitching in his sixth post-season game, Martinez went after his first post-season win by out-pitching Johnson and allowing just four hits over seven innings despite arm and leg ailments. Backed by a frenzied indoor crowd of 58,489 fans, Johnson began with four shutout innings. A throwing error by second baseman Joey Cora provided Cleveland a chance in the fifth, putting Alvaro Espinoza on second base. Lofton capitalized with a line drive single to left off the tiring Johnson. Espinoza scored and gave the Tribe's pitchers a lead they would not relinquish.

In the eighth, Tony Pena delivered another big hit, a leadoff double, and then Lofton took over. The fleet left-handed batter laid down a bunt single sending pinch runner Ruben Amaro, Jr., to third base. Lofton immediately stole second. The "Big Unit's" third pitch to Vizquel bounced off catcher Dan Wilson's glove, bringing Amaro home with Lofton fast behind. Lofton never stopped, blazing around third and sliding past the surprised Johnson with another run. The Indians were energized and the Mariners deflated. Carlos Baerga finished Johnson with a home run to center field.

Julian Tavarez pitched a scoreless eighth and Mesa came on for the ninth. He disposed of Griffey on a ground out and struck out Edgar Martinez. First baseman Tino Martinez walked, but Buhner hit a routine grounder to third. Espinoza's throw to first baseman Herb Perry completed the 4-0 victory and gave the Indians their first American League pennant in 41 years.

As Tribe fans celebrated in Cleveland, the Indians headed for Atlanta. The 1995 World Series would be a rematch, of sorts, of the 1948 World Series between the Indians and the Braves who had since been uprooted from Boston and Milwaukee. Atlanta was back in the World Series for the third time in the 1990s, having lost to Minnesota in 1991 and Toronto in 1992. With pitchers Greg Maddux, Tom Glavine, John Smoltz, Kent Mercker and Steve Avery, Atlanta had a starting rotation reminiscent of Cleveland's great staff of the 1950s.

For the opening game, Orel Hershiser, unbeaten with seven wins in his post-season career, faced Maddux who was making his first World Series appearance. Maddux was dominant, allowing just two hits. Atlanta outfielders made just two putouts all night. Kenny Lofton manufactured a run in the first by reaching base on an error, stealing second, stealing third and scoring on Carlos Baerga's ground out. Atlanta's slugging first baseman Fred McGriff tied the game with a second-inning home run.

The score was still tied when Hershiser ran out of gas in the seventh inning, walking McGriff and right fielder David Justice. Paul Assenmacher walked pinch hitter Mike Devereaux and left a bases-loaded situation to Julian Tavarez. Atlanta took the lead on a fielder's choice and scored again on a successful suicide-squeeze bunt by shortstop Rafael Belliard. In the ninth, Lofton circled the bases again on a single, ground out and throwing error, but Baerga popped out to end a 3-2 Braves victory.

Cleveland took the early lead again in the second game when Eddie Murray belted a two-run homer to left field off Glavine. Atlanta tied the game in the third against Dennis Martinez on a sacrifice fly by third baseman Chipper Jones and a run-scoring single by Justice. The Braves' young catcher, Javy Lopez, untied the game with a two-run homer off Martinez in the sixth. Cleveland scored an unearned run in the seventh, but got no further as Atlanta's bullpen preserved a 4-3 win.

Jacobs Field, and all of Cleveland, was aglow for the return of the World Series. Charles Nagy, in a must-win situation, faced Smoltz. Atlanta scored first, but Tribe bats awoke with four unanswered runs to finish the evening for Smoltz. Relief pitcher Brad Clontz stemmed the tide and Atlanta rallied on solo home runs off Nagy by McGriff and designated hitter Ryan Klesko.

Baerga singled home Lofton in the seventh, but Atlanta rallied again in the eighth. Nagy surrendered a double to Marquis Grissom and a run-scoring single to Luis Polonia. Nagy departed with the Tribe clinging to a 5-4 lead. Polonia scored as Baerga fumbled Justice's grounder. Devereaux then delivered a go-ahead single off Tavarez.

Cleveland needed yet another rally and got one in the eighth inning when Sandy Alomar Jr. laced a double past first base off Atlanta's relief ace Mark Wohlers to score Manny Ramirez with the tying run. Jose Mesa preserved the tie through the ninth inning when first baseman Herbert Perry made an outstanding short-hop catch of Jones's grounder to end the frame.

Baerga began the Indians' half of the eleventh with a double to right-center off Alejandro Pena. Albert Belle was walked intentionally to bring Murray to the plate. His only hit of the World Series had been his home run in the second game, but this time he delivered with a line-drive single to center. Alvaro Espinoza slid home with the winning run for a 7-6 victory.

Omar Vizquel makes a diving grab of a ground ball in Game 1 of the 1995 World Series. Greg Maddux threw a two-hitter as the Braves beat the Tribe, 3-2, at Atlanta Fulton County Stadium. Vizquel was one of only four Indians to hit the ball into the outfield as Maddux retired 19 of 27 batters on ground balls.

Lefty Steve Avery silenced the Cleveland offense—and Jacobs Field—in the pivotal fourth game. A disappointing 7-13 in the regular season, Avery allowed just three hits in six innings. Klesko homered off Indians starter Ken Hill in the sixth, but Belle answered with a line drive into the Atlanta bullpen to tie the score. The Braves finished off Hill in the seventh when Grissom walked and Polonia doubled him home. Justice capped a three-run rally with a devastating two-run single off Assenmacher. Atlanta scored again in the ninth and a solo homer by Ramirez was too little, too late. A 5-2 loss put the Indians a game away from elimination.

The Indians earned a trip back to Atlanta with a 5-4 victory in the fifth game. Hershiser redeemed himself by pitching eight innings and allowing just two runs. Cleveland solved the seemingly-invincible Maddux for seven hits and four runs. Belle started the Tribe's scoring with another first-inning two-run home run into the right field bullpen and Thome ended it with a majestic solo homer to center field off Clontz in the eighth. Mesa gave Indians fans a thrill in the ninth by allowing a long two-run homer to Klesko. "Senor Slam" then ended the 1995 season at Jacobs Field by painting the outside corner with a third strike to Mark Lemke. The magic of Jacobs Field had worked one last time. Another sellout crowd (43,595) celebrated the most magical season in Cleveland since 1948 and hoped for a miracle in Atlanta.

Game 6 of the 1995 World Series was a Fall Classic pitching masterpiece. Tribe bats were silenced again by Glavine. But Dennis Martinez was determined to keep Cleveland in the game, just as he had in the sixth game at Seattle. As the din of the "Tomahawk Chop" reverberated inside Atlanta-Fulton County Stadium, Glavine allowed just one hit in eight innings. Tony Pena had Cleveland's only safety, a bloop single to center in the sixth. Justice, who had publicly challenged Atlanta fans to match the electricity of Jacobs Field, was on the spot in the sixth against reliever Jim Poole. Justice prevailed with a home run for the only run of the game. In the ninth, Wohlers made quick work of Lofton and pinch hitter Paul Sorrento. When Baerga hit a fly ball to Grissom in center, Atlanta had a 1-0 win and its first world championship since coming to Georgia in 1966.

Cleveland had come up two wins short of the ultimate prize in 1995, but had given memories to Tribe fans that many had wondered if they would ever receive again. Despite the World Series loss, the 1995 Indians had earned recognition as one of baseball's best teams ever, having led the AL in team batting average and team earned run average while leading the league in wins.

For Cleveland fans, the disappointment over the World Series defeat turned to shock days later when owner Art Modell announced he was moving the National Football League's Cleveland Browns to Baltimore. For all the times it seemed like the Indians might leave town, few fans ever considered that the Browns, a Cleveland fixture since 1946, would move. Intense civic pressure would help earn Cleveland a new Browns expansion team to begin play in 1999.

From 1996 to 1998, the Indians would have a corner on the Cleveland sports market for the first time since World War II. Cleveland fans responded to their championship baseball club by selling out every Indians home game in 1996 in advance of opening day, a feat never before achieved by any major league club. It ensured a new attendance record (3,318,174) and the Tribe's first season with more than three million in home attendance. Only the Orioles and the expansion Colorado Rockies had higher attendance in 1996.

Eddie Murray is greeted by Albert Belle following Murray's two-run second-inning home run that put the Tribe in front in Game 2 of the 1995 World Series. The Braves won, 4-3, to take a 2-0 advantage.

LEGENDS OF THE TRIBE

Anything short of a repeat trip to the World Series would be a step backwards. The magic of 1995 was a once-in-a-lifetime experience and impossible to repeat. But with a 99-62 record, Cleveland led the major leagues in wins for a second consecutive year, a feat unprecedented in Tribe history. Unlike the cakewalk of 1995, the Indians were challenged by the White Sox into August before pulling away to win the AL Central by 14.5 games. Fittingly, Cleveland clinched its second straight playoff berth with a 9-4 win at Chicago on September 17.

With the best offense in baseball, the Indians' one weak link seemed to be the lack of a dominant number one starting pitcher. Tribe management attempted to fill that hole by signing 30-year-old right hander Jack McDowell, a Cy Young Award winner in 1993 when he won 20 games for the second straight season. McDowell proved to be a disappointment, winning 13 games and pitching just 192 innings after averaging nearly 230 the previous six seasons. Steady Charles Nagy led the team with 17 wins, Orel Hershiser had 15 victories and Chad Ogea added 10. Jose Mesa was no longer invincible, but saved 39 games in 69 appearances. Middle-relief pitchers Paul Assenmacher

Charles Nagy won a career-high 17 games for the second of three times in 1996. The Tribe's most consistent starter that season, he surpassed the 200-inning mark for the first time since 1992 and finished fourth in the balloting for the Cy Young Award.

and Eric Plunk were dependable again. Third-year reliever Paul Shuey was used more frequently, but did not show the consistency to earn the job of closer. For the second straight season, the Indians led the AL in team earned run average.

The Indians' mighty offense dominated the AL again in 1996 despite a noticeable downturn in the performance of veteran Carlos Baerga. Whether due to an ankle injury suffered in the World Series, being out of shape or enjoying too much of the Cleveland nightlife, Baerga's batting average and power production had dropped noticeably since mid season of 1995. His diminished offense accentuated limited range and defensive ability at second base. John Hart acted decisively and stunned the fans on July 29 by trading Baerga and Alvaro Espinoza to the New York Mets for infielders Jeff Kent and Jose Vizcaino. Kent could provide more power at second base and Vizcaino could also play second while providing insurance for Vizquel who battled with a sore right shoulder throughout the season.

Cleveland again led the leasgue with a .293 team batting average and set a franchise record with 952 runs scored and 218 home runs. The Indians tied an AL record by having three players (Albert Belle, Manny Ramirez and Jim Thome) with more than 30 homers and more than 100 RBI each. Belle led the way again with 48 homers and 148 RBI. He became Cleveland's all-time home run leader, ending the campaign with 242 career home runs. Kenny Lofton was also spectacular. His 210 hits were the most by a Indians player since 1936. With 75 stolen bases, he led the AL for the fifth straight season to become Cleveland's all-time theft leader.

The regular-season success of 1995 and 1996 had raised expectations dramatically for fans, media and management, and the Jacobs Field honeymoon was ending with the realities of trying to hold a championship club together in the era of free agency. Belle's contract expired in 1996 and Lofton's in 1997.

Dennis Martinez and Eddie Murray were both unhappy. Martinez spent much of the 1996 season on the disabled list and Murray was traded to Baltimore in July. Wayne Kirby and Jim Poole also left. Familiar faces Julio Franco and Greg Swindell returned. Franco succeeded Paul Sorrento, who departed to Seattle as a free agent, at first base and had a stellar season with a team-leading .322 batting average and 76 RBI. To add spark for the stretch, Hart traded promising outfielder Jeromy Burnitz for veteran infielder Kevin Seitzer. The move seemed to work as Cleveland won 19 of its final 26 games after sluggish play in June, July and August.

Unlike 1995, the Tribe's 99 wins earned them the right to face the wild-card participant in the playoffs, but unlike 1995, Cleveland would start the playoff on the road at Oriole Park at Camden Yards, home of the Baltimore Orioles. Turmoil surrounded the team and its starting second baseman, Robbie Alomar, younger brother of the Indians' catcher. During the final weekend of the regular season, Alomar had spit in the face of umpire John Hirschbeck during an argument, igniting a fierce debate over whether he should be

Albert Belle's 50-homer season of 1995 was followed by 48 in 1996, making him the Indians' all-time home run leader. His 148 RBI led the AL for the third time in his career.

LEGENDS OF THE TRIBE

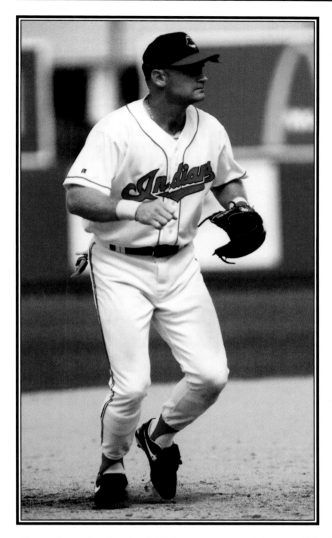

allowed to play in the 1996 post season. Alomar did play and the Orioles shocked the Indians by sweeping both games in Baltimore. Cleveland took the third game, thanks to a dramatic grand slam home run by Albert Belle off Baltimore's intimidating flame thrower, Armando Benitez. The fourth game was a pitcher's duel in Cleveland's favor until Roberto Alomar's clutch hit off Jose Mesa in the ninth inning forged a tie. Alomar put an end to the 1996 Indians with a home run off Mesa in the 12th inning, giving Baltimore a 4-3 win and a 3-1 victory in the series.

The 1996 season was Exhibit A in proof that there are no guarantees in post-season baseball, especially the expanded format introduced in 1995. The season also proved to many that regular-season success was no substitute for a quick exit from the playoffs. In the regular season, the Indians merely needed enough success to win the weak AL Central. In 1997, they would have to do so without Albert Belle or Kenny Lofton. The Tribe's all-time-leading home run hitter defected to the White Sox as a free agent, making him Public Enemy Number One in Cleveland. Before Lofton could take the same exit, Hart dealt the speed burner and Alan Embree to the Braves for Marquis Grissom and David Justice, the villain of the sixth game of the 1995 World Series.

The other major new addition to the 1997 Indians was all-star third baseman Matt Williams, acquired from San Francisco in November 1996 in a trade that sent Jeff Kent, Jose Vizcaino and Julian Tavarez to the Giants.

The Tribe's 1997 lineup was revamped with heavy doses of National League power. Ex-Giant Matt Williams (left), who led the NL with 43 homers in the strike-shortened 1994 season, became the third baseman as Jim Thome moved to first. Outfielder David Justice (right) had averaged nearly 26 homers from 1990-95, but had missed most of '96 with injury when he was acquired in the deal that sent Kenny Lofton to Atlanta.

A stellar defensive third baseman over a 10-year major league career, Williams had challenged the single-season home run record in 1994 before the campaign was cut short by the strike. He finished with a career-high and NL-leading 43.

With the addition of Williams, Jim Thome moved to first base. Julio Franco began the season at second base, but veteran Tony Fernandez emerged as Vizquel's keystone partner, giving Cleveland one of the strongest infields in club history.

A seismic change came to Major League Baseball in 1997 with inter-league play. For the first time, American and National League teams would compete against each other, on a limited basis, in the regular season. The Indians' first inter-league games were scheduled against the NL Central Division—the St. Louis Cardinals, Cincinnati Reds, Houston Astros, Chicago Cubs and Pittsburgh Pirates.

The season would also bring the All-Star Game back to Cleveland for the first time since 1981 and the first time ever at Jacobs Field. David Justice was elected to the starting outfield, but was unable to play due to injury. Jim Thome replaced Justice and joined Sandy Alomar as the Tribe's representatives. Alomar, having a dream season, hit a two-run homer off Shawn Estes in the seventh inning to give the AL a 3-1 victory. He was selected the game's MVP, the first Cleveland player ever to receive the honor and the first player ever to win the award in his home park.

Enjoying a rare injury-free season, the veteran catcher had a career year with 21 homers, 83 RBI and a .324 batting average. Thome led the club with 40 homers while Justice led with a .329

> Sandy Alomar Jr. belts a two-run home run in the eighth inning of the 1997 All-Star Game at Jacobs Field. It gave the AL a 3-1 victory and Alomar the game's MVP award. Alomar's '97 season was his best with career highs in doubles (37), homers (21), RBI (83) and batting average (.324).

batting average. Williams did the same with his 105 RBI. Charles Nagy was the team leader in wins for the fifth time and in strikeouts for the fourth straight season. Jose Mesa struggled to 16 saves, but reliever Mike Jackson, signed as a free agent prior to the season, showed closing ability as well with 15 saves.

August 27, 1997, was Thome's 27th birthday. In his honor, his teammates who typically wore their pants legs down to their ankles exposed their socks to the calf, a more old-fashioned style employed by Thome. With "socks up," the Indians battered the Angels, 10-4, the first of 15 wins in 22 games to assure a third consecutive AL Central championship.

Rookie pitcher Jaret Wright, who made his big league debut on June 24, helped down the stretch with eight wins. Julio Franco's second stint with the Tribe ended when he was released on August 13. With a .301 lifetime batting average, Franco became one of Cleveland's all-time hit leaders—1,272—after returning to the Indians. Hart made another late-season move, trading for infielder-outfielder Bip Roberts from the Royals.

For all its talent, the Indians hovered around the .500 mark throughout the 1997 season. On September 2, they were just 2.5 games ahead of the second-place White Sox. Chicago opted for a late-season housecleaning of questionable timing to many fans and observers. The Indians won five of seven games against Chicago in early September to fend off the second-place club. Cleveland clinched its third straight AL Central title by defeating the Yankees on September 23 and finished the regular season with an 86-75 record.

The 1997 ALDS between Cleveland and New York (the AL wild-card team with a 96-66 record) provided for the most meaningful games between the teams since the 1950s. Four games in the five-game series were decided by two runs or less.

The Tribe took the upper hand in the first playoff game between the two rivals with five first-inning runs off David Cone at Yankee Stadium, three on Sandy Alomar's home run. Cleveland's pitching failed in the sixth inning when Yankees' designated hitter Tim

Raines, shortstop Derek Jeter and right fielder Paul O'Neill hit back-to-back-to-back homers off Eric Plunk (Raines and Jeter) and Paul Assenmacher (O'Neill). The explosion by the Bronx Bombers powered an 8-6 New York victory.

Hargrove sent out Jaret Wright to start the second game. He allowed three runs in the first inning, but followed with five shutout innings. The offense exploded for five two-out runs off Andy Pettitte in the fourth inning. Matt Williams's two-run homer gave the Indians a 7-3 lead in the fifth. Jose Mesa preserved a 7-5 win to tie the series.

The largest single-game crowd ever at Jacobs Field (45,274) was disappointed when the series moved to Cleveland. Hefty New York lefty David Wells scattered five hits and Paul O'Neill hit a grand slam off Chad Ogea to power a 6-1 Yankees win.

Tribe hopes to continue the season rested on the right arm of Orel Hershiser who started the fourth game against Dwight Gooden. The "Bulldog" barely survived the first inning. New York scored twice and only a perfect throw from left fielder Brian Giles to Sandy Alomar cut down another run.

After the first, Hershiser held the Yankees scoreless. But, Cleveland could manage just one run, on a David Justice homer, off Gooden. The Tribe had not scored off New York relief pitchers in the series and when manager Joe Torre brought on closer Mariano Rivera in the eighth, hopes looked bleak. Four outs from defeat, Alomar belted a line drive over the right-field wall. The game was tied. The blow revived the Tribe and the Jacobs Field faithful. Mike Jackson preserved the tie in the top of the ninth.

Torre's other relief star, Ramiro Mendoza, surrendered a bloop single to Marquis Grissom to start the Cleveland ninth. Bip Roberts sacrificed Grissom to second. The magic of Jacobs Field took hold again when Omar Vizquel's hard ground ball back to the box ricocheted off Mendoza and past Jeter into left field. Grissom brought home the winning run and was mobbed by his jubilant teammates. Cleveland's 3-2 victory forced a winner-take-all fifth game.

None of the seven previous post-season series involving the Indians had gone the distance. Not since the playoff game of 1948 in Boston had the Tribe faced a contest like the fifth game of the 1997 ALDS. And just as Boudreau had gambled on rookie Bearden in 1948, Hargrove went with rookie Wright in this crucial game.

Wright again opposed Pettitte and again Cleveland solved the New York lefty in the third inning. Manny Ramirez doubled to score Grissom and Vizquel with the game's first runs. The din in Jacobs Field increased when Matt Williams singled home Ramirez. A sacrifice fly by Tony Fernandez scored Alomar with another run in the fourth.

Leading 4-0, Wright began to fade after four innings. New York scored two runs in the fifth and one in the sixth before mounting another threat in the seventh. An infield single by Jeter off Jackson brought Assenmacher from the bullpen to face O'Neill. When O'Neill hit a hard grounder toward right field, Thome made the most important defensive play of his career. The first baseman dove to his right, snared the grounder, and, on his stomach, threw to Vizquel to force Jeter at second base. Bernie Williams bounced into a 6-4-3 double play and the inning was over.

Hargrove called on Mesa to close out the game. The decibel level in Jacobs Field continued to rise in the ninth as Mesa retired Raines and Jeter.

O'Neill momentarily quieted the crowd of 45,203 with a double to right, but Bernie Williams hit the first pitch from Mesa in the air to left field. Brian

Sandy Alomar Jr. adds still another highlight to his spectacular 1997 season with a three-run homer off New York's David Cone in Game 1 of the ALDS at Yankee Stadium.

LEGENDS OF THE TRIBE

Giles made the catch and jubilation reigned at Jacobs Field. Only once before (the 1920 World Series) had the Indians won a post-season series with a victory in Cleveland. The first ever playoff series between the Yankees and Indians ended with the Tribe victorious and headed back to the ALCS against the Orioles.

In the 1997 ALCS, Cleveland lost its fifth straight playoff opener, dropping a 3-0 decision to Scott Erickson at Camden Yards. The next night, the Tribe trailed the Orioles 4-2 in the eighth inning and faced the fearsome Armando Benitez. Walks to Sandy Alomar and Jim Thome set the stage for Marquis Grissom with two out. Fighting the effects of stomach flu, Grissom hit a Benitez slider over the fence in left-center field. The three-run homer gave Cleveland a 5-4 win and tied the series.

Jacobs Field magic reached its peak when the 1997 ALCS moved to Cleveland. Orel Hershiser and Mike Mussina were brilliant, trading goose eggs into the seventh inning. Mussina had 15 strikeouts and the Tribe turned four double plays behind Hershiser as the Indians and Orioles forged a 1-1 tie.

The game remained tied in the 12th inning when Grissom walked and Tony Fernandez singled him to third against Baltimore closer Randy Myers. As Tribe super fan John Adams pounded his drum in the left-field bleachers, Omar Vizquel came to bat. The squeeze play was in order. On the 2-1 pitch, Vizquel squared to bunt and missed the pitch, but so did Baltimore catcher Lenny Webster as Grissom tiptoed home with the winning run. The catcher and manager Davey Johnson argued to no avail. Nine minutes short of five hours, the longest ALCS game ever ended in a 2-1 Tribe victory.

Baltimore came back with a vengeance against Jaret Wright and took a 5-2 lead in the third inning of the fourth game. With a run in the fourth and a Manny Ramirez homer in the fifth, the Indians pulled close. Singles by Thome, David Justice and Alomar tied the score at 5-5. With the bases loaded, Webster's nightmarish series got worse with another bizarre play at home plate. Reliever Arthur Rhodes bounced a pitch to Grissom. Justice scored as Webster's throw got away from the reliever and Alomar scored too, from second base, as Orioles scrambled around home plate.

The ball gets past Baltimore catcher Lenny Webster on Omar Vizquel's squeeze-play bunt attempt in the 12th inning of Game 3 of the 1997 ALCS. It allowed Marquis Grissom to score the winning run in a 2-1 Tribe victory at Jacobs Field.

Matt Williams and Jim Thome embrace in the infield after Jose Mesa struck out Baltimore's Roberto Alomar for the final out of a 1-0 victory in Game 6 of the 1997 ALCS at Camden Yards. It gave the Indians their second AL pennant in three seasons.

Geneva, Ohio, native Brian Anderson retired 10 of the 12 batters he faced in relief of Wright. The lefty Anderson gave way to right-hander Jeff Juden who turned over a 7-6 lead to Jose Mesa. In the ninth, a lead-off walk to Roberto Alomar spelled trouble and resulted in the tying run when first baseman Rafael Palmeiro singled off Mesa's foot.

Baltimore's rally provided still another heroic opportunity for Sandy Alomar, Jr. Walks to Ramirez and Matt Williams brought Alomar up against Benitez. Alomar came through again, lacing a game-winning hit to beat the Birds, 8-7. The Indians were a win away from another World Series.

Chad Ogea was given the chance to end the series in Cleveland, but the Indians were again unable to provide him any runs. A ninth-inning rally fell short and a 4-2 loss sent the Indians back to Baltimore.

Game 6 of the 1997 ALCS produced gut-wrenching tension. As Mussina mowed down the Tribe once again, Charles Nagy escaped one jam after another to keep the game scoreless. Cleveland managed just two hits through the first 10 innings against Mussina and Myers. Benitez relieved Myers to start the 11th and, with two out, Fernandez forever etched his name into Tribe history with a homer off Benitez over the high right-field wall at Camden Yards to make it 1-0.

Mesa relieved Brian Anderson and opened the bottom of the 11th with a strikeout of Chris Hoiles. Webster grounded out, but Brady Anderson singled to right. A trip to the World Series rested on another match-up between Mesa and Roberto Alomar. Sandy's younger brother worked the count full. Mesa fired a fastball over the inside corner for a strikeout and a 1-0 win. The Indians were American League champions for the second time in three years.

Cleveland's unlikely opponent in the 93rd World Series was the Florida Marlins. The five-year-old expansion club was the NL wild-card team with 92 wins, sweeping the Giants and upsetting the Braves to win the NL pennant. In contrast to Richard Jacobs and the Indians, Marlins owner H. Wayne Huizenga spared no expense to stock his big league club. Huizenga and general manager Dave Dombrowski lured manager Jim Leyland from the Pirates and brought in stars like third baseman Bobby Bonilla, outfielders Gary Sheffield, Devon White and Moises Alou and pitchers Alex Fernandez, Kevin Brown and Al Leiter. Homegrown stars included catcher Charles Johnson and 22-year-old pitcher Livan Hernandez, a Cuban refugee. Florida reached the World Series faster than any expansion team in major league history.

Hernandez faced Orel Hershiser in the Series opener. In the fourth inning, Alou blasted a three-run homer off the left field foul pole to give the Marlins a 4-1 lead. Johnson followed with an awesome blast into the upper deck of Pro Player Stadium. Hershiser suffered just his second post-season loss in 10 decisions, a 7-4 defeat that continued the Indians' streak of series-opening losses.

Chad Ogea pitched Cleveland to a 6-1 win in the second game. The Indians broke a 1-1 tie with three runs in the fifth inning on run-scoring hits by Marquis Grissom and Bip Roberts. Sandy Alomar completed a rout of Brown with a two-run homer in the sixth. Ogea, Mike Jackson, and Jose Mesa scattered eight hits to give Cleveland its first World Series win on the road since 1948.

From the warm weather climate of Florida, the series moved to inclement Cleveland where a 23-degree wind-chill factor existed for the night game on October 21. For five innings, the Jacobs Field magic prevailed as the Indians battered Leiter. Jim Thome's two-run homer gave Charles Nagy a 7-3 lead. But, the "Fish" came back with a two-run home run by designated hitter Jim Eisenreich. Run-scoring hits by shortstop Edgar Renteria and right fielder Sheffield off Jackson tied the game in the seventh.

In the ninth, the Indians came unglued. Three Tribe errors helped Florida score seven runs. Florida closer Robb Nen struggled through the bottom of the ninth as the Tribe scored four runs before he could close a 14-11 victory. The game featured six errors, 11 pitchers, 26 hits and 17 walks. Pompous pundits criticized the Indians, the Marlins, the weather and the play as embarrassments to baseball.

Jacobs Field looked like a winter wonderland before the fourth game that matched rookie pitchers Jaret Wright and Tony Saunders. Manny Ramirez teed off with a two-run homer in the first and Matt Williams capped the scoring with a two-run homer off Jay Powell in the eighth. Every batter in the Cleveland lineup had a hit except Marquis Grissom whose World Series hitting streak ended at 15 games. Wright pitched well and Brian Anderson finished with three shutout innings to complete a 10-3 Tribe victory in the coldest game (38 degrees, 18 degrees wind chill) in World Series history.

In the 1997 finale at Jacobs Field, Sandy Alomar singled home a run in the second and blasted a three-run homer in the third to give the Indians a 4-2 lead. His four RBI gave him 10 in the series and 19 in the post season. After a rocky start, Hershiser retired 10 straight batters and seemed in control in the sixth. Then, Sheffield singled, Bonilla walked and Alou hit a three-run homer that gave Florida a 5-4 lead.

Florida scored again in the sixth. Single runs in the eighth and ninth innings extended the Marlins' margin to 8-4 in front of 44,888 cold, quiet fans at the Jake. Florida starter Hernandez had allowed just three singles after Alomar's home run, but two Florida mis-plays in the ninth aided a three-run Cleveland rally. With the score 8-7, Alomar came to bat as the potential winning run, but Sheffield caught his routine fly ball to end the game. The Marlins took a 3-2 Series lead back to Florida.

Ugly baseball in the Cleveland cold gave way to a gem of a sixth game in Miami. Ogea delivered on the mound and at bat. With the bases loaded in the second inning against Brown, he lined a single to right field to score two runs. Ramirez drove Omar Vizquel home with a third run in the third. In the fifth, Ogea led off with a double to right, becoming the first pitcher since the Tigers' Mickey Lolich in 1968 with two hits in a World Series game. Ramirez drove Ogea home and the Tribe led 4-0.

Weary from running the bases, the Indians' new hero was lifted in the sixth inning with a 4-1 lead in favor of Jackson. With two outs and runners on second and third, Johnson batted for Florida. The catcher hit a hard ground ball headed for left field until Vizquel dove to his right and gloved the ball. Popping up to his feet, he threw across to Thome to retire Johnson and end the inning with one of his greatest plays.

Jackson, Paul Assenmacher and Mesa then combined for four scoreless innings to complete a flawless 4-1 victory. For the first time ever, the Indians would play in the seventh game of a best-of-seven series.

Bip Roberts puts a tag on Moises Alou in Game 5 of the 1997 World Series at Jacobs Field. Alou was one of several free agent signees that helped strengthen the five-year-old Marlins to playoff status.

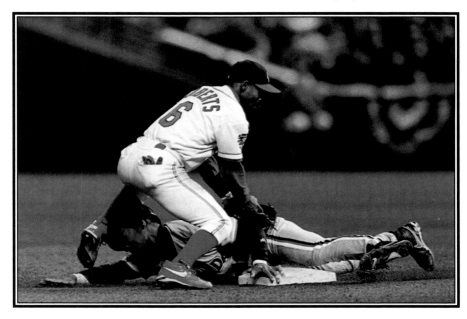

Jaret Wright joined Stan Coveleski (1920) Bob Feller (1948) and Bob Lemon (1948) as the fourth pitcher chosen to start a game that could bring the Tribe a world championship. Mike Hargrove bypassed Nagy who had struggled in the third game.

Tony Fernandez came up big again with a two-run single off Leiter in the third inning of the seventh game. In his best start yet, Wright carried a one-hit shutout to the seventh inning. His only costly mistake of the night was his first pitch of the seventh, a high change up that Bonilla belted into the stands for Florida's first run. Wright struck out Johnson, but when he walked Craig Counsell, Hargrove called on Assenmacher, who retired pinch-hitter Kurt Abbott and White to maintain a 2-1 lead. Jackson and Anderson retired the Marlins in order in the eighth. The Tribe needed three more outs.

Mesa took the hill for the ninth and immediately surrendered a lead-off single to Alou. He struck out Bonilla, but Johnson lined a two-strike single to right and Alou raced to third. Suddenly, all the momentum was with the Marlins. Counsell's hard fly to right sent Ramirez to catch a sacrifice fly that scored Alou and tied the game, 2-2. One out away from the world championship, the Indians were now in a sudden-death situation. Mesa got the final out of the ninth, but gave way to Nagy in the 10th.

The beginning of the end for the Tribe came in the Florida 11th when Bonilla led off with a two-strike single through the middle. Trying to sacrifice, catcher Gregg Zaun popped out to Nagy. Counsell followed with a lazy grounder to the right side. Fernandez moved to the ball, but it rolled under his glove into right field. The error put Counsell on first as Bonilla staggered to third. Eisenreich was walked intentionally to load the bases. With the infield and outfield drawn in, White hit a grounder to Fernandez who threw home to force out Bonilla. One strike later, Edgar Renteria hit a line drive over Nagy's glove into center field to score Counsell with the run that won the World Series. As 67,204 fans celebrated with the Marlins, the Indians were left with one of the most heartbreaking losses in baseball history.

Cleveland's seventh-game loss was also Herb Score's final game as radio voice of the Indians. He had reached legendary status as a pitcher, but also did so as a broadcaster with 34 consecutive seasons behind the microphone for Tribe games, 30 of them on radio stations WERE, WWWE and WKNR. For a generation, Score was the primary link between the Indians and their fans. It was often suggested that Score had seen more bad baseball (a knock on the 1964-1993 Indians), but he was rewarded with a front-row seat to some of the best, most exciting baseball (1994-1997) ever played in Cleveland.

Almost immediately following the World Series, the Indians had to face additional losses, this time in the expansion draft to stock the new Arizona Diamondbacks and Tampa Bay Devil Rays. Cleveland lost the maximum of three players. Brian Anderson was the first player chosen by Arizona. Pitching prospect Albie Lopez and first baseman Herb Perry went to the Devil Rays. Arizona also swung a draft-day deal to acquire third baseman Travis Fryman from the Tigers. The Diamondbacks really had their sights set on Matt Williams who wished to play in Arizona. On December 1, Williams was traded to Arizona for Fryman, pitcher Tom Martin and cash.

Expansion also caused a change in the Tribe's competition in the AL Central. The Milwaukee Brewers transferred to the NL Central and Detroit moved over from the AL East to take Milwaukee's place and make room for Tampa Bay in the East.

The look of the Indians changed dramatically in December when Kenny Lofton came home, signing as a free agent. Also signed was 33-year-old right-hander Dwight Gooden, the once

Rookie pitcher Jaret Wright started Game 4 of the 1997 World Series (below), won by the Tribe, 10-3. He later took a one-hit shutout into the seventh inning of Game 7 before being lifted for Paul Assenmacher.

LEGENDS OF THE TRIBE

brilliant Mets hurler, as a free agent. Lofton made Marquis Grissom expendable and he was traded with Jeff Juden, to the Brewers for pitchers Ben McDonald, Ron Villone and Mike Fetters, who was then sent to Oakland for pitcher Steve Karsay.

Lofton would step right back in as a catalyst in center field and batting lead off. Gooden would replace Orel Hershiser in the starting rotation. McDonald proved to be damaged goods and was sent back to Milwaukee.

Still dissatisfied with his pitching, John Hart made another deal just before opening day, sending prized hitting prospect Sean Casey to the Reds for 32-year-old right hander Dave Burba. A native of Dayton, Ohio, and a former Ohio State hurler, Burba had proved to be a durable starter with Cincinnati in 1996 and 1997. The new pitching rotation would consist of Charles Nagy, Jaret Wright, 22-year-old right-hander Bartolo Colon, Burba and Gooden. Chad Ogea, who had three long stays on the disabled list in 1998, became the only other Tribe pitcher with more than one start. Mike Jackson would supplant Jose Mesa as the closer and save 40 games. Mesa had run into off-field problems and was traded to the Giants with pitcher Alvin Morman and infielder-outfielder Shawon Dunston for reliever Steve Reed and outfielder Jacob Cruz.

The Indians had another fine year in 1998 and went wire to wire in the AL Central, cruising to a fourth straight divisional title, clinching on September 14 against the Twins and finishing with an 89-73 record, nine games better than the second-place White Sox.

Nagy and Burba both had 15 wins followed by Colon (14), Wright (12) and Gooden (8). Manny Ramirez rose to superstar status with 45 home runs and 145 RBI, both totals fourth best in the AL. Jim Thome belted 30 home runs despite missing 35 games with a broken hand. Travis Fryman drove in 96 runs.

The Yankees, however, had a season for the ages, winning 114 games to eclipse the record set by the 1954 Indians for most victories in an AL season (though the .721 win-

Third baseman Travis Fryman (left) and right fielder Manny Ramirez (right) each hit career highs in home runs in 1998. Acquired with pitcher Tom Martin from Arizona for Matt Williams, Fryman hit 28 as one of the Tribe's most consistent run producers. Ramirez hit 45 with 145 RBI to finish sixth in the AL MVP voting.

Dave Burba bolstered the starting rotation after being acquired from Cincinnati prior to opening day of 1998 for first baseman Sean Casey. The 32-year-old Burba won a career-high 15 games and topped the 200-inning plateau for the first time in his nine major league seasons.

ning percentage of the 1954 Indians remained the league record). Following the wild ride of October 1997 and as the 1998 season evolved, the two clear goals for the post season were a rematch with the Yankees and another trip to the World Series.

To achieve its first goal, the Tribe would have to get past the Red Sox in the 1998 ALDS. Boston had lost 13 straight post-season games dating back to the sixth game of the 1986 World Series, but overpowered Jaret Wright and the Tribe, 11-3, to start the 1998 ALDS. Boston first baseman Mo Vaughn drove in seven runs with a pair of home runs and shortstop Nomar Garciaparra added a three-run homer. Pedro Martinez held Cleveland's offense in check and sent the Indians to a defeat for the seventh straight time in the opening game of a playoff series.

Boston seemed to have help as Game 2 began at Jacobs Field. Dwight Gooden got into an argument with home plate umpire Joe Brinkman over his ball-strike calls. Mike Hargrove took up the cause for his pitcher and was ejected by Brinkman just three pitches into the game. Boston took a two-run lead when Garciaparra doubled with the second run scoring on a close play at the plate. When Gooden argued with Brinkman about the play, he was ejected. With 45,229 fans ready to revolt, Dave Burba restored order and held Boston in check. The Indians seemed to be inspired by Brinkman and drove Boston starter Tim Wakefield from the game in a five-run second inning capped by David Justice's three-run homer off John Wasdin. The Tribe's 9-5 victory tied the series.

At Fenway Park, Cleveland got the better of two close contests. Charles Nagy's eight innings of four-hit pitching paced a 4-3 win in the third game. The Indians had just five hits, but four were solo home runs by Jim Thome, Manny Ramirez (2) and Kenny Lofton. For the fourth game, Boston manager Jimy Williams elected to use Pete Schourek as his starting pitcher and save Martinez for a possible fifth game. Schourek responded by pitching a shutout into the sixth inning. A solo home run by Garciaparra was the only run surrendered by Bartolo Colon in five-and-two-thirds innings. The Indians finally broke through in the eighth against closer Tom Gordon. A two-run double by Justice was enough to give the Tribe a 2-1 victory and a rematch with the Yankees.

Words like "invincible" were being used to describe manager Joe Torre's team and New York looked the part by handing Cleveland another series-opening loss at Yankee Stadium. Jaret Wright was bombarded in a five-run first inning and David Wells allowed just three hits through the first eight innings. A two-run homer by Manny Ramirez in the ninth made the final score 7-2.

The second game was to be a pitchers duel between Charles Nagy and David Cone. David Justice homered for Cleveland in the fourth, but New York tied the game in the seventh. It was still tied in the 12th with pinch runner Enrique Wilson on first for the Indians. Travis Fryman bunted to first baseman Tino Martinez, but Martinez's throw hit Fryman and bounced into the outfield. As New York second baseman Chuck Knoblauch argued the play with umpire Ted Hendry, Wilson kept running, stumbling around third and almost crawling home with the go-ahead run. Kenny Lofton then singled home two more runs and Mike Jackson saved the 4-1 victory for Dave Burba.

In Cleveland, Bartolo Colon pitched brilliantly and put the Tribe in the driver's seat. The Indians bombed Andy Pettitte in the fifth inning with home runs by Ramirez, Jim Thome (his second of the game) and left-fielder Mark Whiten. Colon pitched a four-hitter and Cleveland took the series lead with a 6-1 win.

The tide turned against the Tribe when Orlando Hernandez, half-brother of Livan, started the fourth game for New York. "El Duque" overpowered the Indians, allowing just three hits. Dwight Gooden could not match the Cuban right hander and lost a 4-0 decision. After Wright's poor performance in the first game, Mike Hargrove started Chad Ogea who had pitched well in relief in the opener. This time Ogea was routed, allowing four runs before Wright was called on in the second inning. Wells seemed vulnerable, but repeatedly escaped trouble. Mariano Rivera snuffed out the last threat and saved a 5-3 victory for the Yanks.

Back in New York, the Indians needed Nagy and staff to get through the sixth game and provide Colon a chance in the seventh. But Nagy struggled and so did the defense. When third baseman Scott Brosius hit a three-run homer off Nagy in the third, New York led, 6-0, and all Indians hopes seemed lost. Cone sailed through four shutout innings, but the Tribe put up one last fight in the fifth. Thome hit a Ruthian grand slam high and deep into the right-field stands and the Indians were within a run, 6-5.

The Tribe got no closer, however, as Mendoza pitched three devastating innings of one-hit ball. A throwing error by Omar Vizquel, after 46 consecutive post-season games without a miscue, opened the door to three New York runs in the sixth inning. In the ninth, Rivera retired the Indians in order and 57,142 fans at Yankee Stadium celebrated the 9-5 victory to the repeated strains of Frank Sinatra's "New York, New York." Cleveland's two wins in the ALCS were the only post-season defeats suffered by New York in 1998 as the Yankees went on to a second World Series win in three years.

As the Indians went back to the drawing board for 1999, it was apparent that the regular season had become something of a formality. Tribe players knew they dominated the AL Central and had, to a certain extent, played to the level of the division's competition during the 1997 and 1998 regular seasons. Management promised that 1999 would be different and Hargrove publicly announced two goals: 100 wins in the regular season and a World Series victory. Even as the manager set those goals, however, owner Dick Jacobs cast a shadow over the season by announcing his intention to sell the franchise.

Following the 1998 season, Cleveland set its sights on one free agent who could help propel the club past the Yankees. He was Roberto Alomar, signed by the Tribe on November 24, 1998. Joining his brother, Sandy, the 31-year-old second baseman gave the offense an entirely new look and ignited a juggernaut that scored runs at a pace unequaled in franchise history. With Alomar batting third, behind Lofton and Vizquel, Cleveland had three .300 hitters with speed at the top of the order.

The biggest beneficiary of these table setters would be Manny Ramirez who surpassed Hal Trosky's team RBI record of

Jim Thome hits a fifth-inning Ruthian grand slam high and deep into the right-field stands to pull the Indians within a run of New York, 6-5, in Game 6 of the 1998 ALCS at Yankee Stadium. The Tribe got no closer, however, as the Yankees won the pennant, 9-5.

162, set in 1936. Ramirez's 165 RBI were the most by any major league player since 1938 when Jimmie Foxx drove in 175 runs. Led by Ramirez, Cleveland scored a club-record 1,009 runs in 1999, the first time any team had scored 1,000 or more runs in a season since 1950 and only the seventh in big league history to reach the 1,000 mark.

Roberto Alomar (120), Richie Sexson (116), and Jim Thome (108) joined Ramirez with over 100 RBI. Ramirez led the club with 44 home runs followed by Thome (33), Sexson (31), Roberto Alomar (24) and David Justice (21). Robbie Alomar led the AL with 138 runs scored and Ramirez (131), Omar Vizquel (112), Kenny Lofton (110) and Thome (101) also topped 100. Vizquel continued his transformation from a defensive specialist to a two-way threat and tied Ramirez for the team lead with a .333 batting average. Thome achieved the rare distinction of leading the American League in both walks (127) and strikeouts (171).

The keystone combination of Alomar and Vizquel gave the Indians the most acrobatic middle infielders in club history. Each won a Gold Glove award.

Pitching could not match the offense, but Bartolo Colon, Charles Nagy and Dave Burba became three dependable starters. While Colon blossomed, leading the staff with 18 wins, Jaret Wright did not and struggled throughout 1999 with just eight wins. Nagy's 17 victories gave him five straight seasons with at least 15. Burba won 15 for the second straight season. Dwight Gooden, however, won just three and could not be counted on for the post season. Steve Karsay was brilliant as a set-up man, but hurt his arm after a trial in the starting rotation. Veteran lefty Mark Langston got a shot and 41-year-old knuckleballer Tom Candiotti was brought back to try to bolster the rotation.

The bullpen, a great strength in 1995 and 1996, was suspect after closer Mike Jackson. Off-season trades that sent Brian Giles to the Pirates for lefty Ricardo Rincon and Chad Ogea to the Phillies for righty Jerry Spradlin did not provide the relief help that John Hart sought.

In the regular season, the offense was a joy to behold. The Indians fell three victories short of Hargrove's 100-win goal and just one win shy of matching the Yankees for the best record in the AL. To match the fifth-best win total in franchise history, the Tribe overcame major injuries to Sandy Alomar Jr., Travis Fryman and outfielder-designated hitter Wil Cordero, an off-season free agent signee. The injuries provided opportunities for catcher Einar Diaz and outfielder-first baseman Richie Sexson. Both prized prospects came through.

Cleveland led the league in home attendance (for the first time since 1948) with a new team record of 3,468,460. Every regular-season game was sold out again, stretching Cleveland's record-setting streak to 373 games. Since the start of divisional play in 1969, only two other clubs (the 1971-75 Oakland Athletics and the 1991-93, '95-99 Atlanta Braves) could boast of five or more successive division championships.

The Tribe's fifth straight AL Central win earned a third ALDS meeting with the Red Sox who countered

Bartolo Colon became the Tribe's best starting pitcher in 1999, winning a career-high 18 games with 161 strikeouts in 205 innings. His 3.95 ERA made him one of only seven AL pitchers to finish under 4.00.

Cleveland's mighty offense with Pedro Martinez. In the opening game, however, the Boston ace was forced from the contest with a sore back. Reliever Derek Lowe took over a 2-0 Boston advantage against Bartolo Colon to the sixth inning when Jim Thome powered Cleveland into a tie with a two-run homer. Colon sparkled over eight innings and Paul Shuey pitched a scoreless ninth. In the Cleveland ninth, Travis Fryman singled home Manny Ramirez and the Tribe had its first win to start a post-season series since beating Boston in 1995.

Cleveland dominated the second game. With just seven hits, the Tribe scored 11 runs off Red Sox starter Bret Saberhagen and reliever John Wasdin. Charles Nagy, Steve Karsay and Mike Jackson scattered six hits and the Indians took a commanding lead in the ALDS with an 11-1 victory before 45,184 fans.

All resemblance to the 1995 ALDS ended in the middle of the third game. Dave Burba was pitching a one-hit shutout with a 1-0 lead when he was forced from the game with numbness in his right arm after the fourth inning. Jaret Wright relieved Burba and allowed two runs in the fifth and another in the sixth. Cleveland tied the game, 3-3, in the seventh, but Boston broke the game open with six runs in the seventh off Wright, Ricardo Rincon, and rookie Sean DePaula. The 9-3 Red Sox win was a prelude to perhaps the most embarrassing loss in Indians history.

Richie Sexson (left) and Roberto Alomar (right) were offensive stars for the 1999 Indians. In his first full big league season, Sexson hit 31 homers with 116 RBI as a left fielder, first baseman and DH. Alomar stabilized second base after signing as a free agent, then became the first in club history to hit 20 homers (24), drive in 100 runs (120), score 100 runs (138) and steal 30 bases (37) in a season.

Kenny Lofton slides head-first into the bag while attempting to beat out an infield hit in Game 5 of the 1999 ALDS versus the Red Sox at Jacobs Field. He suffered a broken collarbone, but recovered to be in the lineup for opening day, 2000.

Having lost Burba and used Wright, Hargrove went with Colon on three days rest. Bartolo was ineffective on short rest. Karsay, Steve Reed, Paul Assenmacher and Shuey were just as ineffective. The result was a dreadful 23-7 defeat. Boston's 23 runs, 24 hits, and 16-run victory margin were all post-season records.

Still, the fourth-game defeat counted as just one loss. Back at Jacobs Field, the Indians had Nagy ready to start while Boston had to go with Saberhagen. Martinez remained a question mark with his sore back. Both starting pitchers were ineffective in a game that resembled a boxing match. Nomar Garciaparra continued to annihilate Tribe pitching with a two-run homer in the first, but the Tribe countered with three runs on Omar Vizquel's run-scoring double and Thome's majestic homer to center field. Fryman's two-run homer in the second gave Cleveland a 5-2 lead and sent Saberhagen to the showers.

LEGENDS OF THE TRIBE

Boston rallied in the third. With a run home and runners at second and third, Garciaparra was finally bypassed to put struggling left fielder Troy O'Leary on the spot. O'Leary promptly hit Nagy's first pitch for a grand slam over the right-field fence giving Boston a 7-5 lead.

The Indians came back again. Robbie Alomar and Ramirez opened the third with back-to-back doubles for a run and Thome delivered another towering homer to center that turned a one-run deficit into an 8-7 Indians lead. He received a standing ovation after passing Babe Ruth on the all-time list with his 16th post-season home run. Only Mickey Mantle and Reggie Jackson (18 each) had hit more post-season homers than Thome.

Trouble loomed in the Boston bullpen where Pedro Martinez was warming up. When center fielder Darren Lewis doubled to start the fourth, Nagy was replaced by DePaula. Third baseman John Valentin's sacrifice fly to left tied the game, 8-8.

Sore back or not, Martinez took the mound and silenced the Tribe and the Jacobs Field crowd of 45,114. The fans were further silenced when Kenny Lofton was injured sliding headfirst into first base attempting to beat out an infield hit. He suffered a broken collarbone. Improving with each pitch, Martinez did not allow a hit in six innings of relief work.

Shuey relieved DePaula to start the seventh. Valentin singled and took second when Robbie Alomar made another stellar play to retire designated hitter Brian Daubach. With first base open, Garciaparra, the 1999 AL batting champion, was given another intentional pass. O'Leary then hit Shuey's next pitch over the right-field wall for an 11-8 Boston lead.

Like the 1954 World Series, almost nothing went right for the Indians after Burba's injury. Colon and Nagy had not responded when Hargrove altered the pitching rotation. Other than DePaula, the bullpen did not respond. And, when Garciaparra was finally avoided, O'Leary made Cleveland pay. Boston won the deciding game, 12-8, to end the Tribe's season.

The Jacobs era at Jacobs Field concluded on a losing note, but was, arguably, the most successful period in Indians history. With five straight post-season appearances, a sellout streak covering more than four full seasons and a lineup of all-stars, the organization had made Cleveland a baseball town again. The Indians were poised for continued success and further pursuit of a World Series victory in the new millennium. But first, big changes were in store.

The three straight losses to Boston in the 1999 ALDS marked the end of Mike Hargrove's tenure as manager. When Hargrove was a player, Tribe fans and Cleveland media voiced concerns about the club in general, but the Indians' success with Hargrove as manager had put virtually every one of his moves under a microscope.

Hargrove was criticized for the makeup of the playoff roster—and a possible deference to veteran players who may have under-produced or were less than 100 percent healthy, over other players. The manager's detractors criticized his use of pitchers in the 1999 ALDS, especially Jaret Wright in the third game, creating the need to have Bartolo Colon and Charles Nagy pitch

Mike Hargrove became manager when the turnaround of the franchise was only beginning, then became a consistent factor in the success. But three straight losses to Boston in the 1999 ALDS marked the end of his tenure. In 8 1/2 seasons, Hargrove compiled a 721-591 record with five division championships and two pennants.

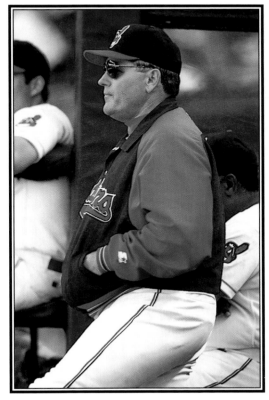

New faces of 2000 were familiar old faces as well. Charlie Manuel (left) had been the hitting coach since 1994 when he succeeded Mike Hargrove as manager. Chuck Finley (right) had pitched 14 seasons with the Angels with 165 career wins when he signed as a free agent in December 1999.

on three days rest in games four and five. Hargrove's supporters suggested that, after Burba's injury, he went for the kill by using Wright in the third game, knowing his two best pitchers were in the wings and that Nagy was 9-1 (including two post-season wins) in his career against Boston.

Strategy aside, the Indians had now been to the post season five straight years without winning a World Series and John Hart determined that it was time for a change. Citing the need for a new voice and a new energy in the clubhouse, Charlie Manuel became Hart's selection to become the new manager beginning with the 2000 season. Manuel had been part of the Tribe organization since December 2, 1987, serving as a hitting instructor at the major league and minor-league levels, and managing Cleveland's top farm clubs from 1990 through 1993. Manuel had been Hargrove's hitting instructor since 1994.

As a player from 1979 through 1985 and manager from 1991 through 1999, Hargrove made his mark on Cleveland baseball from days of little hope to days of championship expectations. With a regular-season managerial record of 721-591, "Grover" trailed only Lou Boudreau's 728 wins among all Tribe managers. Only Boudreau had managed more games for the Indians (1,377) than Hargrove.

Manuel's new boss was Larry Dolan who purchased the Indians early in 2000. A Chardon, Ohio, lawyer, Dolan officially became owner on February 15, 2000. Dolan, and four family trusts, purchased the club for a Major League Baseball-record $323 million, about $283 million more than the Jacobs brothers had paid for the club in 1986. More so than Dick Jacobs, Larry Dolan expressed the sentiments of a fan when he purchased the team, citing shared moments with family at Indians games and keeping score while listening to Jack Graney broadcast Tribe games on the radio.

As the Indians entered the new century and the 2000 season, the club remained a championship contender while retaining their core of longtime fan favorites including Jim Thome, Omar Vizquel, Manny Ramirez, Kenny Lofton, Sandy Alomar Jr. and Charles Nagy. Thome and Ramirez had both climbed onto Cleveland's top 10 all-time home run leaders list and seemed poised to challenge each other for Albert Belle's record. Vizquel had won seven straight Gold Glove awards (six with the Indians), more than any player in American League history, and moved up among Cleveland's all-time stolen base leaders. Lofton kept adding to his club record for stolen bases while moving up among the Indians' all-time leaders in runs scored. Despite spending much of the 1991-1995 and 1999 seasons on the disabled list, Alomar had caught more games for the Tribe than all but three catchers—Jim Hegan, Steve O'Neill and Luke Sewell. Nagy was among the Tribe's all-time leaders in wins, winning percentage and strikeouts.

The organization again trained its sights on one free agent for 2000 and reeled in left-handed pitcher Chuck Finley. A four-time all-star, Finley had spent all his 14 major league seasons with the Angels and was the all-time franchise leader with 165 victories. He averaged nearly a strikeout per inning from 1995 through 1999. Finley was especially adept at beating the Yankees, a problem area for the Indians in 1999.

Cleveland also spent big money on Cuban pitcher Danys Baez. After losing to the likes of Cuban hurlers Livan and Orlando Hernandez, the Indians counted on young Baez to improve a pitching staff that had proven not quite good enough to win a World Series. Baez was one of numerous young talents expected to keep the Tribe in contention on a year-in, year-out basis. Pitching prospects Tim Drew and C.C. Sabathia were first-round draft choices. Russell Branyan was the top power-hitting prospect. Drew, along with Paul Rigdon, Jim Brower, Mark Watson, Sean DePaula and Justin Speier were among the pitchers recalled from the minors when a serious rash of injuries befell the pitching staff in May 2000.

As the Dolan era began, the 1900s had ended and the 100th anniversary of the Indians approached. Cleveland ended the last century with two world championships, five American League titles, five American League Central Division crowns and a century's worth of treasured memories, some joyous and some painful. Two of baseball's most storied teams were the 1920 and 1948 world champions. The 1954 and 1995 clubs were outstanding as well, favorable in comparison to any of baseball's great teams. The 1908, 1940 and 1959 teams were a player, or a game, or a play, away from being champions. The 1997 Indians could have and should have been.

The down times have been frustrating. From 1909 to 1917, from 1927 to 1939, from 1941 to 1947, and, most notably, from 1960 to 1993, baseball enjoyment other than pennant contention had to sustain Tribe fans. Therein lies the core that defines Cleveland Indians baseball. Champions and all-stars are great, better than also-rans and wanabees, but Indians baseball is part of the fabric of Cleveland. In today's fast-changing time, Indians baseball in Cleveland should remain a treasured constant in good times and bad times and great times.

A productive farm system continues to develop talent for future Indians pennant contenders. C.C. Sabathia became the top pitching prospect after being selected in the first round of the 1998 amateur draft.

Year-by-Year Finishes

Season	Finish	Won	Lost	GB	PCT	Manager
1901	Seventh	54	82	29	.397	Jimmy McAleer
1902	Fifth	69	67	14	.507	Bill Armour
1903	Third	77	63	15	.550	Bill Armour
1904	Fourth	86	65	7.5	.570	Bill Armour, Napoleon Lajoie
1905	Fifth	76	78	19	.494	Napoleon Lajoie
1906	Third	89	64	5	.582	Napoleon Lajoie
1907	Fourth	85	67	8	.559	Napoleon Lajoie
1908	Second	90	64	.5	584	Napoleon Lajoie
1909	Sixth	71	82	27.5	.464	Napoleon Lajoie, Deacon McGuire
1910	Fifth	71	81	32	.467	Deacon McGuire
1911	Third	80	73	22	.523	Deacon McGuire, George Stovall
1912	Fifth	75	78	30.5	.490	Harry Davis, Joe Birmingham
1913	Third	86	66	9.5	.566	Joe Birmingham
1914	Eighth	51	102	48.5	333	Joe Birmingham
1915	Seventh	57	95	44.5	.375	Joe Birmingham, Lee Fohl

1920 American League and World Champions

Season	Finish	Won	Lost	GB	PCT	Manager
1916	Sixth	77	77	14	.500	Lee Fohl
1917	Third	88	66	12	.571	Lee Fohl
1918	Second	73	56	2.5	.566	Lee Fohl
1919	Second	84	55	3.5	.604	Lee Fohl, Tris Speaker
1920	First	98	56	(+2)	.636	Tris Speaker
1921	Second	94	60	4.5	.610	Tris Speaker
1922	Fourth	78	76	16	.507	Tris Speaker
1923	Third	82	71	16.5	.536	Tris Speaker
1924	Sixth	67	86	24.5	.438	Tris Speaker
1925	Sixth	70	84	27.5	.455	Tris Speaker
1926	Second	88	66	3	.571	Tris Speaker
1927	Sixth	66	86	43.5	.431	Jack McAllister
1928	Seventh	62	92	39	.403	Roger Peckinpaugh
1929	Third	81	71	24	.533	Roger Peckinpaugh
1930	Fourth	81	73	21	.526	Roger Peckinpaugh
1931	Fourth	78	76	30	.506	Roger Peckinpaugh
1932	Fourth	87	65	19	.572	Roger Peckinpaugh
1933	Fourth	75	76	23.5	.497	Roger Peckinpaugh, Bibb Falk, Walter Johnson
1934	Third	85	69	16	.552	Walter Johnson
1935	Third	82	71	12	.536	Walter Johnson, Steve O'Neill

1948 American League and World Champions

Season	Finish	Won	Lost	GB	PCT	Manager
1936	Fifth	80	74	22.5	.519	Steve O'Neill
1937	Fourth	83	71	19	.539	Steve O'Neill
1938	Third	86	66	13	.566	Oscar Vitt
1939	Third	87	67	20.5	.565	Oscar Vitt
1940	Second	89	65	1	.578	Oscar Vitt
1941	Fourth-tie	75	79	26	.487	Roger Peckinpaugh
1942	Fourth	75	79	28	.487	Lou Boudreau
1943	Third	82	71	15.5	.536	Lou Boudreau
1944	Fifth-tie	72	82	17	.468	Lou Boudreau
1945	Fifth	73	72	11	.503	Lou Boudreau
1946	Sixth	68	86	36	.442	Lou Boudreau
1947	Fourth	80	74	17	.519	Lou Boudreau
1948	First	97	58	(+1)	.626	Lou Boudreau
1949	Third	89	65	8	.578	Lou Boudreau
1950	Fourth	92	62	6	.597	Lou Boudreau
1951	Second	93	61	5	.604	Al Lopez
1952	Second	93	61	2	.604	Al Lopez
1953	Second	92	62	8.5	.597	Al Lopez
1954	First	111	43	(+8)	.721	Al Lopez
1955	Second	93	61	3	.604	Al Lopez

1954 American League Champions

Season	Finish	Won	Lost	GB	PCT	Manager
1956	Second	88	66	9	.571	Al Lopez
1957	Sixth	76	77	21.5	.497	Kerby Farrell
1958	Fourth	77	76	14.5	.503	Bobby Bragan, Joe Gordon
1959	Second	89	65	5	.578	Joe Gordon
1960	Fourth	76	78	21	.494	Joe Gordon, Jimmy Dykes
1961	Fifth	78	83	30.5	.484	Jimmy Dykes
1962	Sixth	80	82	16	.494	Mel McGaha
1963	Fifth-tie	79	83	23.5	.488	Birdie Tebbetts
1964	Sixth-tie	79	83	20	.488	Birdie Tebbetts
1965	Fifth	87	75	15	.537	Birdie Tebbetts
1966	Fifth	81	81	17	.500	Birdie Tebbetts, George Strickland
1967	Eighth	75	87	17	.463	Joe Adcock
1968	Third	86	75	16.5	.534	Alvin Dark
1969	Sixth	62	99	46.5	.385	Alvin Dark
1970	Fifth	76	86	32	.469	Alvin Dark
1971	Sixth	60	102	43	.370	Alvin Dark, John Lipon
1972	Fifth	72	84	14	.462	Ken Aspromonte
1973	Sixth	71	91	26	.438	Ken Aspromonte
1974	Fourth	77	85	14	.475	Ken Aspromonte
1975	Fourth	79	80	15.5	.497	Frank Robinson

1995 American League Champions

Season	Finish	Won	Lost	GB	PCT	Manager
1976	Fourth	81	78	16	.509	Frank Robinson
1977	Fifth	71	90	28.5	.441	Frank Robinson, Jeff Torborg
1978	Sixth	69	90	29	.434	Jeff Torborg
1979	Sixth	81	80	22	.503	Jeff Torborg, Dave Garcia
1980	Sixth	79	81	23	.494	Dave Garcia
1981	Sixth	52	51	7	.505	Dave Garcia
1982	Sixth-tie	78	84	17	.481	Dave Garcia
1983	Seventh	70	92	28	.432	Mike Ferraro, Pat Corrales
1984	Sixth	75	87	29.5	.463	Pat Corrales
1985	Seventh	60	102	39.5	.370	Pat Corrales
1986	Fifth	84	78	11.5	.519	Pat Corrales
1987	Seventh	61	101	37	.377	Pat Corrales, Doc Edwards
1988	Sixth	78	84	11	.481	Doc Edwards
1989	Sixth	73	89	16	.451	Doc Edwards, John Hart
1990	Fourth	77	85	11	.475	John McNamara
1991	Seventh	57	105	34	.352	John McNamara, Mike Hargrove
1992	Fourth	76	86	20	.469	Mike Hargrove
1993	Sixth	76	86	19	.469	Mike Hargrove
1994	Second	66	47	1	.584	Mike Hargrove
1995	First	100	44	(+30)	.694	Mike Hargrove
1996	First	99	62	(+14.5)	.615	Mike Hargrove
1997	First	86	75	(+6)	.534	Mike Hargrove
1998	First	89	73	(+9)	.549	Mike Hargrove
1999	First	97	65	(+21.5)	.599	Mike Hargrove

1997 American League Champions

Top 10: Batting

Games
Terry Turner 1,619
Nap Lajoie.................................1,614
Lou Boudreau...........................1,560
Jim Hegan 1,526
Tris Speaker..............................1,519
Ken Keltner 1,513
Joe Sewell.................................1,513
Earl Averill 1,509
Charlie Jamieson 1,483
Jack Graney...............................1,402

At Bats
Nap Lajoie.................................6,034
Earl Averill 5,909
Terry Turner 5,787
Lou Boudreau...........................5,754
Ken Keltner 5,655
Joe Sewell.................................5,621
Charlie Jamieson 5,551
Tris Speaker..............................5,546
Jack Graney...............................4,705
Bill Bradley...............................4,648

Runs
Earl Averill 1,154
Tris Speaker..............................1,079
Charlie Jamieson 942
Nap Lajoie....................................865
Joe Sewell....................................857
Lou Boudreau..............................823
Larry Doby...................................808
Hal Trosky...................................758
Kenny Lofton 753
Ken Keltner 735

Hits
Nap Lajoie.................................2,046
Tris Speaker..............................1,965
Earl Averill 1,903
Joe Sewell.................................1,800
Charlie Jamieson 1,753
Lou Boudreau...........................1,706
Ken Keltner 1,561
Terry Turner 1,472
Hal Trosky................................1,365
Julio Franco..............................1,272

Extra Base Hits
Earl Averill 724
Tris Speaker..................................667
Hal Trosky....................................556
Ken Keltner 538
Nap Lajoie.....................................536
Lou Boudreau...............................495
Albert Belle...................................481
Joe Sewell......................................468
Larry Doby....................................450
Andre Thornton 419

Doubles
Tris Speaker..................................486
Nap Lajoie.....................................424
Earl Averill 377
Joe Sewell......................................375
Lou Boudreau...............................367
Ken Keltner 306
Charlie Jamieson 296
Hal Trosky....................................287
Bill Bradley...................................238
Odell Hale.....................................235

Triples
Earl Averill 121
Tris Speaker..................................108
Elmer Flick....................................106
Joe Jackson.....................................89
Jeff Heath.......................................83
Ray Chapman.................................81
Jack Graney....................................79
Terry Turner 77
Bill Bradley, Nap Lajoie,
Charlie Jamieson 74

Home Runs
Albert Belle...................................242
Earl Averill 226
Hal Trosky....................................216
Larry Doby....................................215
Andre Thornton 214
Manny Ramirez.............................198
Jim Thome.....................................196
Al Rosen..192
Rocky Colavito..............................190
Ken Keltner 163

Runs Batted In
Earl Averill 1,084
Nap Lajoie.....................................919
Hal Trosky....................................911
Tris Speaker..................................884
Joe Sewell......................................869
Ken Keltner 850
Larry Doby....................................776
Albert Belle...................................751
Andre Thornton 749
Lou Boudreau...............................740

Batting Average
Joe Jackson................................ .375
Tris Speaker............................... .354
Nap Lajoie................................. .339
George Burns .... .327
Eddie Morgan .... .323
Earl Averill .... .322
Joe Sewell.................................. .320
Johnny Hodapp .... .318
Charlie Jamieson .... .316
Joe Vosmik, Hal Trosky............ .313

Total Bases
Earl Averill 3,200
Tris Speaker..............................2,886
Nap Lajoie.................................2,728
Ken Keltner 2,494
Hal Trosky................................2,406
Lou Boudreau...........................2,392
Joe Sewell.................................2,391
Charlie Jamieson 2,251
Larry Doby...............................2,159
Albert Belle...............................1,995

Slugging Percentage
Albert Belle .... .580
Manny Ramirez......................... .576
Hal Trosky................................. .551
Jim Thome................................. .547
Joe Jackson................................ .542
Earl Averill .... .541
Tris Speaker............................... .520
Jeff Heath................................... .506
Larry Doby................................. .500
Rocky Colavito, Al Rosen......... .495

Top 10: Pitching

Games
Mel Harder.....................582
Bob Feller 570
Willis Hudlin 475
Bob Lemon 460
Gary Bell.......................419
Mike Garcia 397
Eric Plunk 373
Stan Coveleski 360
George Uhle...................357
Early Wynn 343

Innings
Bob Feller 3,827
Mel Harder..................3,426
Bob Lemon 2,850
Willis Hudlin 2,558
Stan Coveleski 2,502
Addie Joss 2,327
Early Wynn 2,287
George Uhle.................2,200
Mike Garcia 2,138
Sam McDowell 2,109

Wins
Bob Feller 266
Mel Harder....................223
Bob Lemon 207
Stan Coveleski 172
Early Wynn 164
Addie Joss.....................160
Willis Hudlin 157
George Uhle...................147
Mike Garcia 142
Jim Bagby Sr., Sam McDowell 122

Losses
Mel Harder....................186
Bob Feller 162
Willis Hudlin 151
Bob Lemon 128
Stan Coveleski 123
George Uhle...................119
Sam McDowell 109
Early Wynn 102
Addie Joss.......................97
Mike Garcia 96

Winning Percentage
Addie Joss 623
Wes Ferrell 622
Bob Feller 621
Early Wynn 621
Bob Lemon 618
Mike Garcia 597
Jim Bagby Sr. 589
Charles Nagy 585
Stan Coveleski 583
Bob Rhoads 571

Strikeouts
Bob Feller 2,581
Sam McDowell 2,159
Bob Lemon 1,277
Early Wynn 1,277
Mel Harder..................1,161
Charles Nagy 1,143
Gary Bell.....................1,104
Mike Garcia 1,095
Luis Tiant....................1,041
Addie Joss 920

Walks
Bob Feller 1,764
Bob Lemon 1,251
Mel Harder..................1,118
Sam McDowell 1,072
Early Wynn 877
Willis Hudlin 832
George Uhle...................709
Mike Garcia 696
Gary Bell.......................670
Stan Coveleski 616

Earned Run Average
Addie Joss 1.89
Bob Rhoads 2.39
Bill Bernhard.................2.45
Earl Moore 2.58
Gaylord Perry 2.71
Stan Coveleski 2.80
Luis Tiant......................2.84
Willie Mitchell................2.89
Sam McDowell 2.99
Jim Bagby Sr. 3.02

Shutouts
Addie Joss 45
Bob Feller 44
Stan Coveleski 31
Bob Lemon 31
Mike Garcia.....................27
Mel Harder......................25
Early Wynn 24
Sam McDowell 22
Luis Tiant........................21
Guy Morton, Bob Rhoads............19

Saves
Doug Jones 129
Jose Mesa 104
Mike Jackson 94
Ray Narleski 53
Steve Olin 48
Jim Kern 46
Sid Monge 46
Gary Bell........................45
Ernie Camacho 44
Dave LaRoche 42

Bob Feller

All-Time Roster

A

ABBOTT, Fred...................1903-04
ABBOTT, Paul...........................1993
ABER, Al 1950-53
ABERNATHIE, Bill 1952
ABERNATHY, Ted 1963-64
ABLES, Harry 1909
ADAMS, Bert.......................1910-12
ADCOCK, Joe...........................1963
AGEE, Tommie 1962-64
AGUAYO, Luis...........................1989
AGUIRRE, Hank 1955-57
AKERFELDS, Darrel 1987
ALDRETE, Mike.........................1991
ALEXANDER, Bob......................1957
ALEXANDER, Gary 1978-80
ALEXANDER, Hugh 1937
ALLANSON, Andy 1986-89
ALLEN, Bob................1961-63,'66-67
ALLEN, Johnny 1936-40
ALLEN, Neil...............................1989
ALLEN, Rod 1988
ALLISON, Milo.....................1916-17
ALLRED, Beau 1989-91
ALOMAR, Roberto 1999-00
ALOMAR, Sandy....................1990-00
ALSTON, Del 1979-80
ALTIZER, Dave 1908
ALTOBELLI, Joe ....1955,'57
ALVARADO, Luis 1974
ALVIS, Max 1962-69
AMARO, Ruben 1994-95
ANDERSEN, Larry ....1975,'77,'79
ANDERSON, Brian 1996-97
ANDERSON, Bud 1982-83
ANDERSON, Dwain 1974
ANDREWS, Ivy Paul...................1937
ANDREWS, Nate..................1940-41
ANTONELLI, John 1961
APONTE, Luis 1984
ARLIN, Steve 1974
ARMSTRONG, Jack...................1992
ARMSTRONG, Mike 1987
ARNSBERG, Brad.......................1992
ASHBY, Alan 1973-76
ASPROMONTE, Ken 1960-62
ASSENMACHER, Paul............1995-99
ATHERTON, Keith 1989
AUSTIN, Rick........................1970-71
AUTRY, Martin 1926-28
AVEN, Bruce..............................1997
AVERILL, Earl D. ....1956,'58
AVERILL, Earl 1929-39
AVILA, Bob 1949-58

AYALA, Benny 1985
AYLWARD, Dick.........................1953
AZCUE, Joe..........................1963-69

B

BAERGA, Carlos ....1990-96,'99
BAGBY, James, Sr. 1916-22
BAGBY, James, Jr.................1941-45
BAILES, Scott 1986-89
BAILEY, Steve 1967-68
BAINES, Harold 1999
BAKER, Charles..........................1901
BAKER, Frank ....1969,'71
BAKER, Howard.........................1912
BALL, Neal............................1909-12
BALLINGER, Mark 1971
BANDO, Chris.......................1981-88
BANKS, George 1964-66
BANNISTER, Alan 1980-83
BARBARE, Walter 1914-16
BARBEAU, William 1905-06
BARKER, Len 1979-83
BARKER, Ray 1965
BARKLEY, Jeff 1984-85
BARNES, Brian 1994
BARNES, Rich 1983
BARNHART, Leslie ....1928,'30
BASKETTE, James 1911-13
BASSLER, Johnny 1913-14
BATES, Ray 1913
BAXES, Jim 1959
BAY, Harry 1902-08
BAYNE, William 1928
BEALL, John 1913
BEAN, Belve.................1930-31,'33-35
BEARDEN, Gene 1947-50
BEARSE, Kevin 1990
BECK, Ervin 1901
BECK, George 1914
BECKER, Heinz 1946-47
BECKER, Joe 1936-37
BEDFORD, Gene 1925
BEDGOOD, Phil 1922-23
BEEBE, Fred 1916
BEENE, Fred 1974-75
BEHENNA, Rick 198315
BELL, Buddy 1972-78
BELL, David ....1995,'98
BELL, Eric 1991-92
BELL, Gary 1958-67
BELL, Jay 1986-88
BELL, Roy 1940-41
BELLE, Albert 1989-96
BEMIS, Harry 1902-10
BENGE, Ray 1925-26
BENJAMIN, Stan 1945
BENIN, Henry 1914

BENTON, Al..........................1949-50
BENTON, Butch 1985
BERARDINO, John ....1948-50,'52
BERG, Moe.........................1931,'34
BERGER, Charles 1907-10
BERGER, Louis W. ....1932,'35-36
BERGMAN, Alfred H.................1916
BERNAZARD, Tony...............1984-87
BERNHARD, William 1902-07
BERROA, Geronimo 1998
BERRY, Joe 1946
BERRY, Ken 1975
BESCHER, Robert 1918
BEVACQUA, Kurt 1971-72
BIBBY, Jim 1975-77
BIELECKI, Mike 1993
BILLINGS, John 1913-18
BIRAS, Stephen 1944
BIRMINGHAM, Joe...............1906-14
BISHOP, Lloyd 1914
BISLAND, Rivington 1914
BLACK, Bud ....1988-90,'95
BLACK, Don 1946-48
BLAEHOLDER, George...............1936
BLANCO, Ossie 1974
BLANDING, Fred...................1910-14
BLANKS, Larvell 1976-78
BLAIR, Willie 1991
BLYLEVEN, Bert 1981-85
BOGHTE, Bruce..........................1977
BOCKMAN, Eddie 1947
BOEHLING, Joe...............1916-17,'20
BOHNET, John 1982
BOLEY, Joe 1932
BOLGER, Jim 1959
BOLTON, Cecil 1928
BOND, Walter 1960-62
BONDS, Bobby...........................1979
BONNER, Frank 1902
BONNESS, William 1944
BOOKER, Richard......................1966
BOOLES, Seabron......................1909
BOONE, James 1922-23
BOONE, Ray 1948-53
BORDERS, Pat.......................1997-99
BOSMAN, Dick 1973-75
BOSS, Harley 1933
BOUCHER, Denis 1991-92
BOUDREAU, Lou 1938-50
BOWMAN, Abe 1914-15
BOWSFIELD, Ted.......................1960
BOYD, Gary 1969
BRACKEN, Jack 1901
BRADFORD, Buddy 1970-71
BRADLEY, Bill 1901-10
BRADLEY, John..........................1916
BRAGGINS, Richard...................1901

BRANSON, Jeff 1997-98
BRANYAN, Russell.................1998-00
BRENNAN, Addison 1918
BRENNAN, Tom 1981-83
BRENNER, Delbert 1912
BRENTON, Lynn ....1913,'15
BRENZEL, William 1934-35
BREWINGTON, Jamie 2000
BREWSTER, Charles 1946
BRIDGES, Rocky........................1960
BRIGGS, Dan.............................1978
BRIGGS, John 1959-60
BRISSIE, Lou 1951-53
BROACA, John...........................1939
BRODOWSKI, Dick 1958-59
BROHAMER, Jack ....1972-75,'80
BRONKIE, Herman 1910-12
BROOKENS, Tom 1990
BROWER, Frank 1923-74
BROWER, Jim 1999-00
BROWN, Clint 1928-35, 41-42
BROWN, Dick 1957-59
BROWN, Jackie 1975-76
BROWN, Larry 1963-71
BROWN, Lloyd 1934-37
BROWN, Walter 1927-28
BROWNE, Jerry 1989-91
BUCKEYE, Garland 1925-28
BUELOW, Fred 1904-06
BURBA, Dave 1998-00
BURCHART, Larry 1969
BURNETT, John 1927-34
BURNITZ, Jeromy 1995-96
BURNS, George ....1920-21,'24-28
BURTON, Ellis 1963
BUSBY, Jim 1956-57
BUSKEY, Tom.......................1974-77
BUTCHER, Henry..................1911-12
BUTCHER, John 1986
BUTLER, Bill..............................1972
BUTLER, Brett 1984-87

C

CABRERA, Jolbert ....1998,'00
CAFFIE, Joe 1956-57
CAFFYN, Benjamin 1906
CAGE, Wayne 1978-79
CALDWELL, Bruce......................1928
CALDWELL, Ray 1919-21
CALLAHAN, David 1910-11
CALVERT, Paul.....................1942-45
CAMACHO, Ernie 1983-87
CAMILLI, Lou 1969-72
CAMPBELL, Bruce 1935-39
CAMPBELL, Clarence 1940-41
CAMPER, Cardell 1977
CANDAELE, Casey 1996-97

CANDIOTTI, Tom............1986-91,'99
CARED, Bernie 1978
CARDENAL, Jose.................1968-69
CARDENAS, Leo 1973
CARISCH, Fred 1912-14
CARLTON, Steve........................1987
CARNETT, Ed 1945
CARR, Charles....................1904-05
CARRASQUEL, Chico 1956-58
CARREON, Camilo 1965
CARREON, Mark 1996
CARSON, Walter 1934-35
CARTER, Joe......................1984-89
CARTER, Paul 1914-15
CARTY, Rico 1974-77
CASE, George 1946
CASEY, Sean 1997
CASIAN, Larry 1994
CASTILLO, Carmen 1982-88
CENTER, Earl............1942-43,'45-46
CERMAK, Edward.....................1901
CERONE, Rick 1975-76
CHAKALES, Bob 1951-54
CHAMBLISS, Chris................1971-74
CHANCE, Bob 1963-64
CHANCE, Dean.........................1970
CHAPMAN, Ben 1939-40
CHAPMAN, Ray 1912-20
CHAPMAN, Sam 1951
CHAPPELL, Larry 1916
CHARBONEAU, Joe 1980-82
CHECH, Charles 1908
CHEEVES, Virgil 1924
CHRISTOPHER, Mike...........1992-93
CHRISTOPHER, Russ 1948
CHURN, Clarence 1958
CICOTTE, Al 1959
CIHOCKI, Al 1945
CISSELL, Chalmor................1932-33
CLANTON, Ucal........................1922
CLARK, Allie 1948-51
CLARK, Bryan 1985
CLARK, Dave 1986-89
CLARK, Harvey.........................1902
CLARK, James 1971
CLARK, Mark 1993-95
CLARK, Robert....................1920-21
CLARK, Terry 1997
CLARK, William 1924
CLARKE, Joshua 1908-09
CLARKE, Justin 1905-10
CLARKE, Sumpter 1923-24
CLARKSON, Walter 1907-08
CLINE, Ty 1960-62
CLINGMAN, William 1903
CLINTON, Lou 1965
CLYDE, David 1978-79
CODIROLI, Chris......................1988
COLAVITO, Rocky.......1955-59,'65-67
COLBERT, Vince 1970-72
COLE, Albert...........................1925
COLE, Alex 1990-92
COLEMAN, Gordon 1959

COLEMAN, Robert 1916
COLLAMORE, Al 1914-15
COLLARD, Earl 1927-28
COLLINS, Don 1980
COLLUM, Jackie 1962
COLON, Bartolo 1997-00
COMBS, Merrill 1951-52
COMER, Steve 1984
CONGALTON, William 1905-07
CONNALLY, George 1931-34
CONNATSER, Bruce...............1931-32
CONNOLLY, Ed 1967
CONNOLLY, Joe 1922-23
CONNOR, Joseph 1901
CONSTABLE, Jim 1958
CONWAY, Jack ....1941,'46-47
CONYERS, Herb 1950
COOK, Dennis ....1992-93,'95
CORA, Joey 1998
CORDERO, Wil 1999
COUGHTRY, Marlan 1962
COUMBE, Fred 1914-19
COVELESKI, Stan 1916-24
COX, Ted............................1978-79
CRAGHEAD, Howard...........1931,'33
CRAIG, Rodney 1982
CRANDALL, Del 1966
CREEL, Keith 1985
CRISTALL, William 1901
CROSBY, Ed 1974-76
CROSS, Frank 1901
CRUZ, Jacob 1998-00
CRUZ, Victor 1979-80
CULLENBINE, Ray 1943-45
CULLOP, Henry 1927
CULLOP, Nick 1913-14
CULMER, Wil 1983
CULVER, George 1966-67
CURRY, Tony 1966
CURTIS, Chad 1997
CURTIS, Jack 1963
CYPERT, Al 1914

D

DADE, Paul 1977-79
DAILEY, Bill 1961-62
DALENA, Pete 1989
DALEY, Bud 1955-57
DALY, Tom 1916
DASHNER, Lee 1913
DAVALILLO, Vic 1963-68
DAVIDSON, Homer 1908
DAVIS, Bill 1965-66
DAVIS, Harry 1912
DAVIS, Steve 1989
DAWSON, Joe 1924
DEAN, Alfred.....................1941-43
DeBERRY, Hank 1916-17
DEDMON, Jeff 1988
DELAHANTY, Frank 1907
de La HOZ, Mike 1960-63
DeLUCIA, Rich 1999
DEMETER, Don 1967

DEMETER, Steve 1960
DeMOTT, Ben 1910-11
DEMPSEY, Rick 1987
DENNING, Otto 1942-43
DENNY, John 1980-82
DENTE, Sam 1954-55
DePAULA, Sean 1999-00
DESAUTELS, Gene ....1941-43,'45
DesJARDIEN, Paul 1916
DETORE, George 193011
DEVLIN, James 1944
DIAZ, Bo 1978-81
DIAZ, Einar 1996-00
DICKEN, Paul ....1964,'66
DICKERSON, George 1917
DILLARD, Don 1959-62
DILLINGER, Harley 1914
DILONE, Miguel....................1980-83
DiPOTO, Jerry 1993-94
DOANE, Walter 1909-10
DOBSON, Joe 1939-40
DOBSON, Pat 1976-77
DOBY, Larry ....1947-55,'58
DOLJACK, Frank 1943
DONAHUE, Francis................1903-05
DONAHUE, Patrick 1910
DONOHUE, Peter 1931
DONOVAN, Dick 1962-65
DONOVAN, Mike 1904
DONOVAN, Thomas 1901
DORAN, William 1922
DORMAN, Dwight......................1928
DORNER, August..................1902-03
DORSETT, Brian 1987
DORSETT, Calvin ....1940-41,'47
DOWLING, Peter 1901
DRAKE, Logan 1922-24
DRAKE, Thomas 1939
DREW, Tim 2000
DUFFY, Frank 1972-77
DUNCAN, Dave 1973-74
DUNLOP, George 1913-14
DUNNING, Steve 1970-73
DUNSTON, Shawon 1998
DYBZINSKI, Jerry.................1980-82
DYCK, James 1954

E

EAGAN, Charles 1901
EASTER, Luke 1949-54
EASTERLY, Jamie 1983-87
EASTERLY, Ted 1909-12
ECKERSLEY, Dennis 1975-77
EDMONDSON, George 1922-24
EDMONSON, Ed 1913
EDWARDS, Doc 1962-63
EDWARDS, Hank........1941-43,'46-49
EDWARDS, Jim 1922-25
EELLS, Harry 1906
EGAN, Arthur 1914-15
EGLOFF, Bruce 1991
EIBEL, Henry...........................1912
EICHELBERGER, Juan...............1983

EICHRODT, Fred 1925-27
EISENSTAT, Harry 1939-42
ELLERBE, Frank 1924
ELLINGSEN, Bruce 1974
ELLIS, John 1973-75
ELLISON, George 1920
ELLSWORTH, Dick 1969-70
EMBREE, Alan ....1992,'95-96
EMBREE, Charles........1941-42,'44-47
ENGEL, Joe 1919
ENGLE, Arthur 1916
ENZMANN, John 1918-19
ESCHEN, James 1915
ESCOBAR, Jose 1991
ESPINOZA, Alvaro 1993-96
ESSEGIAN, Chuck 1961-62
ESSIAN, Jim 1983
EUNICK, Fernandas 1917
EVANS, Joe 1915-22
EVERS, Hoot 1955-56

F

FAETH, Tony 1919-20
FAHR, Gerald 1951
FAIN, Ferris 1955
FALK, Bibb 1929-31
FALKENBERG, Fred.........1908-11,'13
FANWELL, Harry 1910
FARMER, Ed 1971-73
FARMER, Jack 1918
FARR, Steve ....1984,'94
FARRELL, John ....1987-90,'95
FELLER, Bob.............1936-41,'45-56
FERMIN, Felix 1989-93
FERNANDEZ,Tony 1997
FERRARESE, Don 1958-59
FERRELL, Wesley 1927-33
FERRICK, Tom ....1942,'46
FERRY, Alfred 1905
FEWSTER, Chick 1924-25
FIELDER, Cecil 1998
FINLEY, Chuck 2000
FIROVA, Dan............................1988
FISCHER, Carl 1937
FISCHLIN, Mike 1981-85
FISHER, Ed 1968
FISHER, Gus............................1911
FITZGERALD, Ed 1959
FITZKE, Paul 1924
FITZMORRIS, Al 1977-78
FLANIGAN, Ray 1946
FLEMING, Les ....1941-42,'45-47
FLICK, Elmer.....................1902-10
FLORES, Jesse 1950
FOILES, Hank ....1953,'55-56,'60
FONSECA, Lew 1927-31
FORD, Ted ....1970-71,'73
FOSSE, Ray ....1967-72,'76-77
FOSTER, Alan 1971
FOSTER, Edward.......................1908
FOSTER, Roy 1970-72
FRANCO, Julio............1983-88,'96-97
FRANCONA, Terry 1988

FRANCONA, Tito 1959-64
FRAZIER, George 1984
FRAZIER, Joe 1947
FREIBURGER, Vernon 1941
FREISLEBEN, Dave 1978
FRIDLEY, Jim 1952
FRIEND, Owen 1953
FRIERSON, Robert 1941
FROBEL, Doug 1987
FRY, Johnson 1923
FRYMAN, Travis 1998-00
FULLER, Vern ....1964,'66-70
FUNK, Frank 1960-62

G

GAFFKE, Fabian 1941-42
GAGLIANO, Ralph 1965
GALATZER, Milton 1933-36
GALEHOUSE, Dennis 1934-38
GALLAGHER, Charlie.................1901
GALLAGHER, Dave 1987
GALLAGHER, Jackie.................1923
GAMBLE, Oscar 1973-75
GANDIL, Charles 1916
GARBARK, Robert 1934-35
GARCIA, Mike 1948-59
GARDNER, Larry 1919-24
GARDNER, Ray 1929-30
GARDNER, Rob 1968
GARLAND, Wayne 1977-81
GARRETT, Clarence 1915
GASSAWAY, Charles 1946
GEIGER, Gary 1958
GENINS, Frank.........................1901
GENTILE, Jim 1966
GEORGE, Charles 1935-36
GEORGE, Lefty 1912
GERKEN, George 1927-28
GETTEL, Al 1947-48
GETZ, Gus 1918
GIL, Gus 1967
GILES, Brian.........................1995-98
GILL, John 1927-28
GINN, Tinsley 1914
GINSBERG, Joe 1953-54
GLAVENICH, Luke 1913
GLEESON, James 1936
GLENDON, Martin 1903
GLIATTO, Salvador.........................1930
GLYNN, Bill 1952-54
GLYNN, Ed 1981-83
GOCHNAUR, John 1902-03
GOGOLEWSKI, Bill 1974
GOLDMAN, Jonah ....1928,'30-31
GOMEZ, Ruben 1962
GONZALES, Rene 1994
GONZALEZ, Denny.........................1989
GONZALEZ, Jose 1991
GONZALEZ, Orlando.........................1976
GONZALEZ, Pedro.................1965-67
GOOCH, Lee 1915
GOOD, Wilbur 1908-09
GOODEN, Dwight 1998-99

GORDON, Don.........................1987-88
GORDON, Joe 1947-50
GOULD, Al 1916-17
GOZZO, Mauro 1990-91
GRABER, Rod.........................1958
GRAHAM, George.........................1902
GRAMLY, Tom 1968
GRANEY, Jack.................1908,'10-22
GRANT, Edward.........................1905
GRANT, George.........................1927-29
GRANT, James.........................1943-44
GRANT, Jim 1958-64
GRASSO, Mickey 1954
GRAVES, Danny 1996
GRAY, Gary 1980
GRAY, John 1957
GRAY, Ted 1955
GREEN, Gene 1962-63
GREGG, David 1913
GREGG, Vean 1911-14
GRIFFIN, Alfredo 1976-78
GRIGGS, Arthur 1911-12
GRIM, Bob 1960
GRIMES, Oscar 1938-42
GRIMSLEY, Jason 1993-95
GRIMSLEY, Ross 1980
GRISSOM, Marquis.........................1997
GROMEK, Steve 1941-53
GROOM, Robert 1918
GROTH, Ernie 1947-48
GRUBB, Harvey.........................1912
GRUBB, Johnny.........................1977-78
GUANTE, Cecilio 1990
GUISTO, Louis.............1916-17,'21-23
GULLEY, Thomas.................1923-24
GUNKEL, Woodward 1916

H

HAGERMAN, Zeriah 1914-16
HALE, Bob 1960-61
HALE, Odell.................1931,'33-40
HALL, Jimmie.........................1968-69
HALL, Mel 1984-88
HALL, Russell 1901
HALLA, John 1905
HALLMAN, Bill 1901
HALT, Alva 1918
HAMANN, Elmer.........................1922
HAMILTON, Jack 1969
HAMILTON, Steve.........................1961
HAMMOND, Walter..........1915, 1922
HAMNER, Granny 1959
HAND, Rich 1970-71
HANEY, Chris 1999
HANSEN, Doug 1951
HARDER, Mel.........................1928-47
HARDY, Carroll.........................1958-60
HARDY, John 1903
HARGAN, Steve 1965-72
HARGROVE, Mike 1979-85
HARKNESS, Fred 1910-11
HARPER, Tommy 1968
HARRAH, Toby 1979-83

HARRELL, Billy ....1955,'57-58
HARRELSON, Ken.................1969-71
HARRIS, Billy 1968
HARRIS, Charles 1951
HARRIS, Joe.................1917, 1919
HARRIS, Mickey.........................1952
HARRISON, Roric.........................1975
HARSHMAN, Jack.................1959-60
HARSTAD, Oscar 1915
HART, William 1901
HARTFORD, Bruce 1914
HARTLEY, Grover.................1929-30
HARTMAN, Bob.........................1962
HARVEL, Luther 1928
HARVEY, Erwin 1901-02
HASSEY, Ron 1978-84
HATFIELD, Fred.........................1958
HAUGER, John.........................1912
HAUSER, Joe.........................1929
HAVENS, Brad 1988-89
HAWKINS, Wynn.................1960-62
HAWORTH, Howard.................1915
HAYES, Frank 1945-46
HAYES, Von 1981-82
HEATH, Jeff 1936-45
HEATON, Neal 1982-86
HEDLUND, Mike.................1965,'68
HEFFNER, Bob 1966
HEGAN, Jim ....1941-42,'46-57
HEIDEMANN, Jack.........1969-72,
HELD, Woodie 1958-64
HELF, Henry.........................1938, 1940
HEMAN, Russ 1961
HEMPHILL, Charles 1902
HEMSLEY, Rollie 1938-41
HENDERSON, Bernard.........................1921
HENDRICK, George 1973-76
HENDRICK, Harvey 1925
HENDRYX, Tim 1911-12
HENGEL, Dave 1989
HENNIGAN, Phil.........................1969-72
HENRY, Earl.........................1944-45
HERMOSO, Angel.........................1974
HERNANDEZ, Jeremy 1993
HERNANDEZ, Jose 1992
HERNANDEZ, Keith.........................1990
HERSHISER, Orel 1995-97
HESS, Otto ....1902,'04-08
HEVING, Joe ....1937-38,'41-44
HICKEY, John 1904
HICKMAN, Charles ....1902-04,'09
HIGGINS, Bob 1909
HIGGINS, Dennis.........................1970
HIGGINS, Mark 1989
HILDEBRAND, Oral...............1931-36
HILGENDORF, Tom 1972-74
HILL, Glenallen 1991-93
HILL, Herb 1915
HILL, Hugh 1903
HILL, Ken 1995
HILLEGAS, Shawn 1991
HINCHMAN, Harry 1907
HINCHMAN, William 1907-09

HINTON, Chuck ....1965-67,'69-71
HINZO, Tommy 1987, 1989
HOAG, Myril 1944-45
HOCKETT, Oris 1941-44
HODAPP, John 1925-32
HODGE, Harold.........................1971
HOFFER, Bill.........................1901
HOFFMAN, Edward 1915
HOGAN, Harry 1901
HOGAN, Ken 1923-24
HOHNHORST, Ed............1910, 1912
HOLLAND, Robert 1934
HOLLOWAY, Ken 1929-30
HOOD, Don 1975-79
HOOPER, Bob 1953-54
HORN, Sam.........................1993
HORTON, Tony.........................1967-70
HORTON, Willie.........................1978
HOSKINS, Dave 1953-54
HOUSTON, Tyler.........................1999
HOUTTEMAN, Art.........................1953-57
HOWARD, Doug 1976
HOWARD, Ivan 1916-17
HOWARD, Thomas 1992-93
HOWELL, Millard 1940
HOWELL, Murray.........................1941
HOWSER, Dick 1963-66
HUBBARD, Trenidad 1997
HUDLIN, Willis 1926-40
HUFF, Mike 1991
HUGHES, Roy.........................1935-37
HUISMANN, Mark 1987
HUMPHRIES, John 1938-40
HUNNEFIELD, William F............1931
HUNTER, Billy 1958
HUNTER, William E. 1912

I

IOTT, Fred 1903
IRWIN, Thomas.........................1938

J

JABLONOWSKI, Pete..............1930-12
JACKSON, Damian 1996-97
JACKSON, Jimmy.........................1905-06
JACKSON, Joe 1910-15
JACKSON, Michael W. 1973
JACKSON, Michael R. 1997-99
JACKSON, Randy.........................1958-59
JACOBSON, Bill.........................1927
JACOBY, Brook ....1984-91,'92
JACOME, Jason 1997-98
JAMES, Chris 1990-91
JAMES, Dion 1989-90
JAMES, Lefty 1912-14
JAMES, William H.................1911-12
JAMIESON, Charles.................1919-32
JASPER, Harry.........................1919
JEANES, Ernest.........................1921-22
JEFFCOAT, Mike 1983-85
JEFFERSON, Reggie 1991-93
JEFFERSON, Stan 1990
JESSEE, Dan 1929

JETER, John 1974
JIMENEZ, Houston....................1988
JOHN, Tommy 1963-64
JOHNSON, Alex 1972
JOHNSON, Bob 1974
JOHNSON, Cliff 1979-80
JOHNSON, Jerry 1973
JOHNSON, Larry D. 1972, 1974
JOHNSON, Lou 1968
JOHNSON, Victor 1946
JOHNSTON, Doc........1912-14,'18-21
JONES, Doug ....1986-91,'98
JONES, Hal 1961-62
JONES, Sam P. 1914-15
JONES, Sam 1951-52
JONES, Willie 1959
JORDAN, Scott 1988
JORDAN, Tom 1946
JOSS, Adrian 1902-10
JUDEN, Jeff 1997
JUDNICH, Walt 1948
JUNGELS, Ken ....1937-38,'40-41
JUSTICE, David 1997-00

K

KAHDOT, Isaac.........................1922
KAHL, Nick 1905
KAHLER, George....................1910-14
KAISER, Bob 1971
KAISER, Jeff 1987-90
KAMIENIECKI. Scott 2000
KAMM, William 1931-35
KARDOW, Paul 1936
KARR, Ben............................1925-27
KARSAY, Steve 1998-00
KAVANAGH, Martin...............1916-18
KEEDY, Pat 1989
KEEFE, David 1922
KEKICH, Mike 1973
KELLEY, Tom 1964-67
KELLY, Bob 1958
KELLY, Pat 1981
KELTNER, Ken ....1937-44,'46-49
KENDALL, Fred 1977
KENNEDY, Bill 1948
KENNEDY, Bob 1948-54
KENNEDY, Vernon...................1942-44
KENNEY, Jerry 1973
KENT, Jeff 1996
KEOUGH, Marty.........................1960
KERN, Jim ....1974-78,'86
KIBBLE, John 1912
KILKENNY, Mike 1972-73
KILLIAN, Ed 1903
KINDALL, Jerry 1962-64
KINER, Ralph 1955
KING, Eric 1991
KING, Jim 1967
KINNEY, Dennis 1978
KIRBY, Wayne 1991-96
KIRKE, Jay 1914-15
KIRKLAND, Willie 1961-63
KIRSCH, Harry 1910

KISER, Garland..........................1991
KITTLE, Ron 1988
KITTRIDGE, Malachi 1906
KLEIN, Louis 1951
KLEINE, Harold 1944-45
KLEPFER, Ed..................1915-17,'19
KLIEMAN, Ed 1943-48
KLIMCHOCK, Lou 1968-70
KLINE, Steven Jack....................1974
KLINE, Steven J. 1997
KLIPPSTEIN, John 1960
KLUGMANN, Joe 1925
KNAUPP, Henry 1910-11
KNICKERBOCKER, William...1933-36
KNODE, Robert 1923-26
KOESTNER, Elmer 1910
KOMMINSK, Brad 1989
KOPF, William, ...1913
KRAKAUSKAS, Joe ....1941-42,'46
KRALICK, Jack....................1963-67
KRAMER, Tom...................1991, 1993
KRAPP, Gene 1911-12
KRAUSE, Harry 1912
KREUGER, Rick 1978
KRIVDA, Rick............................1998
KROLL, Gary 1969
KRONER, John 1937-38
KRUGER, Arthur 1910
KRUEGER, Ernest 1913
KUBISZYN, Jack 1961-62
KUENN, Harvey 1960
KUHN, Bernard 1924
KUHN, Kenny 1955-57
KUIPER, Duane 1974-81
KURTZ, Hal 1968
KUZAVA, Bob 1946-47

L

LaCHANCE, George....................1901
LACEY, Bob 1981
LACY, Osceola 1926
LAJOIE, Napoleon 1902-14
LAMB, Ray 1971-73
LAMBETH, Otis 1916-18
LAMPKIN, Tom 1988
LAND, Grover ....1908-11,'13
LANDIS, Jim 1966
LANGFORD, Elton 1927-28
LANGSTON, Mark 1999
LaROCHE, Dave 1975-77
LARY, Lyn 1937-39
LASHER, Fred 1970
LASKEY, Bill 1988
LATTIMORE, William 1908
LATMAN, Barry 1960-63
LAW, Ron 1969
LAWRENCE, Jim 1963
LAWSON, Roxie 1930-31
LAXTON, Bill 1977
LEBER, Emil 1905
LEE, Cliff 1925-26
LEE, Leron 1974-75
LEE, Mike 1960

LEE, Thornton 1933-36
LEEK, Gone 1959
LEHNER, Paul 1951
LEHR, Norman 1926
LEIBOLD, Harry 1913-15
LEITNER, George.......................1902
LEIUS, Scott 1996
LELIVELT, Jack 1913-14
LeMASTER, Johnnie 1985
LEMON, Bob ....1941-42,'46-58
LEMON, Jim 1950, 1953
LEON, Eddie 1968-72
LEONARD, Joseph 1916
LEVIS, Jesse 1992-95, 1999
LEVSEN, Dutch 1923-28
LEWIS, Mark 1991-94
LEWALLYN, Dennis 1981-12
LIEBHARDT, Glenn 1906-09
LILLIQUIST, Derek 1992-94
LIND, Carl 1927-30
LINDE, Lyman 1947-48
LINDSAY, William 1911
LINDSEY, Jim 1922, 1924
LINK, Fred 1910
LINTZ, Larry 1978
LIPSKI, Bob 1963
LIS, Joe 1974-76
LISTER, Peter 1907
LITTLETON, Larry 1981
LIVINGSTON, Paddy.........1901, 1912
LOCKE, Bobby 1959-61
LOCKLIN, Stu 1955-56
LOFTON, Kenny..........1992-96,'98-00
LOHR, Howard 1916
LOLICH, Ron 1972-73
LOLLAR, Sherm 1946
LOPEZ, Al 1947
LOPEZ, Albie 1993-97
LOPEZ, Luis 1991
LOPEZ, Marcelino 1972
LORD, Bristol 1909-10
LOVULLO, Torey 1998
LOWDERMILK, Grover 1916
LOWENSTEIN, John 1970-77
LUKE, Matt 1998
LUND, Gordon 1967
LUNDBOM, John 1902
LUNTE, Harry 1919-20
LUPLOW, Al 1961-65
LUSH, William 1904
LUTZKE, Walter 1923-27
LYON, Russell 1944

M

MACHEMEHL, Charles 1971
MACK, Ray ....1938-44,'46
MACKIEWICZ, Felix 1945-47
MADDERN, Clarence..................1951
MAGALLANES, Ever 1991
MAGLIE, Sal 1955-56
MAGRANN, Tom 1989
MAHONEY, Jim 1962
MAILS, John.........................1920-22

MAJESKI, Henry 1952-55
MALDONADO, Candy ......1990,'93-94
MANNING, Rick 1975-83
MANTO, Jeff ....1990-91,'97-99
MARIS, Roger 1957-58
MARSH, Fred 1949
MARTIN, Billy 1959
MARTIN, Morris 1958
MARTIN, Tom 1998-00
MARTINEZ, Carlos 1991-93
MARTINEZ, Dennis.................1994-96
MARTINEZ, Tony 1963-66
MATHIAS, Carl 1960
MAYE, Lee 1967-69
MEDINA, Luis ....1988-89,'91
MEIXELL, Merten 1912
MELE, Sam 1956
MELTON, Bill 1977
MERCKER, Kent 1996
MERULLO, Matt 1994
MESA, Jose 1992-98
MESSENGER, Andrew 1924
METIVIER, George 1922-24
METKOVICH, George 1947
MEYER, Lambert 1945-46
MIDDLETON, John 1922
MILACKI, Bob 1993
MILBOURNE, Larry 1982
MILJUS, John 1928-29
MILLIGAN, Randy 1993
MILLER, Edwin 1918
MILLER, Raymond 1917
MILLER, Robert 1970
MILLER, Walter 1924-31
MILLS, Abbott 1911
MILLS, Buster 1942, 1946
MILLS, Frank 1914
MILNAR, Al...............1936,'38-43
MINGORI, Steve 1970-73
MINOSO, Minnie........1949,'51,'58-59
MITCHELL, Dale 1946-56
MITCHELL, Kevin 1997
MITCHELL, Willie 1909-16
MLICKI, Dave 1992-93
MOELLER, Dan 1916
MONACO, Blas.................1937, 1946
MONGE, Sid 1977-81
MONTAGUE, Edward........1928,'30-32
MOON, Leo 1932
MOORE, Barry 1970
MOORE, Earl 1901-07
MOORE, Edward 1934
MOORE, James 1928-29
MORA, Andres 1980
MORAN, Billy...........1958-59,'64-65
MORGAN, Eddie 1928-33
MORGAN, Joe 1960-61
MORMAN, Alvin 1997-98
MORONKO, Jeff 1984
MORRIS, Jack 1994
MORTON, Guy 1914-24
MOSES, Gerry 1972
MOSS, Howard 1946

MOSSI, Don 1954-58	NISCHWITZ, Ron 1963	PERRING, George 1908-10	REGALADO, Rudy 1954-56
MULLINS, Fran 1986	NIXON, Otis 1984-87	PERRY, Gaylord 1972-75	REICH, Herman 1949
MUNCRIEF, Bob 1948	NIXON, Russ 1957-60	PERRY, Herbert 1994-96	REILLEY, Alex 1909
MURCHISON, Thomas 1920	NOBOA, Junior 1984, 1987	PERRY, Jim ....1959-63,'74-75	REILLY, Thomas 1914
MURRAY, Eddie 1994-96	NOLES, Dickie 1986	PETERS, John 1918	REINHOLZ, Arthur 1928
MURRAY, Ray ....1948,'50-51	NORRIS, Jim 1977-79	PETERS, Russ ....1940-44,'46	REISER, Pete 1952
MUTIS, Jeff 1991-93	NUNAMAKER, Leslie 1919-22	PETERSON, Cap 1969	REISIGL, Jacob 1911
MYATT, Glenn 1923-35		PETERSON, Fritz 1974-76	REUSCHEL, Paul 1978-79
MYERS, Elmer 1919-20	**O**	PETTY, Jess 1921	REYNOLDS, Allie 1942-46
	O'BRIEN, Jack 1901	PEZOLD, Larry 1914	REYNOLDS, Bob 1975
MC	O'BRIEN, Pete 1989	PHELPS, Ken 1990	RHOADS, Robert 1903-09
McALEER, James 1901	O'BRIEN, Peter 1907	PHILLEY, Dave 1954-55	RHOMBERG, Kevin 1982-84
McBRIDE, Bake 1982-83	O'DEA, Paul 1944-45	PHILLIPS, Adolfo 1972	RICE, Edgar 1934
McCABE, Ralph 1946	ODENWALD, Ted 1921-22	PHILLIPS, Bubba 1960-62	RIDDLEBERGER, Dennie 1972
McCARTHY, Jack 1901-03	ODOM, John 1975	PHILLIPS, Ed 1935	RIDZIK, Steve 1958
McCOSKY, Barney 1951-53	O'DONOGHUE, John 1966-67	PHILLIPS, Thomas 1919	RIGDON, Paul 2000
McCRAW, Tom ....1972,'74-75	OELKERS, Bryan 1986	PICKERING, Ollie 1901-02	RINCON, Ricardo 1999-00
McCREA, Francis 1925	OGEA, Chad 1994-98	PIERETTI, Marino 1950	RIPKEN, Billy 1995
McDONALD, John 1999	O'HAGEN, Harry 1902	PIERSALL, Jim 1959-61	RISKE, David 1999
McDONNELL, Jim 1943-45	OJEDA, Bobby 1993	PINA, Horacio 1968-69	RITTER, Reggie 1986-87
McDOWELL, Jack 1996-97	OLIN, Steve 1989-92	PINIELLA, Lou 1968	RITTWAGE, Jim 1970
McDOWELL, Oddibe 1989	OLIVER, Dave 1977	PINSON, Vada 1970-71	ROA, Joe 1995-96
McDOWELL, Sam 1961-71	OLSON, Gregg 1995	PITULA, Stan 1957	ROBERTS, Bip 1997
McGUIRE, James A 1901	OLSON, Ivan 1911-14	PIZARRO, Juan 1969	ROBERTS, Dave 1999-00
McGUIRE, James T ....1908,'10	O'NEILL, Steve 1911-23	PLUNK, Eric 1992-98	ROBINSON, Eddie ....1942,'46-48,'57
McHALE, Martin 1916	ONSLOW, Edward 1918	POAT, Ray 1942-44	ROBINSON, Frank 1974-76
McINNIS, John 1922	OROSCO, Jesse 1989-91	PODBIELAN, Bud 1959	ROBINSON, Humberto 1959
McKAIN, Harold 1927	ORTA, Jorge 1980-81	PODGAJNY, John 1946	ROCCO, Mickey 1943-46
McLEMORE, Mark 1990	ORTIZ, Junior 1992-93	POLCHOW, Louis 1902	RODGERS, Wilbur 1915
McLISH, Cal 1956-59	OSTDIEK, Henry 1904	POOLE, Jim ....1995-96,'98-99	RODRIGUEZ, Rick 1988
McMAHON, Don 1964-66	OTIS, Harry 1909	POPE, Dave ....1952,'54-56	ROHN, Dan 1986
McNEAL, John 1901	OTTO, Dave 1991-92	PORTER, Dick 1929-34	ROHR, Billy 1968
McNULTY, Pat ....1922,'24-27	OULLIBER, John 1933	PORTER, J.W. 1958	ROHDE, Dave 1992
McQUILLAN, George 1918	OWCHINKO, Bob 1980	POST, Wally 1964	ROLLINS, Rich 1970
		POTT, Nelson 1922	ROMAN, Jose 1984-86
N	**P**	POUNDS, William 1903	ROMANO, John 1960-64
NABHOLZ, Chris 1994	PADGETT, Ernie 1926-27	POWELL, John 1975-76	ROMERO, Ramon 1984-85
NAGELSEN, Louis 1912	PAGEL, Karl 1981-83	POWER, Ted 1992-93	ROMO, Vicente 1968-69
NAGELSON, Russ 1968-70	PAIGE, George 1911	POWER, Vic 1958-61	ROOF, Phil 1965
NAGY, Charles 1990-00	PAIGE, Satchel 1948-49	POWERS, Ellis 1932-33	ROSAR, Buddy 1943-44
NAHORODNY, Bill 1982	PALMER, Lowell 1972	POWERS, John 1960	ROSELLO, Dave 1979-81
NARAGON, Hal ....1951,'54-59	PAPISH, Frank 1949	PRICE, John 1946	ROSEN, Al 1947-56
NARLESKI, Ray 1954-58	PARKER, Harry 1976	PRUITT, Ron 1976-81	ROSENTHAL, Larry 1941
NASH, Ken 1912	PARRISH, Lance 1993	PYTLAK, Frank 1932-40	ROSS, Don 1945-46
NAYMICK, Mike ....1939-40,'43-44	PARSONS, Casey 1987		ROSEMAN, Claude 1904, 1906
NEEMAN, Cal 1963	PASCHAL, Ben 1915	**Q**	ROTH, Robert 1915-18
NEHER, James 1912	PASCUAL, Camilo 1971	QUIRK, Jamie 1984	ROTHEL, Robert 1945
NEIS, Bernie 1927	PAUL, Mike 1968-71		ROY, Luther 1924-25
NELSON, Dave 1968-69	PAWLOSK1, Stan 1955	**R**	ROZEK, Dick 1950-52
NELSON, Rocky 1954	PAXTON, Mike 1978-80	RABBITT, Joe 1922	RUDOLPH, Don 1962
NETTLES, Graig 1970-72	PEARSON, Alexander 1903	RADATZ, Dick 1966-67	RUHLE, Vern 1985
NETZEL, Milo 1909	PEARSON, Monte 1932-35	RAFTERY, Thomas 1909	RUSSELL, Jack 1932
NEWCOMBE, Don 1960	PECK, Hal 1947-49	RAGLAND, Tom 1973	RUSSELL, Jeff 1994
NEWHOUSER, Hal 1954-55	PECKINPAUGH, Roger ....1910,'12-13	RAICH, Eric 1975-76	RUSSELL, Lloyd 1938
NICHOLS, Rod 1988-92	PENA, Geronimo 1996	RAINES, Larry 1957-58	RUSZKOWSKI, Hank ....1944-45,'47
NICHOLLS, Simon 1910	PENA, Orlando 1967	RAKERS, Jason 1998-99	RUTHERFORD, Jim 1910
NIEHAUS, Richard 1920	PENA, Tony 1994-96	RAMIREZ, Alex 1998-00	RYAN, Buddy 1912-13
NIEKRO, Phil 1986-87	PENNER, Kenneth 1916	RAMIREZ, Manny 1993-00	RYAN, Jack 1908
NIELSEN, Milt 1949, 1951	PERCONTE, Jack 1982-83	RAMOS, Domingo 1988	
NIEMAN, Bob 1961-62	PEREZCHICA, Tony 1991-92	RAMOS, Pedro 1962-64	**S**
NILES, Harry 1910	PERKINS, Broderick 1983-84	RATH, Morris 1910	SALAS, Mark 1989
NILL, George 1907-08	PERLMAN, Jon 1988	REED, Jerry ....1982-83,'85	SALMON, Chico 1964-68
NIPPER, Al 1990	PERRIN, William 1934	REED, Steve 1998-00	SALVESON, John 1943, 1945

SANDERS, Ken.................1973-74	SORRELLS, Ray..................1922	TAYLOR, Ron 1962	VANDE BERG, Ed......................1987
SANDERS, Scott 2000	SORRENTO, Paul 1992-95	TAYLOR, Sam 1963	VANDER MEER, John 1951
SANTANA, Rafael 1990	SOTHORON, Allen 1921-22	TEBBETTS, Birdie 1951-52	VARNEY, Lawrence 1902
SANTIAGO, Jose 1954-55	SOUTHWORTH, William ....1913,'15	TEDROW, Allen 1914	VASBINDER, M. Calhoun............1902
SCHAEFER, Herman 1918	SPEAKER, Tris 1916-26	TEMPLE, John 1960-61	VELEZ, Otto 1983
SCHAFFERNOTH, Joe 1961	SPEECE, Byron 1925-26	TERRY, Ralph 1965	VERNON, Mickey .....1949-50,'58
SCHATZEDER, Dan 1988	SPEED, Horace 1978-79	THIELMAN, John 1907-08	VERSAILLES, Zoilo 1969
SCHEIBECK, Frank 1901	SPEIER, Justin...........................2000	THOMAS, Carl 1960	VERYZER, Tom 1978-81
SCHEINBLUM, Richie.......1965,'67-69	SPENCER, Roy 1933-14	THOMAS, Chester 1918-21	VIDAL, Jose 1966-68
SCHLUETER, Norman................1944	SPIKES, Charlie 1973-77	THOMAS, Fay 1931	VILLONE, Ron 1998
SCHRECKENGOST, Ossee 1902	SPILLNER, Dan 1978-84	THOMAS, Gorman 1983	VINSON, Ernest 1904-05
SCHROM, Ken 1986-87	SPRADLIN, Jerry 1999	THOMAS, Stan 1976	VIZCAINO, Jose 1996
SCHULZE, Don 1984-86	SPRING, Jack 1965	THOMAS, Valmy 1961	VIZQUEL, Omar....................1994-00
SCHWARTZ, William 1904	SPRINGER, Steve 1990	THOMASON, Arthur 1910	VON OHLEN, Dave 1985
SCORE, Herb 1955-59	SPRINZ, Joe 1930-31	THOME, Jim 1991-00	VOSMIK, Joe 1930-36
SCOTT, Ed 1901	SPURGEON, Fred 1924-27	THOMPSON, Rich 1985	VUKOVICH, George 1983-85
SCUDDER, Scott 1992-93	STANGE, Lee 1964-66	THOMPSON, Ryan 1996	
SEANEZ, Rudy 1989-91	STANLEY, Fred 1971-72	THONEY, Jack 1902-03	**W**
SEEDS, Robert ....1930-32,'34	STANTON, Mike 1980-81	THORNTON, Andre .....1977-79,'81-87	WADDELL, Tom ....1984-85,'87
SEEREY, Pat 1943-48	STARK, Monroe 1909	TIANT, Luis 1964-69	WAGNER, Leon 1964-68
SEITZER, Kevin 1996-97	STARNAGLE, George 1902	TIDROW, Dick 1972-74	WAGNER, Paul 1999
SEPKOWSKI, Ted ....1942,'46-47	STEEN, Bill 1912-15	TIEFENAUER, Bob ....1960,'65,'67	WAITS, Rick 1976-83
SEWELL, Joe 1920-30	STEINER, Jim 1945	TIMMERMAN, Tom.............1973-74	WAKEFIELD, Howard........1905, 1907
SEWELL, Luke ....1921-32,'39	STEPHENS, Bryan 1947	TINGLEY, Ron 1988	WALKER, Edward 1902-03
SEXSON, Richie 1997-00	STEPHENSON, Riggs 1921-25	TIPTON, Joe ....1948,'52-53	WALKER, Fred 1912
SEYFRIED, Gordon 1963-64	STEVENS, Dave 1999	TOLSON, Charles 1925	WALKER, Gerald 1941
SHANER, Walter 1923	STEWART, Sammy.....................1987	TOMANEK, Dick ....1953-54,'57-58	WALKER, James 1912,15
SHAUTE, Joe 1922-30	STEWART, Walter......................1935	TORKELSON, Chester 1917	WALKER, Jerry 1963-64
SHAW, Jeff 1990-92	STIGMAN, Dick.....................1960-61	TORRES, Rosendo 1973-74	WALKER, Mike ....1988,'90-91
SHAY, Danny 1901	STIRNWEISS, George............1951-52	TOWNSEND, Jack 1906	WALTERS, Al 1924-25
SHEAFFER, Danny 1989	STODDARD, Tim 1989	TREADWAY, Jeff 1993	WAMBSGANSS, William........1914-23
SHIELDS, Francis......................1915	STOVALL, George 1904-11	TRESH, Mike 1949	WARD, Aaron 1928
SHILLING, James 1939	STOVALL, Jesse 1903	TRILLO, Manny 1983	WARD, Colby 1990
SHINAULT, Enoch 1921-22	STREIT, Oscar 1902	TROSKY, Hal 1933-41	WARD, Preston 1956-58
SHIPKE, William 1906	STRICKLAND, Geo. .....1952-57,'59-60	TROUPPE, Quincy 1952	WARD, Turner 1990-91
SHOFFNER, Milburn 1929-31	STRICKLAND, Jim....................1975	TUCKER, Ollie 1928	WARDLE, Curt 1985
SHUEY, Paul 1994-00	STRIKER, Jake 1959	TUCKER, Scooter 1995	WASDELL, Jim 1946-47
SIEBERT, Sonny 1964-69	STROM, Brent 1973	TUCKER, Thurman...............1948-51	WASHINGTON, Ron 1988
SIMPSON, Harry ....1951-53,'55	STROMME, Floyd 1939	TURCHIN, Edward 1943	WATSON, Mark 2000
SIMS, Duke 1964-70	SUAREZ, KEN................1968-69,'71	TURNER, Chris 1999	WAYENBERG, Frank 1924
SITTON, Carl................................1909	SUCHE, Charles 1938	TURNER, Matt 1994	WEATHERLY, Ray 1936-42
SKALSKI, Joe 1989	SUDAKIS, Bill 1975	TURNER, Terry 1904-18	WEATHERS, Dave 1997
SKINNER, Joel 1989-91	SULLIVAN, Dennis................1908-09	TYRIVER, Dave 1962	WEAVER, Floyd 1962, 1965
SLATTERY, John 1903	SULLIVAN, James 1923		WEBB, James 1938-39
SLOCUMB, Heathcliff...............1993	SULLIVAN, Paul 1939	**U**	WEBBER, Les 1946, 1948
SMILEY, John 1997	SULLIVAN, William 1936-37	UHLAENDER, Ted.................1970-71	WEBSTER, Mitch 1990-91
SMITH, Al ....1953-57,'64	SUMMA, Homer 1922-28	UHLE, George ....1919-28,'36	WEBSTER, Ray 1959
SMITH, Alfred 1940-45	SUSCE, George 1941-44	UJDUR, Jerry 1984	WEIGEL, Ralph 1946
SMITH, Charles.........................1902	SUTCLIFFE, Rick 1982-84	UNDERHILL, Vern 1927-28	WEIK, Dick 1950, 1953
SMITH, Clarence 1916-17	SUTHERLAND, Darrell 1968	UNSER, Del 1972	WEILAND, Robert 1934
SMITH, Clay 1938	SWAN, Russ 1994	UPP, George 1909	WEINGARTNER, Elmer..............1945
SMITH, Elmer ....1914-17,'19-21	SWINDELL, Greg.............1986-91,'96	UPSHAW, Cecil 1974	WELF, Oliver 1916
SMITH, Robert 1959	SWINDELL, Joshua 1911, 1913	UPSHAW, Willie 1988	WENSLOFF, Charles 1948
SMITH, Roy 1984-85		USHER, Bob 1957	WERTZ, Bill 1993-94
SMITH, Sherrod 1922-27	**T**	USSAT, Bill 1925, 1927	WERTZ, Vic 1954-58
SMITH Syd...........................1910-11	TABLER, Pat 1983-88		WEST, James 1905, 1911
SMITH, Tommy 1973-76	TAM, Jeff................................1999	**V**	WESTLAKE, Wally 1952-55
SMITH, Willie 1967-68	TANNER, Chuck 1959-60	VAIL, Mike 1978	WEYHING, August 1901
SNYDER, Cory 1986-90	TASBY, Willie 1962-63	VALDEZ, Efrain 1990-91	WHEELER, Ed...........................1945
SNYDER, Russ 1968-69	TAUBENSEE, Eddie 1991	VALDEZ, Sergio 1990-91	WHISENANT, Pete 1960
SODD, William 1937	TAVAREZ, Julian 1993-96	VALENTINETTI, Vito 1957	WHITEHILL, Earl......................1937-38
SOLTERS, Julius 1937-39	TAVENER, John 1929	VALO, Elmer 1959	WHITEN, Mark..........1991-92,'98-00
SORENSEN, Lary 1982-83	TAYLOR, Luther 1902	VAN CAMP, Al.............................1928	WHITFIELD, Fred..................1963-67

Photography Credits

Legend: L=left, C=center, R=right, T=top, B=bottom.

Allsport: pages 185, 186, 187, 188, 194, 195, 196, 197, 198, 201.

George Brace Collection: pages 10C, 29, 30, 31, 32, 33T, 33B, 41B, 44, 46, 47L, 47R, 49, 51, 52, 54, 56, 57, 62L, 62R, 65L, 65R, 66, 67L, 67R, 68L, 68R, 69, 73, 74, 79L, 99R, 114R, 116R, 118, 120, 123, 125, 127.

Chance Brockway: pages xi, 126R, 129, 130, 132,136,141, 145, 148, 149, 156, 164.

Cleveland State University, Cleveland Press Collection: pages 41T, 48, 58, 60, 76, 79R, 81, 84, 85, 86, 87, 89, 92T, 92B, 100L, 110, 111, 113L, 114L, 115, 116L, 119, 121, 124, 128T, 128B, 140, 142, 150, 152, 153, 155, 157, 162.

Diamond Images: pages ii, ix, xiii, 95L, 96, 97R, 98, 99L, 99C, 100R, 101, 105R, 107L, 107R, 108, 112L, 112R, 174L, 177, 178, 199R, 202, 203L, 203R, 205, 214.

Malcom Emmons: pages 126L, 146L, 159, 163.

Pete Groh: pages 146R, 147, 168, 172.

Ron Kuntz: pages i, iv, xvi, 102, 135, 137, 143, 144, 151, 154, 158, 159R, 167, 169, 170, 171, 173, 174R, 175, 176L, 182, 192, 204.

National Baseball Hall of Fame Library: pages xviii, 2, 3, 4, 5, 6, 7, 19, 37, 77, 82, 83, 88, 95R, 103R, 104, 105L, 139, 208.

RJM Collection: pages xv, 8, 10L, 10-R, 12, 14L, 16, 17L, 18L, 21, 22L, 22R, 26L, 26R, 27, 80, 209, 210.

Herman Seid Collection: pages iii, xiv, 63, 70, 78.

SportsChrome USA: pages vi, x, 183, 189, 190.

The Sporting News: page 36.

Tony Tomsic: pages 160, 165, 184.

Transcendental Graphics: pages xii, 15, 17R, 18R, 20, 24, 28, 35, 38, 50, 53, 59, 61, 64, 72, 75, 90, 91, 93, 94, 97L, 103L, 106, 113R, 117, 122, 131, 134.

Skip Trombetti: pages 176R, 180, 181, 191L, 191R, 199L, 200, 206L, 206R, 207.

Mort Tucker Photography: pages 211, 212.

Western Reserve Historical Society: pages viii 11, 13, 14R, 23, 34, 39, 40, 43, 45, 55.

Bibliography

Books

Anderson, Dave. *Pennant Races-Baseball At Its Best*. Doubleday, 1994.

Boudreau, Lou with Schneider, Russell. *Lou Boudreau-Covering All The Bases*. Sagamore Publishing, 1993.

Carter, Craig (editor). *Daguerreotypes* (8th Edition). The Sporting News, 1990.

Dudley, Bruce. *Distant Drums-The 1949 Cleveland Indians Revisited*. Self-published, 1989.

Eckhouse, Morris (editor). *All-Star Baseball in Cleveland*. Society for American Baseball Research (SABR), 1997.

Eckhouse, Morris (editor). *Baseball in Cleveland*. Society for American Baseball Research (SABR), 1990.

Eckhouse, Morris. *Bob Feller*. Chelsea House, 1990.

Eckhouse, Morris. *Day By Day in Cleveland Indians History*. Leisure Press, 1983.

Eskenazi, Gerald. *Bill Veeck: A Baseball Legend*. McGraw-Hill, 1988.

Feller, Bob with Gilbert, Bill. *Now Pitching, Bob Feller*. Carol Publishing Group, 1990.

Grabowski, John J. *Sports In Cleveland: An Illustrated History*. Indiana University Press, 1992.

Lewis, Franklin. *The Cleveland Indians*. G.P. Putnam's Sons, 1949.

Longert, Scott. *Addie Joss: King of the Pitchers*. Society for American Baseball Research (SABR), 1998.

Moore, Joseph Thomas. *Pride Against Prejudice-The Biography of Larry Doby*. Praeger, 1988.

Murphy, J.M. *The National Pastime-Napoleon Lajoie: Modern Baseball's First Superstar*. Society for American Baseball Research (SABR), 1988.

Pluto, Terry. *The Curse of Rocky Colavito*. Simon & Schuster, 1994.

Reidenbaugh, Lowell. *The Sporting News Selects Baseball's 25 Greatest Pennant Races*. The Sporting News, 1987.

Rhodes, Greg & Erardi, John. *The First Boys of Summer-The 1869-1870 Cincinnati Red Stockings*. Road West Publishing Company, 1994.

Romig, Ralph H. *Cy Young: Baseball's Legendary Giant*. Dorrance & Company, 1964.

Schneider, Russell. *The Cleveland Indians Encyclopedia*. Temple University Press, 1996.

Schneider, Russell J. Frank Robinson: *The Making of a Manager*. Coward, McCann & Geoghegan, 1976.

Schneider, Russell. *The Glorious Indian Summer of 1995*. Russell Schneider Enterprises, 1995.

Schneider, Russell. *The Unfulfilled Indian Summer of 1996*. Russell Schneider Enterprises, 1996.

Seidel, Michael. *Streak: Joe DiMaggio and the Summer of '41*. McGraw-Hill, 1988.

Sowell, Mike. *The Pitch That Killed*. Macmillan, 1989.

Thomas, Henry W. *Walter Johnson-Baseball's Big Train*. Bison Books, 1998.

Thorn, John; Palmer, Pete; Gershman, Michael; Pietrusza, David; Hoynes, Paul. *Total Indians*. Penguin Books, 1996

Tiant, Luis and Fitzgerald, Joe. *El Tiante-The Luis Tiant Story*. Doubleday, 1976.

Thornton, Andre as told to Janssen, Al. *Triumph Born of Tragedy*. Harvest House Publishers, 1983.

Toman, James A. *Cleveland Stadium-Sixty Years of Memories*. Cleveland Landmarks Press, 1994

Torry, Jack. *Endless Summers-The Fall and Rise of the Cleveland Indians*. Diamond Communications, 1995.

Veeck, Bill and Linn, Ed. *Veeck-As In Wreck*. Bantam Books, 1963.

Walsh, Edward J. *Gateway: Blueprint of the Future-Book One: Jacobs Field*. Gateway Press Incorporated, 1994.

Guides

The Sporting News Baseball Guide (aka Official Baseball Guide), 1949 to 2000
The Sporting News Baseball Register (aka Baseball Register)
The Sporting News Official Major League Baseball Fact Book 2000 Edition Cleveland Indians media guides, 1949-2000
Cleveland Indians Post-Season Media Guides, 1995-1999

Reference Books

Total Baseball-Sixth Edition
The Sports Encyclopedia: Baseball 2000
The World Series
Green Cathedrals
Baseball Uniforms of the 20th Century
The Negro Leagues Book
The National Baseball Hall of Fame and Museum Yearbook
The All-Star Game
Diamonds